SIDELINED NO LONGER

ADVANCE PRAISE FOR
SIDELINED NO LONGER

"'Everybody Watches Women Sports'—the catchy T-shirt slogan of today was, like so many seemingly overnight success stories, years, even decades in the making. Karen Rudolph gets to the start of it all and tells all. The fascinating, the factions, the fighting and, eventually, the fruition and fulfillment of what women's athletics could and should be are on these pages. From the legislation (Title IX and the Tower Amendment) to the legends (both athletes and administrators) who made it happen: Rudolph has the story.

"And like Caitlin Clark, Dawn Staley, Alyson Felix, Simone Biles, Katie Ledecky and so many others—the story of *Sidelined No Longer: The Untold Story of Women's College Sports* is too good to ignore."

JOHN ANDERSON
ESPN SportsCenter

"Sidelined No Longer: The Untold Story of Women's College Sports is a powerful and necessary read that finally gives voice to the women who changed the trajectory of college athletics. The book offers an in-depth look at the often-overlooked transition from the AIAW to the NCAA, an era marked by tension, courage, and a bold vision for equity. It uncovers why Division I universities needed a different governance structure to push for critical legislation and Title IX compliance, and how that shift paved the way for the opportunities we now see exploding across women's sports.

"From NIL deals and national sponsorships to sold-out arenas and professional leagues, today's female athletes stand on the shoulders of those trailblazers who refused to be sidelined. The media coverage, endorsement deals, and professional pathways young women now enjoy are not just milestones, they are the result of decades of advocacy, persistence, and leadership. This book reminds us that the current "moment" in women's sports wasn't given; it was earned by those who fought tirelessly to open doors for future generations."

LARISSA ANDERSON
Head Softball Coach, The University of Missouri
Current President of the National Fastpitch Coaches Association

"The fight for fairness and the struggle for acceptance is a lonely and thankless endeavor. Many give up along the way, but then there are some like Jean Cerra and ten other women leaders who fully believed that having one organization oversee intercollegiate athletics would increase public acceptance of and enhance opportunities for participation in women's intercollegiate sports. They were right, and this move to one governing body, the NCAA, was the game-changing moment for the growth we see today. During my time at Missouri, I was fortunate to work with this forward-thinking, skilled administrator, Jean Cerra, who deftly managed the transformation of women's programs while assisting the growth of men's programs at the same time. This story deserves to be told, and these women should be rightfully credited for being part of a movement that paved the way to the success women's sports rightfully celebrate today."

JOSEPH R. CASTIGLIONE
Vice President and Director of Athletics
University of Oklahoma

"The road to the current phenomenal success of women's college athletics has not been an easy one. Throughout the decades-long pursuit of equity, female student athletes and coaches were often denied the advantages that male athletes received and took for granted.

"Pioneers came along and powered a relentless movement. Women like Jean Cerra and the author of this book, Karen Rudolph, whom I met when she was a student athlete at Missouri, and so many more trailblazers paved the way for the status and equity that women athletes enjoy today.

"This book needed to be written. Another victory for student athletes. The work goes on."

DRU HANCOCK
Former Senior Associate Commissioner, Big 12 Conference
Four-time chair or co-chair of the Women's NCAA Basketball
Championships

"Thank you, Karen, for your courage and tenacity in telling the untold story of women's college sports. The vision and commitment of eleven female college administrators during a contentious time in our history virtually changed the direction of women's college sports forever."

BARBARA A. HEDGES
Athletic Director, University of Washington, 1991–2004
Senior Associate Director of Athletics, University of Southern
California, 1973–1991

"Before there were Caitlin Clark and Paige Bueckers—and before dynasties like Connecticut (basketball) and Oklahoma (softball)—there wasn't all that much to capture the fancy of women's college sports fans. Fifty years ago athletics opportunities at the intercollegiate level mostly amounted to club and intramural competition, until Title IX slowly took effect. It was a different time, as first the AIAW and then the NCAA began offering women overdue chances to take the field on the same level as their male counterparts. No one knows this better than Karen Rudolph because she lived it as a two-sport student-athlete at the University of Missouri in the '70s. In her book *Sidelined No Longer: The Untold Story of Women's College Sports*, she paints a vivid picture of the early trials and tribulations women's college sports faced—as told by a list of women's administrators who helped blaze that trail. It's a history lesson for anyone who wants to appreciate just how far Clark and Bueckers and programs like Connecticut's and Oklahoma's have come."

JOHN HEISLER
Former Assistant Sports Information Director, University of Missouri
Former Senior Associate Athletics Director, University of Notre Dame

"Almost every important social change in America steers through at least one inflection point—a moment that points the movement down an irrevocable path. This book tells the untold story of how the success of women's sports today is rooted in a tense overthrow of its founding leadership. It is a fascinating insider's tale of the split that spurred the revolution in women in sports."

GERI MIGIELICZ
Journalist and Professor in Journalism, Stanford University

"*Sidelined No Longer: The Untold Story of Women's College Sports* doesn't just recount a movement, it illuminates the women whose determination redefined intercollegiate athletics forever.

"This book captures the courage, conviction and resilience it took for women to build the foundation of college sports. These women are more than athletic administrators; they are trail blazers and leaders who created opportunities for others that often they were unable to experience for themselves. It's important to know our history to appreciate what it took to get where we are and learn lessons in courage that will help us continue to grow."

BRENDA VANLENGEN
ESPN Commentator
Executive Producer of *If Not For Them*

SIDELINED NO LONGER

THE UNTOLD STORY OF WOMEN'S COLLEGE SPORTS

KAREN S. RUDOLPH

SIDELINED NO LONGER
The Untold Story of Women's College Sports

Copyright © 2025 by Karen S. Rudolph

Book Cover Design by Abigael Elliott
Interior Layout and Design by Stephanie Anderson
Editorial Team: Stephanie Rondeau, Chloie Benton, Gin Glass, Kiska Carr
Cover Photography: (Top) Officers of the women's "M" club show off their letter sweaters for the 1928 University of Missouri yearbook, *The Savitar*. (L-R) Ethel Hunt, Alice Sonnenschein, Louise Hitchcock, and Helen Jenkins. Photo courtesy of the University of Missouri Archives. (Bottom) The University of Oklahoma softball team celebrates a national championship, with star Jayda Coleman featured taking this group selfie. Photo courtesy of Edward Real of the *OU Daily* and used with the permission of the *OU Daily*.

Isbns:
979-8-89165-276-7 *Paperback*
979-8-89165-277-4 *Hardback*
979-8-89165-275-0 *E-book*

Published by:
Streamline Books
Kansas City, MO
streamlinebookspublishing.com

*To "The Title IX Generation" of women athletes
and administrators who set the foundation for what
we see in business, on television, in boardrooms,
and throughout athletic competition today.*

CONTENTS

PREFACE

WRITING THIS BOOK has allowed me to connect the past to the present and show how today's sold-out arenas and stadiums, financial deals, television ratings, and popular professional leagues are rooted in the struggles and triumphs of those early years of women's intercollegiate sports.

This story is personal to me because I lived it. As one of the first women to receive an athletic scholarship at the University of Missouri, I'm grateful to the Association for Intercollegiate Athletics for Women for initially organizing women's sports. I knew what it meant to be evaluated as part of a "pilot program" that had never existed before, to see if women were interested in increased athletic competition. Day after day, throughout each season, we proved that women's sports deserved a permanent place in the collegiate landscape.

With interest in women's college sports exploding, we can all celebrate the beginnings of the journey, told in the unknown stories of women athletic administrators who overcame hurdles and bridged a gap, securing growth opportunities for women athletes.

Sidelined No Longer was created using hundreds of hours of phone and in-person interviews. Material from those interviews is quoted directly in the book. Research material, including letters, newspaper articles, records, and more, is footnoted.

I wrote this book for the women who paved the way, many of whom never got the recognition they deserved, for my teammates, and for every girl who's ever laced up her sneakers without knowing the battles fought on her behalf. This is our story, and I'm proud to be both witness and storyteller.

CHAPTER 1
Foundations

TODAY'S WOMEN COLLEGE athletes are achieving unprecedented success, with historic marks in attendance, revenue, media attention, and so much more. Fans have discovered it's fun to follow women's sports, and the phrase "Everyone Watches Women's Sports" has taken off, ignited by derogatory comments on the internet that no one watches women's sports. Premier athletes Sue Bird, Alex Morgan, Simone Manuel, and Chloe Kim, along with Jessica Robertson and others, collaborated on a sports media company—Togethxr (pronounced Together)—to promote women's sports and dispel that notion. When South Carolina basketball coach Dawn Staley wore a hoodie touting that "Everyone Watches Women's Sports" during a game versus Louisiana State University, the sweatshirt sold out before the end of the telecast, serving notice to sports fans everywhere that women are changing the sports world, and indeed are changed by athletic participation.

Trailblazing pioneers who are now retired have seen generations of girls play sports and use that experience to learn leadership skills and become doctors, lawyers, chief executive officers, and professional athletes. To them, the current achievements are the

1

exclamation points on everything they dreamed and imagined, the summation of what they fought and sacrificed for. There are sold-out venues, nationwide media coverage, coaching salaries in the millions of dollars, and women in sports in commercial ads modeling brands and plugging products.

Today, fans are crowding into football stadiums to see women play sports. At the University of Nebraska, ninety-two thousand volleyball fans flooded into Memorial Stadium in August 2023 to watch the Cornhuskers play Omaha, attracting the largest-ever attendance at a women's stand-alone sporting event. The growing popularity drives the development of women's professional volleyball leagues. The newest, Major League Volleyball, has attracted $100 million in funding with a January 2026 launch date.

In October 2023, fifty-five thousand Iowa women's basketball fans cheered as national player of the year Caitlyn Clark began her senior campaign in a preseason exhibition game against DePaul in Kinnick Stadium. The game set an all-time attendance record for women's basketball and raised over $250,000 for an Iowa City children's hospital. Together, the two events authenticated the popularity of women's sports. More advances immediately followed.

By March 2024, Oklahoma University opened its $50 million softball stadium and training complex, Love's Field, which quickly sold out of season tickets. The impressive 4,200-seat stadium, the Taj Mahal of college softball facilities, reflected the Sooners' dominance in the sport: four consecutive national championships beginning in 2021.

Joe Castiglione, athletic director at Oklahoma since 1998, commented that women's sports are the healthiest they have ever been and are continuing to grow.

"Now we have data. We have ratings. We have attendance numbers. You see the interest level in women's sports exploding.

We're proud at the University of Oklahoma to be on the forefront with our new stadium. There are more people who want tickets than the stadium can hold."

In recent years, the softball Women's College World Series has drawn bigger television audiences than the men's College World Series. In 2024, the women's basketball national championship game surpassed the viewership of the men's title game.

The explosion is reflected across the board in women's sports.

The Women's National Basketball Association capitalized on women's team successes during the 1996 Atlanta Olympic Games. Started as a summer league the next year, the WNBA filled a unique gap for basketball fans after college and professional seasons ended. Unfortunately, players frequently had to seek off-season opportunities overseas to augment their salaries. The financial rewards outweighed the challenges to family life, but the 293-day incarceration of Brittney Griner in Russia spotlighted the risks of cultural and political differences. More than twenty-five years after the league's founding, a couple of WNBA stars joined a powerful group of investors to offer an alternative to overseas employment. Napheesa Collier and Breanna Stewart, former teammates at the University of Connecticut, balked at the continuing disruption. They had earned gold medals for the United States women's team at the 2024 Paris Olympics but wanted better financial options for their careers.

Basketball's 3X3 competition had proven popular after being included in the Tokyo Olympic Games; perhaps they could develop a three-on-three women's professional league that allowed women to play stateside and supplement their WNBA salaries. That league, called Unrivaled, opened up in January 2025 with a two-month season in Miami. It offered the highest average salaries in women's sports history ($222,000). All thirty-six players received an equity ownership stake. With innovative rules and court setup, the league attracted a key sponsorship with a nationally known beauty brand, Sephora, which provided a makeup room to glam up before interviews or after practices and games.

Gymnastics and women's soccer also were at the forefront. The National Collegiate Athletic Association approved name, image, and likeness deals for college athletes in 2021. Known as NIL, it allowed Louisiana State University gymnast Olivia "Livvy" Dunne to earn over $10 million during her college career, the top-ranked female athlete in NIL compensation and number four overall. Corporate sponsors saw fresh opportunities to promote women athletes, invest in development, and promote equality.

In 2021, the women's activity clothing company Title Nine donated $1 million to the players' association for soccer's Women's National Team, seeking to close the wage gap between women's and men's salaries. Missy Park, the owner and chief executive officer of the California company, sought to correct the inequity and started a "Kick In for Equal Pay Fund" to support the women's team through other corporate sponsors and individuals. She vowed to match donations up to an additional $250,000.

Park named her company for a landmark 1972 law known simply today as Title IX. Through that, women and girls gained equal access to education and sports. Park was disturbed that the US Soccer Federation paid the women who had dominated international play far less than the men's squad. To her, a win on the soccer field translated into wins in the workplace.

"We want women to lead, and to risk, and to own—and to do it on equal footing, on an equal playing field," Park told *Glamour Magazine* daily newsletter writer Macaela MacKenzie. "Money matters—it's how we connote value in this society."[1]

Soccer continued its prominence in women's sports by adding an impressive new stadium in Kansas City, Missouri, in March

2024. CPKC Stadium, home to the National Women's Soccer League team, the Kansas City Current, opened as the first privately financed venue built exclusively for women's soccer. The team, with investors like Brittany and Patrick Mahomes as well as Angie and Chris Long, sold out every home match in the 11,500-seat stadium that inaugural season.

Media today extols the virtues of investing in women's sports. Organizations and businesses are developing around a model of promoting just women's sports. Entrepreneur Haley Rosen named her company exactly that—Just Women's Sports. Critics told her that it was a charity, not a real business. She has attracted $13 million in startup funds from prominent professional athletes who, like her, are convinced there is a hunger for women's sports content. Similarly, sports bars dedicated to women's athletics have cropped up, including the nation's first in Portland, Oregon, called the Sports Bra. The concept drew Alexis Ohanian, cofounder of Reddit and husband of tennis star Serena Williams, as a major investor who wanted to franchise the idea.

Despite the success and popularity seen today, the landscape of women's athletics looked vastly different a few decades ago. Early trailblazers of the 1970s could only dream of packed stadiums, media interest, and financial investment that many of today's athletes experience. That decade of college sports was dominated by constant adjustments to Title IX, and the governance of women's college sports was at a crossroads. Three different organizations vied for prominence: the well-known and powerful National Collegiate Athletic Association that governed men's sports, the organization for small colleges known as the National Association of Intercollegiate Athletics, and an all-women's group: the Association for Intercollegiate Athletics for Women.

AIAW members believed that their unknown and little-heralded organization had a mandate to continue building what they initially had developed with little support solely by women and for women. It was aligned closely with female physical educators who deliberated on how far and how fast their athletics programs could and should grow. AIAW had a limited and idealistic vision for women's sports that opposed athletic scholarships and recruiting. To them, merging with any of the men's organizations was not in the best interests of what the physical educators wanted: a strong, independent women's program, unlike men's intercollegiate athletics. But not all women wanted to stay in AIAW. Over time, a minority within the group emerged whose desire for change would prove pivotal.

Eleven women, working as Division I administrators alongside men in combined athletics departments, saw a different path. Among them was the University of Missouri women's athletic director, Jean Cerra. She and her colleagues at major universities with men's NCAA sports realized that their schools would never reach compliance with Title IX until their women athletes received benefits comparable to those of the men. And AIAW was holding them back.

Title IX compliance required that individual institutions—not AIAW—ensure equal opportunities for their women's programs when compared to the men's. The large schools faced a near-insurmountable hurdle because men's budgets were enormous compared to the smaller schools. But the smaller colleges and their administrators were AIAW's most powerful voting bloc, unwilling to vote for modifications in rules that accommodated the differences. They continually ignored the large schools' distinctive needs.

Cerra, hired at Missouri in 1976, epitomized that struggle. National organizations for women athletic administrators were nonexistent. For her and many other women, acceptance into the sports culture would come from advocating strongly for increased opportunities while limiting antagonism. Cerra's approach reflected a sense of humor and sensible solutions based on competence, intellect, and ability from the neck up, not opportunities dependent on gender from the neck down.

Although largely unknown today, these hidden figures in the women's sports world laid the foundation for the full inclusion of women into college sports, which became a springboard into professional opportunities. This is the untold story of that history when trailblazers enacted change that moved women's sports forward into a golden era. It's time to recognize those hidden figures who fought to open up those opportunities as quickly as possible for succeeding generations of girls and women.

CHAPTER 2
Early Rules and Restrictions

1880s to 1950s

TOWARD THE END of the nineteenth century, women balked at Victorian-era expectations to stay home because they were too refined or dainty to compete in sports. Restrictive clothing like hoop skirts, bustles, and corsets clashed with the fun, freedom, and challenge of sports competition. By 1893, the women of Smith College in Northampton, Massachusetts, welcomed the chaos and creativity of basketball, a new sport devised two years before and twenty miles away in Springfield by Dr. James Naismith. Gym teacher Senda Berenson lessened the physical impacts by dividing the court into three sections, with two to three players assigned to each section. No player could cross the dividing lines. Dribbling rules were changed regularly over the years so that players could dribble once or as many as two or three times. Defenders had strict rules against batting the ball in an opponent's hands and had to guard with their hands directly above their heads. The Smith College women's intramural contest earned recognition as the first women's basketball game.

Even with those limitations, the lively and unpredictable sport spread within two years to the West Coast. In one of the first women's intercollegiate basketball games, Stanford defeated the University of California, Berkeley by a score of two to one. A lively crowd of seven hundred women at San Francisco's Page Street Armory cheered enthusiastically. Men were not allowed to watch.

Stanford, remarkably, was coed when most private universities were single-sex. When it opened in 1891, nearly a quarter of the 555 students were women. Lou Henry was among those early coeds and served as president of the Women's Athletic Association. After graduating, she married future national government leader and United States President Herbert Hoover, whom she had met at Stanford.

Lou Henry Hoover favored a woman's right to vote but disdained and actively opposed women's competitive sports, which emphasized physical training and athletic development. Instead, she supported a more generalized and inclusive recreational approach. The concept of sports for all, with the motto "A sport for every girl and every girl in a sport," became her group's mantra during the Roaring Twenties. Hoover used her platform as the wife of a cabinet member (Herbert Hoover was Secretary of Commerce from 1921 to 1928) to collaborate with physical educators and women's groups such as the Girl Scouts, which she led as national president. Many physical educators and powerful women like Hoover opposed the development of women's sports.

Physical education leaders characterized their crusade as promoting women's best interests and protecting women's health. They forbade women from running ninety-four feet, the full length of a basketball court, because of the potential damage to players' reproductive organs. Meanwhile, in field hockey, women played an entire 100-yard field with no such restrictions. The women's basketball players persisted despite the opposition. The sport grew more popular, and national championships were organized through the Amateur Athletic Union by the 1920s.

The educators backed a competing organization to the better-known and more firmly established AAU, the National Amateur Athletic Federation, developed after World War I to promote youth fitness levels and combat readiness. Its Women's Division discouraged women from receiving recognition and awards or traveling for competition. Its leaders felt that women athletes should be satisfied with limited competitiveness and publicity and that qualified women should take immediate charge of women's athletics. In a true power play, only those women who supported the Women's Division philosophy were deemed qualified.

Hoover spearheaded the Women's Division in the years after World War I, emphasizing that sports were essential for one's health and that all young girls should participate without competing vigorously. Hoover promoted her views and gained an even bigger platform as First Lady when her husband was elected to a single term in the White House.

During what historically is known as the golden age of sports, men's athletics became associated with corruption, gambling, and increasing crime during the Prohibition era. Athletes faced incredible pressure to accept bribes to lose games. Those under-cover payments mocked the ideals of fair play, and amateurism was challenged. Shockingly, the 1919 World Series was marred by a scandal in which eight members of the Chicago White Sox conspired to lose major league baseball's fall classic.

The idealistic Women's Division repudiated women's competitive sports and sought to protect women from the intense demands of athletic training by restricting those opportunities and instituting special "girls' rules." The slow and boring limitations decreased participation and spectator interest; impeding that interest protected women from the vices influencing men's sports. The ongoing conflict foreshadowed future philosophical battles fifty years later to control women's college sports.

Throughout the 1920s and into the 1930s, Women's Division representatives traversed the country and were featured in newspapers and on the radio disparaging women's sports competition. Instead, they offered play days that brought girls and women together at a host school to enjoy a full day of sports and games: kickball, volleyball, basketball, floor hockey, track, and more. Participants were placed in random groups from every school or organization and played for forty-five minutes or so before changing activities. The day of recreation and socializing was promoted as an acceptable alternative, with competitiveness and physical training discouraged. Cooperative play was the intention, and punch and cookies were frequently served afterward. Sometimes, there were awards recognizing the best in each sport, plus the "Athlete of the Day." Play days continued until the 1970s.

In 1925, the Women's Division, aligned with an educational group, resolved to outlaw school competition. Led by physical educators like nationally known Blanche Trilling of the University of Wisconsin, the groups pressured high school sports associations to disband girls' athletics and tournaments. Most did.

Sidelining women's competitive amateur and Olympic sports, then in their infancy, was another focus. Pressure from the Women's Division stopped the AAU women's national basketball tournament for two years.

Refuting the Claims of the Idealistic Women's Division

DESPITE THE PHYSICAL educators' attempts throughout the 1920s to tamp down women's sports, a small subset within the group wanted more for women's athletic competition. AAU organizers defied the Women's Division and re-started the national tournament. They promoted travel, granted awards, and increased national recognition for the best players, honoring a first AAU All-American team.

The Women's Division stubbornly clung to its values. It blasted women's participation in the upcoming 1932 Los Angeles Olympic Games and advised young women athletes to pursue what they considered socially acceptable avenues like dance, swimming, and tennis.

The AAU and the Amateur Olympic Association, the forerunner of the US Olympic and Paralympic Committee, retorted that thousands of girls and women deserved to try out and compete. Had they failed, one of the country's greatest female athletes, Babe Didrikson, would not have won gold in two track and field events and silver in a third. Ultimately, seventy-four American women participated in the Xth Olympiad along with four hundred men.

When the Great Depression disrupted the national economy during the 1930s, encouraging moments carried women's sports through some dark times. In a book entitled *Dust Bowl Girls,* author Lydia Reeder revealed the largely unknown story of women's basketball and education told through Reeder's great-uncle, Sam Babb, and her grandmother, Lydia May Babb Thomas. Babb recruited young women with basketball scholarships during the Depression years to tiny Oklahoma Presbyterian College in Durant, Oklahoma, trying to build the school's enrollment and provide college educations for women.

He fundraised and coached the team through numerous hardships to eighty-nine straight wins and consecutive AAU national championships. The team won its first national title by defeating the Dallas Golden Cyclones and legendary star Babe Didrikson, who dominated the Olympics later that summer. The team and the school faded into near-obscurity but, in a remarkable way, carried small-town women's sports dreams through a difficult era.[2]

Limited Opportunities for Trailblazers

Competitive women's sports spiraled downhill with a triple whammy of national challenges: continued opposition from the Women's Division, the Great Depression, and World War II. Those influences lasted for decades and added to the dismay of women who are in their seventies and eighties today. But that lack of opportunity gave rise to brazen trailblazers who instituted reforms to elevate women's college sports.

One was Ann Marie Rogers, an athletic administrator who served the University of Alabama and the University of Florida for nearly thirty years. Florida renamed its competitive aquatics center, home to Olympic gold medalists like Tracy Caulkins, Dara Torres, Ryan Lochte, and others, in her honor. She recalled that she and others were annoyed and confused about their lack of sports opportunities. Rogers's explanation added to the chagrin of her many friends who are in their eighties today: The women physical education teachers did not believe in women's competitive sports for many reasons. Rogers herself wanted the chance to compete so much that at Michigan State University, she and a group of friends paid their own way to collegiate competitions in archery and sailing held at nearby universities.

Merrily Dean Baker was another trailblazer, but she experienced vastly different women's college sports competitions. Though close in age to Rogers, Baker recalled her own youthful sports experiences with swimming, field hockey, and gymnastics in the Philadelphia suburbs in the 1960s. When she enrolled at Pennsylvania's East Stroudsburg State College, she was shocked to find out that many of her new friends had never had the chance to play.

Baker's grandmother had played bloomer girl basketball in long skirts and puffy-sleeved blouses shortly after its invention, memories preserved today in cherished black-and-white team photographs. Baker was inspired to enact change and ultimately directed athletics programs at a handful of major universities while becoming one of the first women to work at NCAA headquarters. She noted that social acceptance had changed over generations; her generation was called derogatory names, like "tomboys," while her daughters were called athletes.

When World War II erupted, it surprisingly brought new opportunities for women in sports. The Women's Division no longer existed, its values absorbed into another national organization, the American Alliance for Health, Physical Education, and Recreation. When men were called to military duty, women provided much-needed labor on the farms, in factories, and as players on the nation's ball fields.

After two years of war, Major League Baseball was forced to cancel play, so Philip Wrigley, whose family owned the Chicago Cubs and became rich selling chewing gum, filled the void by forming women's professional baseball teams in the All-American Girls Professional Baseball League. More than six hundred women ultimately played in the league, which operated for ten years and attracted nine hundred thousand spectators at its peak. Women's sports were growing in a manner unknown to previous generations.

The league's story was depicted years later in the popular feature movie *A League of Their Own,* starring Geena Davis and Tom Hanks. The impact of that women's professional league inspired future women's athletics trailblazers like Rogers and Barbara Hedges, who guided athletic departments at the University of Southern California and the University of Washington for over three decades. Hedges's role model was her older sister, Flossie Anderson Ballard, whose softball prowess with the semi-professional Phoenix A-1 Queens during the 1940s earned her an invitation to try out for the AAGPBL. Flossie had joined the factory lines along with thousands of other women whose husbands served in the military, but when she and her best friend were offered a chance to go to Chicago and play in the league, they declined.

"They didn't have the courage to get on the train," said Hedges, mystified still today that her sister turned down such an opportunity. "They needed an escort, or a person to help them." That disappointment motivated Hedges to expand opportunities for future women athletes. She worked closely with John McKay and Dick Perry at the University of Southern California, then moved to the University of Washington in 1991 as the first woman to head an entire athletics program in one of the five most-prominent athletic conferences.

Rogers similarly was inspired by the women's pro baseball league and the local affiliate, the Grand Rapids Chicks. They won two league championships over rivals with colorful names like the Rockford Peaches, Fort Wayne Daisies, Peoria Redwings, Springfield Sallies, Kenosha Comets, and Kalamazoo Lassies. Rogers enthusiastically watched the entertaining games as a child with her family but found limited athletic opportunities for herself. She hungered to compete and made her father hit her grounders every night, preparing for chances that never really came. She and so many other pioneers overcame that minimal playing background to transform women's college sports, helping younger women go from the bleachers to the ballfields to the board rooms.

Through the 1950s, women physical educators nationwide generally opposed women's intercollegiate athletic contests and tolerated only incremental changes. The men's college sports culture willingly went along and kept control of campus facilities and budgets. Nevertheless, college women longed for athletic competition, and by the end of the decade, the national physical education organization amended its bylaws to accept the possibilities of women's intercollegiate athletics, with the terminology that they *may* exist. A few years later, the language and support evolved further, stating that it was *desirable* that intercollegiate athletics programs exist for women. More changes were coming as women's intercollegiate athletic competition was seen as serving the best interests of women. By the mid-1960s, college women and their physical education instructors blazed new paths on the playing courts and athletic fields. One early leader was a young woman from the Tampa, Florida, area: Jean Cerra.

CHAPTER 3
Jean Cerra's Journey

1950s and 1960s

JEAN CERRA'S HOMETOWN of Ybor City, Florida, an ethnic neighborhood of Tampa, brought together families from different areas of Spain along with numerous Italian and Cuban immigrants at the end of the nineteenth century. Jean's maternal grandparents were from the Asturias region of Spain and had immigrated to the United States through Cuba.

Immigrant families stressed family culture and traditions through organizations like *Centro Asturiano de Tampa*, with roots in Northern Spain, or *Centro Español* for those from Galicia, west of Asturias, or even the Italian Club. The clubs boosted cultural groups coming to Tampa and Ybor City, which all lived together but socialized within their own clubs. Those traditions remained unchanged for many years.

Her hometown, nicknamed Cigar City in its heydays, produced half a billion hand-rolled cigars in factories that had few windows above the factory floors, keeping the interior dark and dank. However, political upheaval throughout Cuba curtailed supplies of the world's premier tobacco, and without those products, Ybor City's cigar industry faltered as owners moved production to Central America. Plus, smokers' preferences changed to cheaper cigarettes, adding to the city's economic woes.

Jean's hometown was reminiscent of many areas of the United States in the 1950s, with small towns and cities alike buzzing with the post-World War II baby boom. She grew up as the youngest of three children, with an older sister, Elena, and a brother, Emilio Jr. The neighborhood kids frequently played marbles and cork ball on the quieter side streets. With a makeshift bat from a broom handle and a ball made from a wine cork wrapped tightly with several layers of white adhesive tape, players needed good hand and eye coordination to be successful. Fielders never knew which direction the ball would bounce.

As Jean entered high school and prioritized academics, music, and athletics, she walked frequently after school with friends to the main business district of Ybor City, Seventh Avenue. Her grandfather had started a Cuban bakery only a few blocks from her small private high school, Our Lady of Perpetual Help Academy, known as OLPH. The high school, with 140 students and only a handful of boys, was small, so there were few clubs available, but there was one called Sodality, a faith-based student government group where older students welcomed younger ones in a traditional tapping ceremony. Jean built a lifelong friendship with the junior who tapped her, Genelle Fernandez Garverick. Both enjoyed sports and many school activities and later majored in physical education at a pivotal time that transformed women's college athletics.

Jean recalled that interscholastic sports like volleyball, basketball, and softball began in the ninth grade with games against teams from other Catholic schools. She also played on city recreation teams for Mercedes "Moochine" Fernandez, Genelle's mother. The one-time Tampa Sportswoman of the

Year, Moochine worked as a city playground director at DeSoto Park, just minutes away in Palmetto Beach. When Genelle was a child, Moochine and her fastpitch softball team played on Sunday afternoons at renowned Al Lang Field against the area's many retired former major leaguers. From her prime seat in the dugout, Genelle saw how much fun the former pros had playing against the ladies and longed for her own opportunities.

During the 1950s, playgrounds like DeSoto Park were funded locally and offered extensive recreational activities that included sponsoring popular year-round sports leagues for both men and women. City newspapers frequently printed articles about women's sports, and Genelle kept enough to fill several scrapbooks. As Genelle entered high school, Moochine's brash assertiveness created one amazing opportunity when she recruited girls for a week-long youth sports trip to Havana. Jean, who was two years younger, didn't meet the age qualification. Moochine fundraised all the money for airfare and uniforms through her strong Tampa-area connections. Genelle, now in her eighties, soaked in the memories, calling it a great experience for the DeSoto Park playground kids who had never traveled before to fly to Havana.

"At the time in Cuba, you were either very wealthy or very poor," recalled Genelle about those pre-Castro days. "We played on great fields that were very well kept, against girls from very wealthy families, and we stayed in people's beautiful homes. Our girls were in awe because they didn't come from those kinds of backgrounds. We beat the Cuban girls in everything: volleyball, basketball, and even kickball. Then the boys wanted to play us and we beat them, too!"

The DeSoto Park teams often dominated the city championships because Moochine had an eye for talent. One day, she saw Jean and Genelle playing together at school and recruited Jean to join her program, boosting Jean's confidence in her athletic abilities and competitive desires. According to Genelle, Jean was a good sport who encouraged everyone, and her five-foot, ten-inch height helped her star in volleyball and basketball.

But Jean added much more in terms of leadership by encouraging younger team members and demonstrating the power of building a team together. While women's sports throughout the country experienced everything from indifference to outright discrimination, the OLPH girls received lots of encouragement to play sports, and people watched their games. Those positive experiences may have saved Jean from the pains of discrimination but also increased her desire to amplify sports benefits for younger women.

Education Brings a Foundation

Jean graduated from high school in 1963 as class salutatorian and enrolled at the newly opened University of South Florida, which had been founded less than a decade before in Tampa. She chuckled that it was like the thirteenth grade because all her high school friends went there. Soon, she realized that she wanted more challenges in her life. One day during her second semester, Jean announced that she intended to transfer to Florida State University the following year. Her horrified friends objected, insisting that she stay at USF. After all, she had no friends at FSU.

She agreed; she knew no one, but it was important for her personal growth to gain some independence and meet new people. She said she always knew that she would be a teacher because the only two options available then to women were either teaching or nursing.

The 1960s proved to be a great time to be a physical education major. Not only were PE credits mandatory, but so were class uniforms. Students checked out the cap-sleeved one-piece tunics daily from "the cage," a window adjacent to the locker rooms that stored equipment and washed the outfits for the next day. Today, similar outfits with mid-thigh shorts and snap fronts are making a comeback as rompers or "onesie" fashion items, although they were scorned by generations of women for their association with required physical education classes. The cotton clothing differed significantly from today's easy-care, stretchy tech fabrics and was uncomfortably stiff from being commercially starched. The PE majors were issued white uniforms to distinguish them from regular students.

Jean loved the activity classes and was challenged by some more than others. Jean passed her hardest unit, gymnastics, with the help of an older PE major who lived in the same off-campus apartment complex and served as a type of house mother. She lived in the apartment below Jean and banged on the ceiling to let her know they could practice. Jean was relieved to pass the class with a C grade. She laughed that it was the only C she ever had in college. That preparation proved beneficial during student teaching when her supervising instructor assigned her to teach gymnastics. She did particularly well in that lesson because she spent so much time preparing.

"I was probably the worst person for those skills that you could find," said Jean about teaching that unit. Her solution was to recruit experienced kids for demonstrations. "It took everything for me to do a headstand!"

Golf, a required class for physical education majors, also proved helpful. Her father played frequently and gave her a set of clubs one weekend when she was home from college. Jean found the technical sport frustrating and joked that she was terrible, mostly because she was uninterested in learning it. Within a few years and with opportunities for coaching and practice time, Jean grew more comfortable on the golf course.

Student Teaching and a First Job

Florida State University was a premier teacher training institution, and hundreds of teachers, including physical education majors, graduated from it. Student teachers were assigned all over the state. Jean drew a high school assignment in the Miami area, nearly five hundred miles away. Supervision was coordinated through the cooperating teacher, who filled out forms and did critical evaluations.

As Jean started her student teaching stint, she quickly learned whether her hard work and preparation had paid off. Her supervisor was gone for the first two weeks, so Jean had the high school classes solo. Other staff supervised her in the interim as she worked to gain her teaching credential.

Jean taught the next year in the Miami Dade County Public Schools with Pat Donatelli at Kinloch Park Junior High School, now called Kinloch Middle School. Donatelli, a longtime educator and administrator, met Jean after requesting recommendations from Florida State's physical education department leaders for a staff vacancy. They endorsed Cerra, who already was in the Miami area. Donatelli was quickly impressed and nodded to the principal with a thumbs up that Jean was a strong candidate.

"I could tell that she was very intelligent. She was very easy to talk to and calm. She liked to laugh easily," said Donatelli, adding that Jean performed amazingly well on her own. "I felt like she would be good to work with. And she was."

Donatelli praised Jean's teaching abilities and recalled two key areas in their working relationship. The first area was in-class organization and preparation. The school principal hammered the teachers to write more extensively in their black lesson plan books and carry them to all the activity classes. Donatelli hesitated because the notebooks were quite bulky and she needed her hands free to demonstrate skills and games. The PE staff wanted to comply, but they were not typical classroom teachers. Jean thought about it and the next day brought a smaller brown grade book with note cards tucked inside outlining the skills to be taught. Donatelli caught on right away.

"It made sense; it was a good adjustment. Jeannie was just capable. You didn't have to explain things to her in great detail, because she was a good listener who would understand quickly and come back with something to add."

Donatelli explained that the second key area in their working relationship was Jean's adjustment to teaching throughout the day with classes grouped by ability. Students were grouped by ability long before other schools did that, requiring extensive planning and preparation to accommodate the students' core schedules. It also required flexibility. Jean met this obstacle head on.

There were plenty of other challenges at the urban school, including language barriers between students and teachers. In the 1960s, the school was divided evenly between white, black, and Cuban students in the area south of Miami International Airport, which is now called Little Havana. Both Jean and Donatelli spoke Spanish and were frequently called to the office to help with disciplinary issues caused by miscommunication. Jean elaborated on those turbulent years.

"Those kids were going right into the schools without speaking much English. My Spanish speaking was pretty bad; street Spanish really and more like 'Spanglish.' Sometimes children could leave Cuba but not their parents, so the children were placed with close relatives or with a Catholic family," Jean said and cited the critical urgency in getting children out of Cuba. "They weren't letting the boys out once they reached age fourteen."

Jean taught just one year of middle school before departing to the University of Iowa to work full time on an advanced degree. She took a leave of absence from her teaching position, intending to return. Jean's department chair at Kinloch Middle School lamented the loss of an outstanding teacher after a single year of working together.

"I was very sad to lose her," said Donatelli. "She didn't need any encouragement for things like that, earning higher degrees. She was always in high gear for things that she got interested in. She leaves a footprint wherever she's been. And in our school, it was a good one." They remain lifelong friends despite working together for just a single year.

Donatelli's loss soon would become Iowa's gain.

CHAPTER 4

Obstacles Become Opportunities

1967–1973

JEAN PILED HER belongings into her car for the two-day drive to Iowa City and, accompanied by her father, Emilio, found an available two-story four-plex typical of college-town student housing. Leaving the familiarity of Florida behind bolstered Jean's personal independence, along with adjustments to a small Midwest city dominated by a football-focused Big Ten university. Family members were mystified that she wanted to leave Florida.

"Hispanic women stayed close to home. Latin girls didn't move out of the area, away from family. It was a big trip and a long way from my family. My dad couldn't even pronounce Iowa. He'd say, 'Eye-OHHH-wuhhh,' like it was a foreign country," Jean said with a laugh, emphasizing the middle syllable.

A love for math and science drew Jean to the University of Iowa, known for its science-based physical education curriculum. Jean was particularly interested in a newly emerging field of biomechanics tabbed the "study of human movement." The department's historic achievements since its founding a hundred years before also appealed to her. It was led by M. Gladys Scott, a physical education pioneer who earned Iowa's first doctorate in women's physical education in the mid-1950s. A generation of physical education teachers was trained with her textbooks, including *Analysis of Human Motion: A Textbook in Kinesiology* and *Research Methods Applied to Health, Physical Education, and Recreation.*

Scott raised St. Bernard puppies in her spare time and knew other area breeders, including one with standard poodles. She suggested that Jean get one of the poodle puppies to help her cope with having no family nearby and having a social life limited by teaching, studying, and doing basic life necessities. Jean happily accepted the recommendation and, in gratitude, named the puppy after the renowned educator.

Jean missed eating her familiar Cuban food, a blend of Spanish and Mediterranean flavors, like black beans and rice, with an emphasis on seafood. It was impossible to find anything similar in Iowa City. She longed for the bread from her grandfather's bakery in Ybor City. In the Midwest at the time, if Cuban food was like Spanish food, then Mexican food must be the same thing. Friends pointed out a newly opened Taco Bell restaurant. Admittedly, it fell short of Jean's standards.

Cold weather created other adjustments for the Florida native. Jean snuggled under the covers in the dark early one chilly November morning, hoping the house magically would warm up and delay the cold trudge across the freezing floor. Then, a series of phone calls broke the stillness. Graduate assistant friends screamed at her, even though she was still groggy and sleepy, to run outside because they knew that she had never seen snow. She leaped out of bed in her pajamas and flung herself into the white powder, catching the melting snowflakes on her tongue and laying on her back like a child while creating snow angels.

Grad School Classes

Those difficulties were minimal compared to her hardest personal challenge: dealing with Iowa's segregated men's and women's physical education departments. They were located on opposite sides of campus, separated by the Iowa River, and divided philosophically. The waterway seemed to be a line of demarcation between two departments with similar goals for physical fitness but very different approaches. Men's physical education and intercollegiate athletics at Iowa were under one umbrella. Women's PE and, by the early 1970s, women's intercollegiate athletics were under a separate one. The structural separation gave the women a strong sense of confidence in organization and independence in grading.

Men's physical education at Iowa utilized a standard and well-known A-to-F grading scale. Women's physical education applied a unique but confusing scoring system, with the department's goal being a perfect academic bell curve. Students were assigned grades as numbers from two to nineteen, low to high. At the semester's end, the teaching assistants stayed late into the night with Dr. Margaret Fox, the instructor in charge, to process grades with appropriate numbers of low, average, and high scores.

A lot of subjectivity determined the final individual outcome, with the graduate assistants estimating whether a student earned an eleven, twelve, or another score. The grad assistants were perplexed, explaining to the students what their scores meant under that unique and novel scoring system. Potential complaints were brushed aside. No questioning of the grading system was allowed because their degrees depended on complying with it, she said.

The academic split between men's and women's physical education frustrated Jean further when interests in math and science attracted her to a graduate-level biomechanics course taught by Dr. Louis Alley, a national leader in men's physical education. Jean sought to understand more in an innovative area that explored human movement and even considered pursuing a doctorate in the field. The women's physical education department initially denied her request to pursue coursework across the river in the men's physical education department.

After much discussion amid Jean's protests, the women's PE department allowed Jean to take the course since the biomechanics class was unavailable in their own course offerings. But they insisted that it would count only for elective credit beyond the degree requirements, not academic credit. She begrudgingly accepted the decision, sighing that "never the twain shall meet," realizing that Iowa diplomas specified its degrees as either men's or women's PE.

Jean completed her master's degree in 1969 and continued teaching as an instructor while interacting with Iowa's impressive cast of women's physical education leaders, nationally known and recognized for contributions to the University of Iowa and various organizations. They included Yvonne "Bonnie" Slatton, Peg Burke, Dr. Jeanette Scahill, Fox, and Scott.

Possibly the most influential to women's college sports would be fellow grad student Christine Grant, who completed her master's degree a year after Jean and gained her doctorate four years later. Grant's leadership skills led to a thirty-year tenure as Iowa's director of Intercollegiate Athletics for Women. Iowa's women's athletics program grew like many across the country through enthusiastic support by women's physical education leaders. Those physical education leaders backed an educational model for athletic competition that reflected deeply ingrained views that women's sports should be pure. They rejected the commercialized NCAA, which had expanded through corporate sponsorships, fan support, media interest, and television.

Seeking Equal Access

Spurred on by a national fervor for equal opportunity and battles against racial and gender discrimination, college women athletes, coaches, and instructors organized during the 1960s. The Commission on Intercollegiate Sports for Women was formed in 1966 and was renamed the Commission on Intercollegiate *Athletics* for Women (CIAW) the following year. What initially seemed like a simple name change indicated a bigger focus: expansion for women's athletics.

The national physical education organization supported the programs with a budget drawn from dues-paying individual memberships. That funding approach became problematic as women's college sports evolved and grew. The physical educators had a different goal than those who wanted women's competition to be unhampered by restrictions on athletic scholarships, recruiting, and more.

During that period, physical education leaders approached the NCAA about organizing women's college sports. To their dismay, the NCAA balked, asserting that it was a men's organization developed by men for men. Rebuffed, the women set to work organizing numerous women's postseason events. If sports had educational benefits for boys, and they did, then girls deserved equal access. A structure was needed.

Over the next few years, the women's association, the CIAW, developed championships in eight sports, beginning with swimming and diving, followed by basketball, gymnastics, softball, and outdoor track and field the next year. By the third year, badminton, golf, and volleyball championships were added. Some of the national competitions were held in conjunction with other organizations, like fastpitch softball's Women's College World Series, originally cosponsored by the Amateur Softball

Association in Omaha, Nebraska. Tournaments have been held for the last four decades in Oklahoma City, Oklahoma.

Additional developments reflected growing social and public acceptance. Over a period of three years, women's college basketball finally got the long-sought rules changes and had transformed from a three-on-three half-court game to allowing two rovers to cross the center line. Women's basketball graduated to a five-on-five full-court game in 1971.

Joan Cronan, longtime University of Tennessee women's athletic director and a legendary trailblazer, recalled those years when she taught physical education and coached women's basketball. The team was funded through the intramural budget and called a club sport. It played two games prior to her arrival. She vowed to change that and proclaimed that the team would play anyone within driving distance. A newspaper article about the new coach gave her a chance to laugh at herself years later for making the outrageous claim that someday women's basketball would get so big it was going to have a whole state college tournament.

Ordering team uniforms was one of her first tasks, and she researched what was available. Sitting at her desk in the basement of Alumni Gym, an older basketball facility at the University of Tennessee, she recalled the frustration.

"They weren't making many women's uniforms. I could get men's uniforms," she said but dismissed those as an option because of the fit and the deeper armholes on the jerseys. "And I could get white uniforms with Tennessee orange letters and numbers. But nobody was making Tennessee orange uniforms. I had to come up with another color that I thought looked good with orange and white."

Without a survey, without permission from a committee or boss, and without any hoopla, Cronan chose a Carolina blue to accent the orange and white. The alternate color for Tennessee's women's basketball uniforms has generally been attributed to legendary coach Pat Summitt's inability to order school colors, but it was Cronan who initially used it even before Pat arrived on campus. Today, it's called Summitt Blue in the Hall of Fame coach's honor.

"It's amazing to see the uniform choices we have today," said Cronan. "We've used the color constantly since 1968, and since Pat's death in 2016, we've really brought it back big time."

Cronan coached the team for two years, then moved to the College of Charleston. For three consecutive years, rule changes dictated her coaching strategies as the game moved from half-court to full-court. After a few years, Cronan became the women's athletic director and helped the school earn recognition as the top small-college women's athletic program in the country.

Entering the 1970s, women's intercollegiate sports beyond basketball also were on the rise. Golf notched the longest record for women's college championships. It held annual *individual* women's championships prior to World War II, but it wasn't until the spring of 1970 that the University of Miami won the first women's national intercollegiate *team* golf title. The development of a national association dedicated to organizing women's sports loomed on the horizon. Enthusiasts looked back proudly at the progress, with a growing track record of women wanting more competitive sports opportunities.

For years, physical education departments had organized intramural play, where students competed against other students on the same campus, courtesy of the Latin root word meaning *within the walls*. But enthusiasts embraced new verbiage: *extramural* competition, involving travel between institutions for sports competition

Jean Cerra blossomed amid the growth of women's intercollegiate sports in the late 1960s, particularly as Iowa Women's

Recreation Association members represented the school in extramural contests like field hockey, basketball, fencing, riflery, and golf, traveling to other schools and hosting tournaments on campus. Based on her own enjoyable experiences, Jean relished influencing and developing women's intercollegiate athletic competition.

"There were few professional women around who knew anything [about coaching] or had the necessary experience [in athletic administration]. In our generation, we weren't raised to aspire to those positions," she said, clarifying, "Those jobs for women didn't exist."

Graduate assistants like Jean were frequently assigned coaching duties, mostly volunteer positions, because of limited budgets. Sometimes, the grad assistants earned comp time— compensation via a reduction in the teaching load instead of financial remuneration. Fewer classes conceivably freed up time for coaching. PE majors were expected to teach everything in the course book.

"You were a jack-of-all-trades," said Jean. "You had to do everything: teach, coach, referee, be the groundskeeper. You lined the fields before your games. You did whatever you had to do. There *was* no help. There was no organized women's athletic program. You just filled in, and, hopefully, you had some competency."

Since Jean was from Florida, it was assumed that she knew how to play and, more importantly, teach golf skills. She was picked since she had played the most golf. Back then, Jean said, if you were a PE teacher, you were expected to coach whatever was assigned. Availability, not competency, was the most important quality.

"Not that I was very good," she said with a laugh. "When I started coaching golf, I soon realized I needed someone who knew a helluva lot more than I did." She reached out to the National Golf Foundation, which sent Ann Casey Johnstone to headline the women's clinics. Johnstone, the golf coach at all-women's Stephens College in Columbia, Missouri, was a renowned teaching professional who had been named the national coach of the year a few years prior. The clinic was a success, and Cerra and Johnstone bonded over golf.

Iowa's 1969 women's golf team had five experienced players who knew the game from organized high school competition. But they faced other challenges besides Jean's coaching inexperience, like being prevented from playing on the school's main course, known then as Upper Finkbine.

The club pro saw the women's team unloading golf bags, intending to practice on the university course. He ran out to the parking lot and asked what they were doing, so Jean introduced herself as the new women's golf coach and said they wanted to play a practice round. The golf pro replied no, sorry, women weren't allowed on that golf course. Instead, he suggested Lower Finkbine, a rougher course close to the railroad tracks and frequently flooded by the Iowa River. It was later redeveloped into a student recreation area.

The next year, they were able to practice at Upper Finkbine with help from one player's father, who happened to be in the state legislature.

"But only on Mondays when they were doing course maintenance," clarified Jean.

Today, the beautiful course is home to Iowa's men's and women's teams. Decades afterward, former Hawkeye basketball star Caitlin Clark had no problem getting tee times and marveled about using the course for cross-training purposes, practicing how to control mental and emotional responses to each shot, skills that she found useful in basketball.

A Childhood Friend Guides Growth at Purdue University

While Jean dealt with ongoing challenges in Iowa City, unbeknownst to her, childhood friend Genelle Fernandez Garverick, a grad student at Indiana's Purdue University, found herself as a recreation director beginning in 1969 in a department that oversaw women's extramural sports. Purdue funded its extramural program through student recreation fees under the management of men's physical education and athletics. Garverick said they had enough money for team travel in vans and buses, with mainly the physical education staff serving as coaches. They received small stipends from a recreation budget wholly independent of the women's physical education department.

Garverick speculated that early on, women's physical education leaders at Purdue recognized their budget would be unable to afford the expenses of extramurals, concluding there was more money available for women's sports under the recreation department. That administrative structure helped growth at Purdue, along with good fields and a newly built campus facility, the Co-Recreation Gym, that was available to women's extramurals.

"Purdue's administrative structure was very different from other places we used to visit," Garverick recalled. "We understood where they were coming from, but women's athletics were not going to be anything unless there was more money. It wasn't going to happen. It was a different ballgame for us than for schools limited to women's physical education budgets."

While running that fledgling women's sports program, Garverick attended a national organizational meeting in Estes Park, Colorado, that brought together women's college sports enthusiasts. Garverick noted passionate West Coast leaders from the University of Southern California and the University of

California, Los Angeles who would prove pivotal in expanding women's sports. Their approach differed from the Midwesterners.

"They expressed really strong support for women's extramurals, urging their colleagues to get going," said Garverick. "It was historical. Women involved in extramural sports from all over the country came together to talk about possibilities, about joining men and seeing what would happen." She also recalled that some schools at the conference thought collaborating with men's athletics would be their downfall and spoke against joining them. Garverick returned from that conference inspired about women's college sports and seeking to influence the many ongoing issues.

"I think many women really feared working with men, that we might be second-class citizens," Jean's childhood friend remarked. "The leaders from the California schools were really into it but the Midwest schools just were not."

Within a year, Garverick's experience and perspective would be lost when she left that position as her husband, Allen, accepted a professorship at the University of Missouri.

CHAPTER 5

Title IX Transforms College Sports

1972

THE FIGHT FOR women's college sports in the 1960s reflected battles across the country for racial and gender equality. Congress responded to the national debate and passed laws like the 1965 Civil Rights Act, guaranteeing minorities and underrepresented groups equal access to education and employment. Those guarantees were enhanced further by Title IX, the Patsy Mink Equal Opportunity in Education Act, signed into law by President Richard Nixon on June 23, 1972:

> No person in the United States shall, on the basis of sex, be excluded from participation in, be denied the benefits of, or be subjected to discrimination under any educational program or activity receiving Federal financial assistance.[3]

Title IX opened up admissions for women into law schools and medical schools and in business and engineering in ways that previously were nonexistent. Jean explained that there may have been a few token women pursuing those areas, unlike today, when a majority of candidates for medical degrees and law degrees are female.

The same month that President Nixon signed the Title IX legislation, the Commission on Intercollegiate Athletics for Women, which had been funded by dues-paying individual physical educators and had jump-started women's intercollegiate competition, transferred leadership for women's college sports to the Association for Intercollegiate Athletics for Women (AIAW). Dominated by a physical education philosophy, its approach to sports governance differed from the NCAA. Carole Oglesby, just beginning her career at the University of Massachusetts after being an assistant professor at Purdue, was elected as the organization's first president.

AIAW's formal constitution was approved by hundreds of cheering, exultant women at a November 1973 Delegate Assembly in Overland Park, Kansas. The all-women's association opposed athletic scholarships based on skill, off-campus recruiting, and enhanced benefits, like books, tutoring, room and board, and other perks, unless they were available to all students. AIAW delegate assemblies usually attracted only one female administrator and offered members only one competitive division that encompassed community colleges to huge, football-focused universities. Two opposing views of sports administration were set to clash throughout the 1970s.

Conflicts Arise Over Women's Athletic Scholarships

AIAW decided in its first months that institutions that gave athletic scholarships to women in any sports area would be ineligible for membership. Leaders felt that the policy exemplified educational values and enhanced AIAW's unique and noble vision of women determining the direction of their own college sports programs. However, the policy sparked criticism that it limited women's opportunities.

Decades before AIAW governance, corporations, businesses, and colleges sponsored basketball teams in the Amateur Athletic Union and recruited players with inducements ranging from educational scholarships to employment. The AAU had no limits on recruiting or scholarships. The Wayland Baptist Flying Queens from Texas flew to games all over the country and awarded basketball scholarships, along with other colleges like Nashville Business College, Iowa's Parsons College, Ouachita Baptist from Arkansas and John F. Kennedy College in Nebraska. The AIAW declared the programs ineligible for its championships and recommended that they compete in the AAU.

JFK College in Wahoo, Nebraska, with fewer than two hundred students, became a footnote to that history and ruling. The Patriettes softball squad played hundreds of games over the summers and traveled extensively from coast to coast. Buoyed by that advantage, the team won the first three Women's College World Series from 1969 to 1971. Although the JFK softball team reportedly refrained from offering athletic scholarships, the school was banned from AIAW competition, and the softball team was unable to defend its titles. The three-peat remained unequaled for fifty years until broken by the University of Oklahoma, which claimed four straight NCAA fastpitch titles starting in 2021.

Regulation was needed to ensure equitable and fair competition. AIAW's decision was initially to ban all athletic scholarships, recruiting, and enhanced benefits. But women leaders who thought that their athletes should receive all the same benefits that men had in order to grow women's college sports opposed it. Those leaders pointed to the Title IX legislation as a legal remedy.

Title IX Reshapes College Athletics

Linda Estes, the outspoken University of New Mexico women's athletic director in 1973, was among many in her generation unable to compete in interscholastic or intercollegiate sports because of the prevailing physical education philosophy of "play days," which emphasized social fun and not competition. When Title IX passed, she realized that the question of expanding women's athletics had become a legal one.

"I always loved sports. I always thought it was unfair that the boys had all these sports, but the girls didn't," Estes said. "However, I never thought about it in terms of it being *illegal* until Title IX was passed."

Estes recognized early in her career that there was a battle for *control* of women's sports. She pointed to personal involvement in a New Mexico court case that future Hall of Fame golf pro Nancy Lopez waged in 1972 during high school against the state athletic association. It had prevented her from playing on the high school *boys'* golf team even though her school had no girls' team. Lopez had won the US Girls Junior national championship during the summer and wanted to continue competing. She was represented by Roberta Ramo, a young lawyer with the American Civil Liberties Union. Estes was the only physical educator to publicly speak in court to support the lawsuit. Other physical educators feared that a countersuit would allow males to play on female teams.

Ramo, with Estes's encouragement, presented a novel application of Title IX: The lawsuit claimed that the New Mexico Activities Association discriminated against tax-paying parents who had daughters but no sons. Lopez and Ramo prevailed. Lopez played on the boys' team, winning two New Mexico high school boys' interscholastic state golf titles. The court case served notice nationally that Title IX was applicable to high school and college athletics.

Working closely with Ramo—who later became the first woman president of the American Bar Association—on the Lopez court case transformed Estes. She understood from the person she called "the smartest person I ever met" that discrimination against women's sports was foremost a legal issue. That approach to the application of Title IX was referenced later by advocates all over the country. But, Estes realized, there were no guarantees with Title IX. She summarized the ongoing national controversies during the 1970s as the implications of Title IX were hashed out.

"I naively thought there were guarantees and that when it passed, my problems were over. I'm not going to have to fight anybody. But Title IX didn't guarantee anything," Estes said. She equated the law with a fifty-five-mile-per-hour speed limit. "It doesn't matter unless somebody enforces it. We all realized that we had to see that Title IX was enforced. And that was a long, hard battle that is still going on."

A Firebrand Shakes Up the Status Quo

With the light bulb moment from that experience, Estes focused on other national issues, scrutinizing areas that were sexist, outmoded, or illegal. She questioned why an all-women organization like AIAW referred to the *chairman* of the committees more than thirty different times in an early handbook. Estes fired off a letter to AIAW leadership, excoriating the group for lacking more inclusive language, such as a chairperson or chairwoman. She also took issue with early regulations that required female chaperones for male-coached women's teams, denied subsidizing athlete recruiting, or set higher academic standards for women scholarship athletes. In that letter, Estes declared that AIAW promoted a philosophy that discriminated on the basis of sex. Estes denounced the group's declaration that no participant shall be allowed to attend an association national championship without supervision by a female chaperone.[4]

"They were just backward in terms of equality. To me, they weren't promoting women's sports; they were controlling it. They thought that they were the protectors and knew what was best."

The letter she sent to AIAW leadership described a University of New Mexico situation in which Estes had hired a male coach for the women's swim team. Estes said that the AIAW was adamant that any women's team with a male coach *had* to have a woman chaperone accompany them if they traveled.

"Even if I had unlimited funds, I have no intention of insulting that man's integrity by insisting that a woman accompany the team on trips," she wrote in that letter. "I object to the regulation because it is archaic, stupid and more importantly, *illegal.*"

Estes also critiqued early academic standards, particularly for scholarship athletes, which might force institutions to establish higher grade-point averages for female athletes than for male athletes. At her university, an attempt was made to set the required grade-point average for scholarship women athletes at 2.5. Estes closed her missive by blasting recruiting rules, which stated that institutions or representatives may not subsidize visits of prospective students or their families to the college campus. The firebrand pointed out that the visits of male athletes to college campuses were reimbursed and that coaches were allowed to visit the prospect's home.

"To prohibit the same benefits (whether you regard them as benefits or not) from being available to female athletes is *illegal,*" declared Estes in the fall of 1973. "Please bring the AIAW regulations into line with the law. I strongly recommend that the AIAW officers consult a lawyer regarding the legality of some of their regulations."[5]

In follow-up correspondence the next day, Estes wrote to Mary Rekstad, the lone AIAW executive, about the upcoming AIAW delegate assembly, the organization's first. Estes foresaw increased press coverage and demanded that the delegates "not waste time arguing over issues in which the law gives the final answer rather than the AIAW." She stressed that all AIAW regulations that result in discrimination based on sex should be eliminated.[6]

AIAW President-Elect Morrison wrote back following the delegate assembly and dismissed the descriptions for committee chairpersons as an oversight and differed with Estes over the direction of women's college sports, squashing Estes's legal emphases. To Morrison, the bigger issue seemed to be women's independence in developing women's college sports.

"Legality is certainly a factor but to opt for something just because a man has it negates my value as a self-determining female," Morrison wrote.[7]

Estes's feud with physical educators continued for years, and she joked that a physical education organization called the Division of Girls and Women in Sports stood for "Don't Give Women Sports." The AIAW didn't fare much better, with Estes laughing that it meant "Association for Interfering with Athletics for Women."

"When I first heard about the AIAW and when it first started, I thought it was a good idea," said Estes, still an advocate for women's equality today. Estes assailed AIAW as controlling and overprotective. "But I didn't know that they were going to be so reactionary. I still feel that way. Their attitudes held it back. They had this physical education attitude that had come down for years. They weren't going to change the perspective that they were the protectors; that they thought they knew what was best."

The Kellmeyer Lawsuit Advances Athletic Scholarships

Within the ranks of women's athletics were two divergent points of view: one held by many large Division I universities that said female athletes should have *all* the same opportunities as male athletes. The other promoted a kind of maternal protectionism and objected to a culture of scholarships, pressure, and an arms race for talent prevalent in men's intercollegiate athletics. The latter group demanded autonomy to develop women's sports in the way they saw fit.

Six months after AIAW's 1972 founding, the organization underestimated its members' fervency. Student activists wanted women to have the right to receive athletic scholarships and remain eligible for college championships. The association stubbornly clung to its beliefs that athletic scholarships were unwelcome and unnecessary. With the association unwilling to alter its stance, tennis players and coaches in South Florida sued the physical education organizations and presented their case. Empowered by the thirty-seven words of Title IX, fighting for equal opportunity under the law, the plaintiffs argued that institutions were denying females the same opportunities given to their male counterparts by forbidding athletic scholarships.

The lawsuit was named for Fern Lee "Peachy" Kellmeyer, a college tennis coach who would go on to work closely with Billie Jean King at the Women's Sports Foundation. After numerous meetings over several months, the AIAW, at the direction of the national physical education organizations, settled the Kellmeyer case, changed its policy, and removed discriminatory language from its bylaws. The new policy was put to a vote by AIAW members, who approved it overwhelmingly. The philosophical gap between the women in leadership and those at the grassroots level was exposed, as 80 percent of member institutions voted for women's athletic scholarships.

The 1973 Kellmeyer lawsuit never went to court, but the conflict illuminated upcoming philosophical battles as the AIAW was pried off its physical education pedestal. The court case reflected societal changes and foreshadowed the association's initial loss of power and control over women's intercollegiate athletics. It underscored that discrimination against women in sports came not only from the male-dominated society but also from female physical educators.

Linda Estes remained perturbed that the organization's news-letter inferred that the law had forced the change, not because it was the *right* thing to do for women. The association's media releases begrudgingly accepted the decision. Questions remained about how the athletic scholarships would be paid for, and AIAW leaders asked if the pursuit of athletic scholarships was simply out of envy for the men's programs rather than a legal issue.

"AIAW didn't want scholarships, I can tell you that. I felt women should have scholarships," said Jean Cerra, who admitted that she certainly was envious that those opportunities didn't exist for her and pointed out the legal necessity to comply with Title IX. "The physical education leaders were adamantly opposed. They were for Title IX in every way, except for scholarships."

Congress required that schools meet Title IX obligations by 1979. Ahead were even greater changes as the women leaders promoted sports opportunities for a younger generation of women. Imminent reorganization pitted the forces of big money and commercial sports colliding with AIAW's physical education ideals of woman-run and women-centered sports.

CHAPTER 6
No Guarantees

1971–1976

JEAN CERRA WAS teaching activity classes and coaching Iowa's golf team when she received an invitation from Ann Casey Johnstone to visit Stephens College in Columbia, Missouri. On the day Jean arrived, Johnstone quickly greeted her at the college's golf course. Physical education department chair Dorothy "Dottie" Jones was preparing to tee off, and Johnstone wanted Cerra to join her in a round of golf. By the eighth hole, Jones was so impressed that she offered Jean a future teaching position at Stephens.

"Plus," recalled Cerra years later with a laugh, "she said Stephens needed a volleyball coach and there wasn't anyone else on the faculty who could do it."

Hired in 1971 as the coordinator of Physical Education at Stephens College after that fortuitous golf course meeting, Cerra taught classes that she loved, developed a physical education curriculum, and coached volleyball. Teaching courses like kinesiology and physiology of exercise brought her more professional satisfaction than the activity classes at Iowa.

The school gym where she coached was antiquated. Located on the second floor behind a theater, the little box was accessed through a dedicated staircase. Court lines hugged the walls, leaving no room for spectators. The gym was an afterthought located behind the stage, in reality, a much more prominent venue that showcased Stephens's theater, music, and fashion programs. The college also wanted to expand student enrollment through developing a physical education major program under Cerra's leadership. Having the talents of a woman like Jean Cerra to build its athletic program was a bonus.

"You didn't get extra money to coach. You had a full teaching load and were expected to coach," she explained, noting that private schools prioritized faculty spending personal time with students and contracts stipulated that half of the professors' responsibilities were advising. Her demanding schedule left little time for those required duties, but somehow she managed.

Her $12,000 annual salary seemed like a lot at age twenty-five after spending four years as a grad assistant and instructor. Teaching PE majors' classes while in her mid-twenties boosted her career to a level typically unavailable to those without a doctorate. Johnstone watched out for her and mentored Jean's career development. After winning six Iowa Women's Amateur Golf titles, Johnstone had turned professional and won enough prize money to put her husband through pharmacy school. Les Johnstone was a pharmacist at the Missouri Medical Center, and the couple were pillars in the Columbia community.

Cerra's career blossomed at the historic women's college, organized in 1833 as Columbia Female Academy. It was the oldest women's college west of the Mississippi River, founded only twelve years after Missouri became a state and six years before the University of Missouri enrolled students.

Like many young adults, Jean was focused on career-building when hired at Stephens and was excited to learn from new colleagues about the benefit package. However, when she went to apply, the personnel department informed her that she was too young to be included in the retirement plan; there were restrictions on contributions until a staff member reached age thirty.

While at Stephens, Cerra refined officiating skills for volleyball and basketball, previously developed as a grad assistant at Iowa. Most schools had no budget to pay anyone in those early years of women's college sports. The women's coaches sometimes slipped her ten bucks for expenses, hardly enough to pay for gasoline or meals. There were bigger personal benefits beyond the pay, however, like learning to react quickly and decisively, administering justice while striving for fair play, and staying neutral. Years later, those refereeing skills aided the development of her administrative abilities, according to those who worked closely with her.

"I felt I had a level head. When you're an official, you just react. I never thought about whether I was making the call on the white team or the blue team, for or against one team or another," she reflected. "Officiating taught me to try to do what's right and stick to that decision. I learned to take charge of something in a very fair manner."

Cerra defended referees as simply reacting to what they see, baffled that some people think referees are biased. She said she loved managing games, making the calls, and observing players' self-control or lack thereof. Respectful players mirror the team environment and coach's philosophy, she said, adding that coaches want the responsibility for engaging with the officials, with their student-athletes reflecting positively on the program.

Teaching at Stephens During the Early 1970s

Jean's course load included some activity classes, like archery and golf, but the most meaningful were the classes where prospective teachers learned teaching methods. One particularly tough class was a 7:30 a.m. kinesiology class that emphasized memorizing reams of scientific information about muscle origins and insertions. The students needed to commit to rigorous daily progress with an unfamiliar Latin-based vocabulary. In order to be prepared, she set her alarm clock for two or three hours earlier than usual on those mornings. To instill that necessary academic discipline, Jean announced on the opening day that each class would start with a ten-point quiz. The quizzes were easy from her perspective, building on what she had taught in the preceding class.

"Just very simple, spit it back to me," she chuckled. "I needed them to keep up with me, because they were going to get more complex information the next day."

The first day of the quizzes, only two or three students reached class on time. Most strolled in ten or fifteen minutes late. By the time some of them arrived, the quiz was over, and those students got zeros. Cerra's class had high standards. Her teaching methods required students to correctly spell complex terms. If the students misspelled the names of the muscles, for instance, she marked the answer wrong. To her, it was black and white, like correctly spelling a person's name; if misspelled, then it wasn't their name.

"After the third or fourth class, I'd walk in at seven thirty, and they were all seated at their desks, quizzing each other," she said, praising the students for earning perfect tens, mirroring those high standards. "That's the way it is with people: If you set the bar high, people meet it. And if you set it low enough, they'll meet that, too. My job was to give them something for their money. They were paying expensive tuition, so they better leave there with a good education."

Longtime Southern Illinois University-Carbondale golf coach Diane Daugherty was one of those Stephens College students and vividly recalls Cerra's classes. She competed on Stephens's nationally ranked golf teams in the mid-1970s before becoming a top-ten money winner on the Ladies Professional Golf Association Futures Tour. When knee issues sidelined that dream, she pursued coaching, her success earning her a 2016 induction into the Salukis Hall of Fame.

"That's the kind of teacher you want," Daugherty professed. "Forty-some odd years later, I'm pretty proud that I can remember all the bones and most of the muscle insertions and origins." Cerra's kinesiology course was the hardest college class she ever took, she said, adding with a laugh that she still could name all 206 bones because of her.

"She taught that class like we were going to be brain surgeons. Because of that I can trace a drop of blood through all the arteries and veins to the big toe and back. That was our final. She was fair, but demanding. You knew you'd better come prepared or it might be embarrassing."

Daugherty enrolled at Stephens with encouragement from golf coach Ann Casey Johnstone, who awarded her a $500 scholarship. Daugherty qualified for the collegiate individual national championships her freshman year and helped Stephens's golfers to a top-ten national ranking the next three years.

"We didn't have a men's team to compare ourselves to," Daugherty remarked, noting obvious travel and budget disparities between men's and women's programs that were prevalent at the time. "At some schools the men might be flying everywhere and staying at the Hilton. We thought we were high rollers back in the day, and yet it's nothing like it is today. We were staying four to a room at the Motel 6 and eating fast food."

AIAW Develops Women's College Sports

For the most part, Cerra and other coaches worked with whomever showed up through open tryouts advertised on campus fliers. AIAW rules reflected physical education standards and forbade staff from being reimbursed for off-campus recruiting and home visits, while student-athletes had to pay their own way to see potential campuses. But because of Title IX, those rules began to be questioned by some of the female leadership, including Jean.

"I felt like I was on the cutting edge of what was happening in women's sports, for the betterment of young athletes," Cerra asserted. Steering that influence and development during such a transitional period gave her the confidence that she could accomplish anything she wanted, and she built networks with AIAW colleagues while leading committees, doing seminars on Title IX, coaching, and officiating. She was seen as level-headed and thoughtful.

"She was very effective," said fellow trailblazer Linda Estes of New Mexico. "She worked in a very clever way, she worked smart, she worked quietly."

AIAW conducted postseason playoffs via state, regional, and national tournaments. Schools paid all their own expenses to attend championships, unlike the better-funded NCAA.

"In those early AIAW years, winning reflected the quality of your athletes and the individual who was coaching," noted Cerra. "You didn't have scholarship kids. You weren't recruiting.

Whoever you got, it was the luck of the draw. So, you had to build a team with whatever talent you had. Good coaching was the dominant factor for winning teams."

Undoubtedly, there were no blueprints or roadmaps. Communication was challenging, and often women were unable to meet counterparts in similar roles throughout the country unless they served together on national committees. AIAW regional and national meetings provided networking opportunities. Smaller schools like Stephens and state teachers' colleges like Southwest Missouri State, now known as Missouri State University, in Springfield, Missouri, had significant early advantages in women's college sports because strong leadership in physical education departments attracted the best athletes, who enrolled to pursue physical education degrees.

In Missouri, the strongest developing programs were the former teacher training institutions: Southwest Missouri State University, Central Missouri State University (now called the University of Central Missouri), Northwest Missouri State, Northeast Missouri State (now Truman State), and Southeast Missouri State. All AIAW member schools, including Stephens, competed in one general division for the first few years until small schools like Stephens College formed their own division.

"SMS (Missouri State) had the best athletes, because they had the biggest physical education program in the state," recalled Debbie Duren, a 1973 Missouri State graduate, about her alma mater's early dominance. Duren coached a pair of Mizzou teams, beginning with volleyball before adding softball and recalled tremendous rivalries with Southwest Missouri. "The teachers and athletes were dedicated, drawing a lot of good people who had both motivation and ability and were interested in athletics. They were going to be the future coaches who pursued physical education. Because of that they often would have better teams."

Duren joked that Cerra's Stephens team and the University of Missouri regularly were left to battle for second place. As a physical education student in Springfield, Duren learned field hockey in a class. Soon, she was on the school team.

"Everybody played field hockey. They always needed women athletes to compete against other schools. If a coach didn't have enough players on a Saturday, she'd make a few phone calls and fill out her roster.

"A lot of people ask me if there are official records of who played [then] on the teams, and there aren't. We really weren't too worried about qualifications or if someone was making grades," noted Duren, who pointed out that participation was based on trust when she was in college, with little if any rules enforcement since no one had scholarships. "We were trying to give all our female athletes a chance to play."

AIAW's Foundation and Philosophy

AIAW's 1972 official inception coincided with one of the most remarkable legislative endeavors in US history: Title IX. AIAW evolved under two professional physical education organizations, which managed the association's finances, approved policies, and contributed office space, personnel, and supplies. Both were nonprofit 501(c)3 organizations. Nothing was allowed to impact that status, according to the 1974 AIAW Handbook of Policies and Operating Procedures. The larger physical education umbrella group was the American Association for Health, Physical Education, and Recreation (AAPHER), and its subsidiary was the Division for Girls and Women's Sports (DGWS).

AIAW's Washington, DC, offices anchored its very existence to the development of Title IX, with codes of ethics for coaches, players, administrators, officials, and spectators. The physical educators criticized the excesses in men's sports, which they perceived as emphasizing winning at all costs. AIAW instead promoted what it termed a student-centered approach that balanced travel and competition and claimed that its disapproval of athletic scholarships protected the ongoing development of women's athletics. AIAW leaders debated how athletics programs related to the educational functioning of institutions and stressed that men's athletics should consider AIAW's values-driven concepts, limited athletic scholarships, and recruiting.

Carole Oglesby had a pivotal role in AIAW's expansion, first serving as Commissioner of Championships for the Commission on Intercollegiate Athletics for Women (CIAW), which provided AIAW's foundation, then was elected as AIAW's first president. Her physical education mentors were adamant about the foundational philosophical differences between the early women's organizations and the NCAA. One mentor insisted that she follow physical education doctrine and agree with her that the women's organization would never provide athletic scholarships. Instead, the physical educators wanted what they called programmatic funding tied to educational values, with equal funding with men's programs and provided because of its educational basis, not individual awards through ability-based athletic scholarships.

"We loved scholarships on the basis of other things; just not on the basis of athletic ability," Oglesby recalled.

Her duties included planning the momentous inaugural 1973 AIAW Delegate Assembly in Kansas City, where women from all parts of the country eagerly gathered to promote women's intercollegiate sports. Oglesby wrote the AIAW constitution, which she proudly claimed had enshrined the physical education philosophy. She acknowledged the influence of previous generations of physical educators who rejected any and all development of women's intercollegiate competition, but this new organization, the AIAW, would attempt to thread that needle and institute women's competitive sports with a physical education emphasis.

"We were trying to prove to all of the naysayers, including women who were strong leaders in physical education, that we were able to create an organization that enshrined the philosophy that they supposedly believed in, taking it to the elite [competitive] level. Everybody was incredibly proud, so proud. Everybody who attended was in favor," Oglesby recalled. She described AIAW's first delegate assembly as a raucous and enthusiastic all-women's gathering.

Despite no direct reference to athletic competition in the original thirty-seven words of Title IX, its mandates were applied to athletics since most institutions of higher learning received some sort of federal financial aid. The bumpy road full of legal potholes forced AIAW into defending against numerous Title IX lawsuits, including NCAA attempts to exclude its revenue-producing sports, mainly football and men's basketball, from the law's reach. Increasingly, AIAW resented the NCAA for its multiple attempts to water down Title IX and override women's control. Sharon Taylor, a longtime coach and athletic director at Lock Haven University in central Pennsylvania, recalled the heady times.

"Many of us, especially in the East, saw that the NCAA had shut the door to women's sports. We started this organization that was almost impossible to believe could have even gotten off the ground. We built something great." She and others wanted their own women-centered organization, fearing that they would be an afterthought in a male-dominated system that had opposed Title IX. She pointed out that growing interest in women's sports by the end of the 1970s had attracted some significant new revenues. She wondered if that made it a potential takeover target for the powerful NCAA.

Lock Haven, one of many smaller colleges within a day's drive of AIAW's Washington, DC, headquarters, enthusiastically embraced the joint AIAW and physical education philosophy. Campus general funds, which included student fees, budgeted line items, and limited fundraising, typically supported competitive athletics at the smaller schools. That arrangement contrasted with the huge dollar amounts available at the much bigger, football-oriented universities further west. By 1977, women's athletic scholarships allowed tuition, fees, room, and board while male scholarship athletes received those benefits and more, including books, gifts, allowances, per diem expenses, recruiting costs, laundry, and tutoring services. The larger universities were concerned with Title IX mandates and agonized over how to reach compliance if women athletes were unable to receive all the same benefits as male athletes. AIAW's one-size-fits-all method of governance seemed to set up the larger schools to fail in their efforts to comply with Title IX.

AIAW charged each institution a $150 membership fee to fund the national office, run championships, and pay any legal expenses necessary to sustain the organization. The organization had limited sources of revenue other than institutional dues because of its status as a nonprofit.

AIAW intended to nurture women's sports through the guidance of professional physical educators, stressing each individual's well-being and enrichment through participation. The organization's belief was that each participant's experience should be equal, without regard to the size of the school or its budget, the popularity of the sport, the competitive division, or if an athletic scholarship was involved. Inclusiveness and fairness were to be balanced with the academic mission of the institution. AIAW criticized most athletic department budgets as out of control, excessive, and unsustainable and, therefore, should be limited.

University of Missouri Funds A 1973–74 Pilot Program

Meanwhile, three blocks down College Avenue from Stephens College, University of Missouri Chancellor Herbert Schooling championed women's sports and recognized the legal and political implications of Title IX. After meeting with advocates from the women's golf team in the fall of 1973 and with a two-year $60,000 allotment from the state legislature, he awarded $15,000 for the first year to support travel, coaching, and competition in eight sports overseen by the women's physical education department. The pilot program sought to answer a key Title IX question: Did college women at Missouri and other institutions want more sports opportunities?

Clearly, the answer was yes. Women, unaware at the time that the administration considered their teams an experiment, responded. Athletes tried out for and competed on eight teams: volleyball, golf, field hockey, swimming, basketball, track and field, softball, and tennis. Regarded at first as extramurals, the pioneering program was directed by Dr. Marilyn Markel, with support from early coaches like Laverne Wade, who also served as the AIAW voting representatiave, Marilee Howell, Ellen Scheer, and Diane Lyon. That fall, Wade's volleyball team qualified for the Region VI tournament in Minnesota.

Freshman Lisa Borcherding Housson recalled that the team flew there on a puddle jumper plane from Columbia to St. Louis, then to Des Moines and into Minneapolis-St. Paul. Housson's first-ever plane flight was memorable, with frothy turbulence magnified even more by the team's seat assignments in the back of the plane. While it was the first time the university had paid for women to fly to a competition, there was another hiccup: The women had to buy their own uniforms since funding came through in the middle of the season. Unfortunately, the local sporting goods store didn't stock enough of Mizzou's traditional black and gold school colors.

"They were actually red, white and blue," Housson scoffed. She was frustrated that the school could purchase airline tickets but not team jerseys. "We weren't exactly fully funded, because the entire team couldn't go." Eight players made the travel team as Missouri finished fifth. Housson recalled a black-and-white photo in the local newspaper that showed the team practicing in those uniforms inside old McKee Gym, sometimes called the Women's Gym.

The 1974–75 women's athletics budget swelled to $45,000 under Dr. Marilyn Markel, the women's physical education department chair. With that budget, Missouri hired women's coaches from outside the physical education department for the first time, including Duren, a Columbia native who replaced Wade in volleyball. The recent college graduate and Wade played summer fastpitch softball together, and Duren laughed about a seemingly meager salary offer, knowing she had family resources nearby, including her father's big summer vegetable garden.

"Laverne Wade told me I should apply for the volleyball coaching job at Mizzou. I'd get paid $2,000. I wasn't concerned about the pay because I was married and had someone who could put bread on the table."

A hiring committee that included the head of women's physical education and designated women's athletic director, Dr. Marilyn Markel, also selected Alexis Jarrett to coach three sports—basketball, softball, and track and field—oversee sports information for all eight sports and serve as women's assistant athletic director. All of these jobs were combined for a $7,500 salary.

Jarrett had been teaching in Esko, Minnesota, after graduating from the University of Minnesota-Duluth, also the alma mater of former Mizzou football coach Dan Devine. Jarrett had attended a 1969 Missouri-Air Force Academy football game in Columbia during the fall of her senior year and pitched a story to the school newspaper about Coach Devine, his connection to UM-D and his success as a top-level coach. With the story approved, Jarrett called Missouri's athletic department. Surprisingly, Devine answered the phone. The "local-boy-makes-good" interviews became a prominent two-part series for the *UMD Statesman*. That season, the football Tigers went 9–1, won the Big 8 Conference title, and earned an Orange Bowl berth against Penn State. The connection proved pivotal when Jarrett later applied for Missouri's women's coaching and administrative positions.

Jarrett's sister-in-law, who worked in public relations for the University of Missouri Medical Center, had submitted Jarrett's name without her knowledge. Her background skill set seemed like a good match for the job description. It included teaching a variety of subjects (journalism, geography, English, and physical education), coaching cheerleaders and band majorettes, and officiating and organizing girls' volleyball, basketball, and track competitions in church and community leagues.

Bob G. Woods, the dean of the College of Education, was on that 1974 search committee and contemplated Jarrett's background. The two-part story on Devine caught his attention, and he asked Jarrett if she thought Coach Devine would remember her from the article written five years before. With a nod of her head, she answered that she thought he would. Woods excused himself from the interview and phoned the Hall of Fame coach, who by then was the head coach and general manager of the National Football League's Green Bay Packers. When Devine endorsed Jarrett, Woods returned to the interview room, and after additional discussion, the committee offered her the job.

Jarrett grappled with accepting the offer, which had packed numerous responsibilities into one position in order to justify a full-time salary. She wanted clarification about the numerous roles. The committee emphasized that the job included all of the titles listed: assistant athletic director, sports information director for women, and basketball, softball, and track coach. The journalism element was crucial to the program. None of the women on the physical education staff were interested. After all, they had tenure without the pressures of starting and developing a program from scratch. Jarrett returned to Esko to ponder the job offer.

Jarrett leaned toward saying no, as her friends and university professors warned her that the job was impossible. But many women at the time took on similar roles, coaching numerous sports while teaching and running intramurals.

As she was nearing the deadline to give Missouri an answer, she received a phone call from Devine. A trusted teaching colleague of hers at Esko High School recognized her ability to multi-task and said the Missouri position was perfect for those skills. That colleague, Coopen Johnson, was also one of Devine's closest friends and had mentioned to him about Jarrett's reticence to take the position. Perhaps a phone call from Devine would be beneficial. It was.

Devine recognized the difficult job description and advised her to take the position in a new women's athletic program. That statement made an impact on Jarrett. She agreed to Missouri's offer starting in mid-August.

"It's pretty hard to turn down Dan Devine," Jarrett reckoned, awed at the endorsement even though they had never met in person and had spoken only by phone. Jarrett's office was a cubbyhole in McKee Gym with two desks for herself and a secretary, a file cabinet, a storage cabinet, and a single phone line for the seven coaches. There was a lot of work to do assisting Dr. Markel, including preparations to host the AIAW Region VI volleyball tournament in November.

Schools fulfilled hosting obligations despite sometimes having inadequate facilities as championships in all sports rotated throughout a seven-state area. The participating schools adjusted and worked with what was available because everyone faced the same challenges. Unfortunately, the volleyball matches couldn't be played inside the cavernous Hearnes Arena, recently opened as the home of Mizzou basketball, because there were no receivers for volleyball standards on the arena's rubberized tartan court. It was impossible to install them that quickly without potentially damaging the gray molded rubber floor. The design for the building had incorporated zero accommodations for women's sports or women's teams. Later, Jean Cerra would have to do extensive research to convince men's basketball coach Norm Stewart and the facility manager that installing the metal plates would have no adverse effect on basketball.

"You knew there were going to be some challenges, but you just worked through them," observed volleyball coach Debbie Duren, with a nod to the enthusiasm developing around women's championships. "We thought it was a great thing for all teams to come together in one common space and play in the mid-1970s. It was novel."

The Hearnes Fieldhouse was the only facility option for the Tigers. McKee Gym was too small, with a floor warped from its location above a swimming pool. Brewer Fieldhouse, home of Mizzou men's basketball beginning in the 1920s, had been reconfigured as an intramural and recreational facility. There was a small practice court on the fourth floor above the Hearnes Arena, but it had no available spectator seating.

Instead of competing on the Hearnes Arena floor, teams played on green artificial turf in the Hearnes Fieldhouse, with coaches fearing that their players would get rug burns. Organizers set up side-by-side courts on the rough green carpet and hung protective netting from the ceiling to separate them. Court lines were taped down. There were no women's locker rooms available. Spectator bleachers were an afterthought. Athletes and runners who jogged on the indoor all-weather track encircling the playing site added to the circus-like atmosphere.

At those regional championships, Mizzou hosted future Big Eight Conference foes like Nebraska, Kansas, and Iowa State, as well as Minnesota, Southwest Missouri State, and St. Louis University, plus a trio of small school competitors like Fort Hays (Kansas) State, Augsburg (Minnesota) and St. Cloud (Minnesota). Teams played a best-of-three format to fifteen points, with timed matches and only the serving team able to score, a two-point margin required to win. Today's college teams play under rules that challenge athletic skills, with the best of five sets to twenty-five points and the fifth set shortened to fifteen. Every serve determines a point.

Duren coached Missouri volleyball for six seasons, and by 1978, the team achieved school records that still stand today, including single-season matches played (58) and wins (37). She also coached softball for four seasons.

Stephens College Volleyball

Stephens, with a top peak enrollment approaching two thousand women, initially battled more or less equally with powerhouse schools like Southwest Missouri and the University of Missouri. Cerra, in her third year there, conducted volleyball team tryouts. She found a gem of a player when an athletic California beach girl named Dana Caston Moore strode confidently onto the court.

Jean described how college volleyball was transitioning from earlier rules where players received the ball by almost lifting it with open hands before passing it overhanded to a teammate. Players were allowed two consecutive hits. Jean called that version, which she had learned in Ybor City's recreation leagues, "slap-handed volleyball." Aspiring female athletes like Moore approached the game differently in a power game, passing the received serve or spike attempt by contacting it on the forearms, known today as "bumping" the ball.

Moore played club volleyball for former national team coach Pat Zartman and the Manhattan Beach Trojans. A powerhouse in United States Volleyball Association circles, the club won a national title a few years later behind Flo Hyman and Elaina Roque, two of volleyball's all-time greats.

"When you grew up in the 1960s in Manhattan Beach, all you did was play volleyball on the beach and ride bikes on the Strand," Moore observed. "I had some amazing opportunities that girls didn't have in other parts of the country."

Moore saw a brochure during her senior year touting Stephens College and was intrigued. She knew she wanted to get away from home and thought she would end up at a California university. She longed to see the Stephens campus, enticed by the pamphlet's pictures of the luscious ivy-covered red-brick buildings, and without money for a plane ticket, agreed to keep stats for an older club volleyball team in exchange for a lift to St. Louis. The last leg of her self-financed "recruiting trip" was a solo bus ride to Columbia with a short walk to campus. Undeterred by the complicated itinerary from Southern California to Texas and the Midwest cemented her desire to attend Stephens. Moore felt at home immediately.

Convincing her parents to fork over private school tuition was problematic but possible with family savings. Moore described herself as a typical first-generation college student without good study skills, more than ready for new college experiences and unsure about continuing to play volleyball after training fervently for six years. Her mom insisted that she throw her knee pads and gym shoes into her luggage despite her reluctance. She agreed while doubting that they would be needed. Like it so often happens, mothers know best. Unexpectedly, her passion for the game was reawakened, and that August, even though she was ambivalent about trying out for the Stephens volleyball team, Moore nevertheless showed up and found that she liked the players. However, their skill levels needed some work.

"I remember thinking I was better than everybody there," Moore said cautiously, realizing that those competitive club experiences prepared her for team leadership. "I brought that level of experience that other kids didn't have because I was used to seeing the Olympic tryouts and top-level competition," Moore said. "I loved the game. I was loud when I played. I was always a natural leader so I was able to bring that group of women together on the court."

After the tryouts concluded, Jean posted the team roster on a sheet of brightly colored cardstock. Moore's memories of that remain fresh today and include the attractiveness of Cerra's handwriting. It made an impression.

"She had the coolest handwriting ever and I loved it, especially how she wrote the letter 'G' for G. Jean Cerra," she said and laughed, the letter *G* an initial for Cerra's first name, Gloria. Moore responded less positively to the team uniforms, which were disappointing to the California athlete who was used to first-class apparel on her club team.

The first year, they had to provide their own uniforms: horrible white shorts, navy and white tops, shoes, and knee pads. The next year, the team inherited all-purpose polyester sleeveless jerseys from the basketball team. Moore was aghast. Wearing basketball-style uniforms frustrated the players so much that they added long-sleeved turtleneck shirts underneath despite some discomfort.

"Basketball uniforms were unacceptable," declared Moore, resolute about creating a particular volleyball style. "And in Missouri, it was hotter than hell in the fall."

Moore's leadership extended beyond the court, where she was voted team captain all four years, to student government, where, as a senior, she served as president. She and Stephens's classmates marched and carried signs at Missouri's state capitol in Jefferson City to support the Equal Rights Amendment. Protestors screamed at her that if the Equal Rights Amendment passed, pregnant women would be serving on the combat lines. Ultimately, the amendment fell three states short of ratification. Moore would go on to a successful career in college coaching and administration, moving to Duluth, Minnesota, with her husband Jim, and is now semi-retired from College of St. Scholastica.

"Being at Stephens shaped so much of how I felt about the world and how women should be treated. Our professors urged us to be vocal and to believe in ourselves. I think we would win volleyball games on Jean Cerra's knowledge. For all I know, she wrote the rule book," Moore laughed, "because she knew it inside and out, all the technicalities." Sometimes, that meant pointing out particular rules to referees, with resulting decisions in Stephens's favor.

Moore called her coach a taskmaster with great attention to detail, always willing to learn and modify her teaching and coaching. Sometimes, that necessitated recruiting club volleyball guys from Mizzou, like Mike English and Phil Shoemaker, to scrimmage the team. Cerra remained impressed by those young men and later, when she was at the University of Missouri, hired English as head volleyball coach and Shoemaker as an assistant. Both would go on to successful coaching careers in college volleyball.

But it was Moore who most influenced Cerra's coaching, as Jean worked to learn the power game and hone her coaching instincts, analyzing what was needed, motivating the team, and adjusting strategies. Stephens became a small-college regional volleyball powerhouse, finishing as runners-up in the Missouri small-college state championships before winning the small-college state title twice in the early seventies.

"Jean was such a pioneer while getting us to understand that we were a clean slate because we hadn't experienced much. It was hard for their generation to balance work and family. Those women who were mostly single put their whole lives into making it better for women coming after them. She would have done whatever it took for any of us. Jean became a champion for us. She advocated for the things we wanted, like the uniforms," Moore reflected. "Later I realized how instrumental she was in women's athletics. I'm grateful that the physical education department set the precedent that we can stand up for and believe in ourselves."

Cerra taught and coached at Stephens on a series of probationary contracts before attaining tenure, which provided protections for professors' academic freedom and guarded individuals from unfair dismissal. Instructors applied during their fifth year through a lengthy and detailed review process, which Cerra passed. Her future looked secure and bright at age thirty-one with tenure and finally qualifying for the school retirement plan.

Career Growth Means No Guarantees

By spring 1976, Missouri Chancellor Dr. Herbert Schooling wanted the men's and women's athletic departments combined into one department of intercollegiate athletics, with both housed in the primary athletics administration building, the newly built Hearnes Multipurpose Center. The search was on to locate qualified candidates for a director of women's athletics. Jean thought she was ready. She had gotten to know Dr. Schooling when she was the chair of a Stephens faculty committee that sought his advice on a faculty unionization issue.

"I could see that women's sports were emerging," she recalled. "I felt that I could do that job or I wouldn't have applied. It was a risk at the time because I was giving up my security of tenure."

Again, she turned to trusted friend and adviser Ann Casey Johnstone at Stephens and disclosed her desire to apply for the Missouri job. Ann was dismayed at potentially losing Cerra to the much larger institution and encouraged Cerra to remain at Stephens. Unperturbed, Jean pressed on, knowing the potential for professional growth was substantial. Cerra wanted more information about the position and if there was a preferred candidate. She asked if Ann knew Missouri Director of Athletics Mel Sheehan. Ann replied, yes, they were both members of the same country club.

"I didn't know anything about him, but I realized there weren't very many women who had any kind of collegiate administrative experience," Cerra said. "So, I asked Ann to see what he thought about the opening."

Johnstone talked to Sheehan, who inferred that he had somebody in mind but nevertheless encouraged Jean to apply. Jean figured that she didn't have anything to lose. She was respected at Stephens but hoped for increased pay. Cerra believed it was a good job to advance her career and was interviewed. A few weeks later, in May, she got the unexpected news.

"I was surprised when I got the job. When Mel Sheehan called me, I mentioned to him that I thought he had someone in mind. He told me that he did," Cerra said, perplexed that she had received the job offer. "He told me that he liked the way I answered one question."

And what was that question, she asked. He replied that it was the tenure question. Cerra carefully explained the dialogue.

"He asked me why would I want to leave a job where I had tenure and job security, for one where I was going to be on an annual contract, one year with no guarantees. It was a performance-based contract with no guarantees of renewal and he said that I was going to be disliked from the time I walked into the administrative building.

"My answer to him was that if I need tenure to keep a job, I shouldn't have it," she recounted with a laugh, adding, "And if I'm good, I don't need tenure."

Cerra offered the story years later when she spoke at a University of Missouri dinner in the fall of 2022 that commemorated the fiftieth anniversary of the historic Title IX legislation. At that Celebration for Women's Sports, she recalled Sheehan's description of her hiring in much stronger words, emphasizing that if she took the job, she would be the most hated person in the department.

"It was more like the sense of being unpopular, or something to that effect," she elaborated, refusing to take it personally. "They were just against the women transitioning into the men's athletic department and draining all the money. The NCAA and all the men's programs were fighting Title IX; they were suing so that Title IX would not apply to them."

Although teaching colleagues at Stephens or in Missouri's physical education department might have wanted her to push for the security of tenure, Cerra envisioned a different future for women's sports, one that reached beyond its physical education roots.

"I didn't have that much interaction with the women's PE department once I went to Mizzou," she admitted. "I knew them all. But it wasn't like I had to enlist their help or involve them with the things that I had to do in the athletic department."

For the physical education staff, women's sports were evolving quickly. Perhaps too quickly, Cerra speculated. In some aspects, the women's physical education staff seemed relieved to delegate the competitive aspects of women's sports because most held a much different philosophy. In so many other ways, the tiger that would become women's college athletics was unleashed.

"[Athletic Director] Mel [Sheehan] was being honest with me when he said I was going to face pressures in the department. He was saying that I was going to have resistance. It wasn't going to be a cake walk," she acknowledged. "I knew that. I'm a realist. I understood that they disliked what I represented. There were no guarantees."

Cerra described intercollegiate athletics at the time as a men's club where women were unwelcome. The change was shocking to men because athletics previously were a male bastion. With no hesitation toward Sheehan's assessment that she would be disliked, Jean got to work. A few years later, after she had gotten to know Sheehan better, she graciously portrayed him as an educator at heart, influenced by his background as a St. Louis-area superintendent of schools. This set him apart from many other athletic directors at the time, former big-name coaches who frequently were offered administrative positions when they left the sidelines.

Cerra balanced the concerns of both women's athletics and nonrevenue men's sports with patience and steady leadership. That meant supporting all college athletes while turning critics into allies. That perspective was foremost as she entered the challenges of athletic administration at a large university in the 1970s.

CHAPTER 7
The Tiger Awakens

1960s, 1976–1977

DAYS BEFORE THE public announcement of Jean's hiring, *Columbia Daily Tribune* sports writer Greg Haney expressed both hopes and concerns regarding women's athletics in the Sunday edition. An early May 1976 headline blared *Women's Sports: How far will dollars go?* A week after the article appeared, Missouri announced its choice of the Stephens College coach and educator to lead its women's athletic programs. Jean moved to her new position across town on June 1. Local newspapers gave it little fanfare beyond a few column inches. Along with Jean's pay raise to $30,000 came more pressures and an avalanche of urgent decisions.

"I was dealing with so many new challenges. I was learning as I was going along," Jean said. "I was doing what I needed to do to learn as much as I possibly could about how things operated, because all that was foreign to me. My generation didn't go into athletic administration because that career option didn't exist. We were physical educators. You didn't go to school to learn sports administration because there weren't any options for employment."

Charts in Haney's five-column full-page spread compared women's athletic budgets and scholarships beginning in 1975 at fourteen Division I universities, including Missouri and all the Big Eight schools, along with the University of Southern California, Ohio State University, Indiana, Illinois, Iowa, and Arkansas. Haney's research covered the previous two years.

Ohio State's $200,000 budget topped the charts, expanding by 50 percent the next year. Kansas University's budget was nearly $50,000 less but led the 1975 Big Eight totals, with Nebraska's spending surpassing all of its conference rivals the following year. USC led the surveyed schools in athletic scholarships, topping $100,000. Ohio State's scholarship budget showed the greatest growth, going from zero to nearly equaling Southern Cal's by 1976.

Missouri's operating budgets ranked in the middle. Arkansas's women's athletic budget was under $50,000 both years, the lowest among the schools surveyed. Lagging student interest apparently hindered the amounts granted from the school's general fund and administered through the women's physical education department. Arkansas's women's athletic director Ruth Cohoon called men's college athletics a big business fighting for the entertainment dollar and cautioned against women getting into that.

"We have a different philosophy than the 'win all costs' attitude some men have," Cohoon remarked in Haney's article. Her budget was a pittance compared to that of Arkansas's former football coach-turned-athletic director Frank Broyles, who kept the men's and women's athletics programs separate from 1974 until his retirement thirty years later.

Haney's article portrayed the changing role of women in sports from spectator to participant in 1976 and explored wide-ranging viewpoints and philosophies. University of Iowa women's athletic director Christine Grant urged supporters to evaluate athletics like other educational programs on campus, not by wins and losses. According to Haney, Grant wanted a more reasonable, student-oriented future for women athletes.

Haney questioned Missouri's actual support for women's sports when the Board of Curators two weeks earlier had approved expanding the football stadium and installing artificial turf while scrapping plans to create much-needed on-campus softball and field hockey facilities. The board rejected a proposal to convert a football dressing and training facility west of Memorial Stadium for the women to use. As a result, Missouri's softball team was forced to play on city recreational fields until 1981, when a field was scraped together near the university's A. L. Gustin golf course.

The *Tribune* article also spotlighted recruiting. AIAW rules limited tryouts to each school's campus and disallowed off-campus recruitment and visits to a prospect's home. Kansas women's basketball coach and athletic director Marian Washington grumbled that some schools were breaking those rules, which were applied inconsistently during AIAW's earliest years with no enforcement arm similar to the NCAA. AIAW schools expected competitors to follow guidelines out of a sense of moral fairness.

Haney's closing paragraphs speculated about the soon-to-be-hired candidate to oversee Missouri's women's sports program, hoping for the selection of someone who would serve the women athletes and coaches, not just the wishes of the male-dominated athletic department. Haney concluded that women deserved nothing less than men in terms of equal opportunity.[8]

Major Schools Answer a Survey

In the article, the women's athletic director at the University of Southern California, Barbara Hedges, applauded her school's response to Title IX. Hedges described how USC had fundraised

$25,000 initially for its women's program and praised how well both men's and women's programs worked together. Women's athletics were housed in the physical education department during Hedges's first year at USC. But with no money in the PE budget to support women's sports, women's athletics was moved to a combined athletics department in Heritage Hall. Hedges worked alongside men's athletic director John McKay and absorbed the department's helpful fundraising advice. Years later, Hedges pointed out that USC men's athletics had always excelled at fundraising to cover the cost of athletic scholarships for the private school's expensive tuition and fees. The athletic department's head of donor relations educated her on how to put together and structure a board and what to ask for in dues, helping her develop very necessary skills. Hedges parlayed those into becoming the athletic director at the University of Washington in 1991, one of the first female athletic directors overseeing a major Division I football-playing university belonging to one of the NCAA's top five conferences.

She laughed years later that she had the kind of personality that liked to raise money and soon identified a core base of supporters who similarly were frustrated at the lack of women's competitive opportunities. She reached out to the university community, and supporters responded. And together, they laid the foundation for successful fundraising groups like the Women's Trojan Club and the Women of Troy, which were patterned after the men's groups and focused on scholarship dollars.

"Alumni and friends of the university put pressure on USC to comply with Title IX," she was quoted as saying in the *Tribune* article, adding that the law had caused an awakening on the public's part. "I'd like to think we'll go beyond it."

She recalled that USC's athletic department had avoided divisive things like removing funds from the men's programs to support women's athletics. Instead, with Hedges's leadership, the women elevated their program by creating new revenue streams.

"What it comes down to is this: USC has made a commitment to women's sports," Hedges noted. "I've never felt that Title IX was pushing USC. Right now, it's only a question of how much money USC can generate."[9]

Funding was the first hurdle toward building a great women's athletic department, and she tackled it with zest. Within three years, she convinced the USC comptroller's office to front the program $30,000 to purchase a luxury vehicle for a fundraising raffle. Players and staff members all pitched in and sold the opportunity tickets. Membership in the Women's Trojan Club was an added bonus, along with a potential tax deduction. Everyone in the department was shocked when the Women of Troy quadrupled their money, bringing in over $120,000. Hedges laughed while recalling that USC offered a luxurious Mercedes-Benz to the private school's supporters instead of a lower-priced average American-made sedan or family car.

"They never believed we could do anything like that," said Hedges with a chuckle, adding that the overwhelming success increased not only the budget but the women's standing and stature within the department. "We just needed their support."

Jean Jumps into Athletic Administration

At Missouri, there were no other women in athletic administration. Cerra wasn't lonely; she was too busy. There were coaches to hire, policies to get in place, schedules to be made, and travel requisitions to make. With all that, she focused on one glaring area: inadequacies in the Hearnes Multipurpose Building, also known as the Hearnes Center.

Named for former Governor Warren Hearnes, it served as headquarters for Missouri intercollegiate athletics and, like similar on-campus athletic facilities across the country, was constructed in the 1960s solely for men's intercollegiate sports. Huge appropriations funded it: $8 million in taxpayer obligations and $3 million in revenue bonds. Combined, that equates to nearly $100 million in today's dollars. The arena featured a novel rubbery sticky basketball floor called a tartan floor, which was trendy at the time because of decreased maintenance costs but was later replaced with a hardwood floor because of the disproportionate number of ankle sprains.

One side of the huge boxy building was a thirteen-thousand-seat arena. The other was a fieldhouse with a full 400-meter track, plus a carpeted area for a variety of sports and batting cages. For years, Hearnes housed the entire athletic department staff, including coaches and support personnel in all the men's sports, even football. There were no available offices. One office would open up in late August, but until then, Cerra needed a desk somewhere. Mizzou sports archivist Bob Brendel recalled that head football coach Al Onofrio, along with men's and women's basketball head coaches Norm Stewart and Joann Rutherford, occupied the premier window offices that looked down into the huge fieldhouse. The entire women's coaching staff crammed into one office at the end of a meandering narrow hallway lit by incandescent light.

Potential space for Jean was available across the hall from long-serving MU coach emerita Tom Botts, John "Hi" Simmons, and Don Faurot. The trio had successful careers in track, baseball, and football, respectively, and, following retirement, were destined for Missouri's Intercollegiate Athletics Hall of Fame. Cerra agreed to the office and squeezed in a fourth desk alongside three football graduate assistants. It was cozy, but the new women's athletic director dismissed the low-key welcome.

"They didn't put the football graduate assistants on the window side," she said as she shook her head and laughed, unwilling to make waves and unperturbed that the new position initially didn't earn her certain perks like an executive office with a window. Ultimately, the situation helped her build collegiality with the football staff in a way that might have been impossible in an isolated, front office-type administrative space. The grad assistants soon became some of Cerra's staunchest supporters.

Pete Hoener, one of those football grad assistants, had a lengthy coaching career, twenty years in college and twenty years in the National Football League, finishing with the Washington Football Club, now known as the Commanders. Another was Dave McGinnis, who also rose to the NFL coaching ranks with the Tennessee Titans, St. Louis Rams, and Arizona Cardinals. Hoener said the move to incorporate Jean wasn't surprising; they were well aware that women's athletics were coming in and applauded Jean's professional approach.

"We really didn't think about it too much at the time. We were just young and happy to have any office space at all. It was a lot different then—you worked full-time hours for part-time pay," Hoener offered. "It just didn't seem like a big deal to be in the same office. They told us that Jean was coming in, and we said, 'let's go to work.'"

Turning Animosity into Respect

With her desk and phone set up, Cerra tackled the program's pressing needs. Over the summer, she explored every nook and cranny of the Hearnes Center, searching for space to provide a women's locker room. Nothing seemed adequate. School was starting within weeks, and there was a lot to do for the teams before the students returned.

"I think people were very respectful of me; nice, courteous, professional. I can't say there was any tension. They may not have been happy that I was there," Cerra recalled. "They certainly weren't happy with the circumstances with concerns over funding or what they thought was going to happen."

The men's nonrevenue sports, known today as Olympic sports but at one time called minor sports, objected that funding women's sports might siphon off any remaining crumbs from their small budgets. Cerra earned the coaches' support over time through professionalism and preparation.

"Were they unhappy about having the women there? Sure, yeah. I understood that and respected the feelings and objectives they had internalized. I was patient and tried to work with them through all the changes in a way that would earn their respect. I always got along well with the guys. The men grew up and competed all those years without ever thinking about women doing the same."

Cerra's reputation as firm but not abrasive deflected issues that Sheehan had raised in her hiring interview about being the most disliked person within the department. She said she'd stand her ground without resorting to unnecessary personal attacks or demeaning others. Ordinarily, she was able to work around the one or two difficult men who were critical of the women's presence.

"It wasn't so much disliking me as a person, but not being in favor of the women's programs that were being forced upon them. Fortunately, I didn't have to deal with them that much. Their criticism was like water off my back. I felt like I had great support from the football staff and the guys who were working with me. I never felt there was antagonism."

National Success for Women's Basketball

Women's basketball drew the most attention during Cerra's first year. The team looked strong and returned a core group of players, including a trio of thousand-point scorers in Suzanne Alt and future Missouri Intercollegiate Athletics Hall of Fame members Sharon Farrah and Nancy Rutter Huerd, plus power forward Beth Hokamp Fauser. Coach Joann Rutherford signed three outstanding freshmen, two of whom would become thousand-point scorers, Julie Maxey Ferguson and Cindy Kiser Tudehope, a speedy five-foot, eight-inch guard and all-American shot putter. The core group, along with Kathy Stevenson Turpin, proved to be among Missouri's all-time best, earning a spot in the sixteen-team AIAW national tournament and winning one Big Eight Conference tournament title, along with two runners-up finishes during the next few years.

Scoring came without the benefit of a three-point line, shot clock, or smaller women's basketball utilized today. Players then used a regulation men's basketball known today as a size seven. The standard size six women's or junior-sized basketball, an inch smaller and two ounces lighter, was introduced in the short-lived Women's Professional Basketball League and approved for NCAA play in 1984, an innovation that made the game quicker with increased shooting range and enhanced ball-handling skills.

In Rutherford's first year at Mizzou, 1975–76, the twenty-seven-year-old coach complained that her team returned out of shape and overweight after a semester break in which only two games had been scheduled in six weeks between late November and mid-January. The demanding but frustrated coach scheduled nine games in nine days the following season during the winter holidays, barnstorming through Kansas, Texas, and Oklahoma in a white fifteen-passenger school van pulling a U-Haul trailer for team equipment and luggage. Opponents included a national champion junior college squad from Oklahoma, Seminole State College, and two-time national small-college champion Phillips University. Those programs gave Missouri its only losses on the nine-game road trip. The team suffered through a flu bug and dealt with a blizzard before returning home long enough to do laundry and play yet another game the next day.

Benefiting from the challenging road trip and pushed by Rutherford, Mizzou improved. Conditioning in practices included running the arena steps, hitting every stair while encircling the entire seating area. Up to the D Section in the rafters, then down to the arena floor, until players completed the entire circuit around the spectator seats.

A week after the road trip concluded, the team piled into a charter bus for a twelve-hour drive on Interstate 70 to Boulder, Colorado, for the Big Eight Women's Basketball Tournament. Players eagerly threw pillows and gear into the overhead storage bins. The journey came with an added surprise: stopping in Lawrence, Kansas, to pick up the rival Kansas Jayhawks because neither program had enough budget money for the seeming luxury. The Tigers finished third, besting Colorado, losing to Nebraska, and then defeating their travel partner from KU for third place.

By February, Missouri was on a roll and faced the nation's fourth-ranked team, William Penn College—the regional's top seed in the AIAW Region VI tournament in Decorah, Iowa. The underdog Tigers avenged a ten-point loss at William Penn in the November season opener and clawed their way to the program's first victory over a top five team, defeating William Penn, 85–70.

The Tigers then nipped Central Missouri, 71–69, before falling to nemesis Kansas State, which had built a strong basketball program. The AIAW Region VI performances earned

Mizzou a wild-card invite to the sixteen-team national tournament hosted by the University of Minnesota in Minneapolis. There, Missouri won one of three games, with a first-round loss to powerhouse Southern Connecticut, before beating the host Gophers and losing to number twelve Baylor, which eventually won the consolation bracket.

That 1976–77 season, Missouri went 28–12, notching school records for program wins and games played that still stand today. In a footnote to history, the team's accomplishments remain obscured in Missouri athletic department records, possibly because they were set under AIAW governance. In a similar way, Lynette Woodard's AIAW scoring record of 3,649 points set at Kansas during the late 1970s generally received little attention or acceptance until broken by Iowa's Caitlin Clark in 2024.

By Cerra's second year, Mizzou won the Big Eight Conference tournament in Lawrence, Kansas, beating Woodard and the host squad and top-twenty-ranked Jayhawks. That season, the AIAW changed basketball's playoff format, installing championships similar to the men's NCAA Final Four concept. After winning the AIAW Region VI title, Mizzou, nationally ranked at number thirteen, advanced to the AIAW's Midwest Satellite III Championships, losing to number three North Carolina State, led by coach Kay Yow, then beating Ohio State in a consolation final. Notably, Wayland Baptist, which became eligible to compete in the AIAW as the women's organization accepted increased scholarship benefits, beat North Carolina State to reach the Final Four held in Los Angeles.

Photo Album

In 1975, the Stephens College volleyball team, coached by Jean Cerra, won the AIAW (Association for Intercollegiate Athletics for Women) Missouri small college state championship. Dana Caston Moore is seated in the front row, wearing number 31, while Jean Cerra is in the back row, right side.

Jean Cerra demonstrates passing techniques to her 1975 Stephens College volleyball team.

Stephens College volleyball coach Jean Cerra emphasizes hand position at this 1975 match.

The Council of Collegiate Women Athletic Administrators was renamed the National Association of Collegiate Women Athletic Administrators a decade after its 1979 founding. Today it's known as Women Leaders in Sports. This 2002 composite picture honors those founders.

The University of New Mexico's Linda Estes served the Loboes as associate athletic director and director of women's athletics for over thirty-one years, beginning in 1971.

Jean Cerra was an associate athletic director at the University of Missouri from 1976–1985.

University of California Los Angeles Senior Associate Athletic Director Judith R. "Judie" Holland was a former AIAW President who served UCLA from 1975–1995.

Photo courtesy of Women Leaders in Sports

Mary Hill, San Diego State University, became one of the first women nationally to lead an athletic department with Division I football.

Photo courtesy of Women Leaders in Sports

Barbara Hedges was hired in 1973 as the co-ordinator of the Women's Athletic Program at the University of Southern California before being named senior associate director of athletics responsible for both men's and women's programs.

Photo courtesy of the University of Missouri Archives, C:1/139/9 Box 12

Jean Cerra, pictured on-court at the University of Missouri's Hearnes Center, was featured in a 1984 Missouri Alumnus Magazine article.

Photo courtesy of the University of Missouri
Archives, Mizzou Review, 1978–79

*Jean Cerra, University
of Missouri*

The University of Southern California Women's Athletics Board is pictured with the Mercedes Benz convertible used in a 1984 fundraiser. Athletic Director John McKay is shown in the driver's seat and is surrounded by various notables like John Naber (fifth from left), Cheryl Miller (sixth from left) and Mike Garrett (second from right).

PHOTO ALBUM

Jean Cerra addresses graduates at the 2014 commencement ceremonies for the University of Missouri.

Dean of the College of Education and Human Development Daniel Clay is pictured in 2014 with Jean Cerra at the university's commencement exercises.

In 2016 Jean Cerra was selected for Barry University's Wall of Honor and recognized as a "Professor Emerita," a lifetime honor.

Jean Cerra and Kathy Stephenson Turpin enjoyed a moment at the 2016 Barry University Wall of Honor ceremony in Miami Shores, Florida. Cerra was the women's athletic director at the University of Missouri when Turpin played basketball collegiately. Cerra later hired Turpin in athletic administration at Barry University.

Photo courtesy of Jean Cerra

Jean Cerra was honored as a "Title IX Trailblazer" by the Southeastern Conference in spring 2022.

Photo courtesy of Mizzou Athletics

In September, 2022, Jean Cerra was a featured speaker at the University of Missouri's Celebration of Title IX and Women's Sports Banquet.

Photo courtesy of Mizzou Athletics

Former University of Missouri Athletic Director Desirée Reed-François welcomed Jean Cerra at the Celebration of Title IX and Women's Sports Banquet in September, 2022.

Photo courtesy Women Leaders in Sports

(L-R) Sandy Barbour, Jeanne Lenti-Ponsetto, Dee Todd, Cathie Schweitzer, Jean Cerra, and Patti Phillips at the Women Leaders in Sports 2023 Lifetime Achievement Awards in New Orleans. Phillips is the chief executive officer while Barbour was the master of ceremonies. Cerra and the other women received Lifetime Achievement Awards.

University of Missouri alumni, including Author Karen S. Rudolph, Jean Cerra and 3-time Division I athletic director Cheryl Levick, greeted each other at the 2023 Women Leaders in Sports Convention. Levick received the organization's Lifetime Achievement Award in 2025.

CHAPTER 8

National Leaders Speak Out

1970s
The University of New Mexico

WHILE JEAN SETTLED into athletic administration at Missouri, comfortable even without the protections of tenure, University of New Mexico women's athletic director Linda Estes confronted critics within her department and championed equality for women during some contentious philosophical fights. Among the most progressive and strongest early voices supporting women's college sports, a self-proclaimed "bomb thrower," Estes complained that some colleagues were late to recognize that inclusion in college sports was about not only equality but legality.

Shortly after the 1973 Kellmeyer case forced the AIAW into permitting women's athletic scholarships, Estes announced that eight grants would be awarded to women at her school. Physical education colleagues were appalled and demanded that campus President Ferrel Heady fire her. Their educational philosophy advocated for a purer form of sports competition, one untainted by the money and commercialization seen in men's college sports. Approving women's athletic scholarships seemed to be a worrisome step, and the physical educators objected vigorously.

"He didn't fire me," proclaimed Estes, grateful to have the school president's support. "Instead, he moved women's athletics out of the PE department and into the athletics department." The outspoken Estes, unlike Jean Cerra, remained on the tenure track and saw it as a protection. Estes's budget grew from $4,000 to $3 million by the time she retired in 2000 after thirty-plus years at New Mexico.

"I put my boxing gloves on every day that I went to work," said Estes, who boldly embraced positions for equality earlier than most of the public's acceptance levels, reassured that with the protection of tenure she always could fall back on teaching. One time she rejected an athletic director's demands to dismiss a coach who was gay. "It was a big fight, but with tenure they couldn't touch me. If I hadn't had tenure, I would have been history."

Estes admired Jean's positive approach toward speaking her views clearly but firmly. The two had met at AIAW delegate assemblies and generally voted on the same side. Within a few years, they collaborated in developing an organization of college women athletic administrators, drawn together to resolve issues facing Division I institutions.

"Jean worked effectively and quietly. Her role was much stronger than people realized," Estes proclaimed.

The University of Alabama

Throughout the country, other women's college sports proponents faced not only discrimination but overt blowback. Ann Marie Rogers described derogatory rhetoric she received at Alabama. Her career started at all-women's Smith College in Northampton,

Massachusetts, where everything from playing fields to tennis courts belonged to the women. It was a joy to work there as a young faculty member and she supported student leaders who urged her to organize women's intercollegiate athletics.

Soon, she was hired by Merrily Dean Baker at Princeton University to coach tennis but wanted even more career challenges. She wrote hundreds of schools and scoured the *Chronicle of Higher Education* for potential jobs. A breakthrough came while working at a summer golf camp in New Hampshire when she impressed the camp director, who also was a University of Alabama golf coach. Alabama needed a woman to lead its fledgling women's program, and perhaps Rogers, then known as Ann Marie Lawler, was interested.

"When I came to Alabama, it was definitely different from being at Smith College," she said, slowly shaking her head. Hired in 1974 in the Office of Student Affairs with a budget of $75,000, Ann Marie's first task was deflecting offensive student opinions, mainly voiced by male students who claimed that nobody wanted to see women's sports. The student newspaper printed numerous letters to the editor about her hiring, astounded that her budget might take away from football. Some were hostile, others disgusting. Some males congratulated other males on previous criticisms and offensive comments, seemingly trying to top one another's insults. They exaggerated false claims about Title IX, calling it another attempt on the part of big government to meddle in the affairs of the states. To them, women's sports were expensive and a worthless continuation of the social experimentation that had gone on in the country for too long.

She quoted one particular derogatory description word for word.

"At Alabama, women's sports were not very well accepted in the beginning. They wanted to call the women's teams 'the

Crimson Tits' instead of the Crimson Tide," she recalled about the rude comment, then quoted another. "'Does anyone think a team of tomboy, Billie Jean King prototypes can ever draw the thousands upon thousands of fans that Alabama football attracts? I sure as hell would not and will not pay $7 to watch a girls' volleyball game. The program is serving only the needs of a small minority of the women's libbers on campus and I can think of plenty of worthwhile projects that that seventy-five grand could go toward.'"

Rogers worked hard to turn around those opinions and held an ace in her pocket: former Alabama quarterback and football hero Joe Namath. While on campus, he had received help from three sisters who brought him meals and cooked for him. He donated $50,000 to the women's program and named three scholarships after them.

"That was a lot of money back then. We just kept working at it. Even though the students didn't feel that we should be there or even have a program. We kept doing as much as we could to help the situation and build our reputation." The women's coaches steadily built community connections and rapport, organizing children's sports clinics for Girl Scouts and other youth groups.

Four years after Rogers arrived, intercollegiate athletics merged into one department. The school president wanted legendary football coach and athletic director Bear Bryant to oversee both men's and women's programs since football dollars funded each one. She speculated that they were just going to let her go and add her duties to Bryant's, who apparently had the final say despite his disinterest in the position. After all, he had a football team to coach. But to Rogers, it was her life, and she dug in, fighting to keep her job.

Finally, he agreed that the added duties were no problem and assigned his personal assistant to collaborate with Rogers, who now was called an assistant athletic director instead of women's athletic director. By the mid-1980s, Rogers relocated to the University of Florida as associate athletic director and senior women's administrator.

Colorado State University

Elsewhere, Mary Hill faced similar issues as women's college sports evolved. She was unsure about what to do after growing up on a farm and graduating from high school in Brookfield, Missouri, in the late-1950s, so she married a local. Three years later, the couple divorced. Unwilling to return to the family farm, she enrolled at Northeast Missouri State Teachers College, now known as Truman State, in nearby Kirksville. While there, one of her instructors encouraged her to participate in a track and field play day at the University of Missouri, and with little training or preparation, she placed in three events: shot put, discus and javelin. After earning her degree, the spunky competitor parlayed those successes into a graduate assistantship in 1968 at Texas Woman's University as a field events coach, helping the school win two out of the first three women's college outdoor track championships.

After four years in Denton, Texas, Hill was hired to teach physical education, coach the track team, and be an assistant in intramurals at Colorado State University. When everyone else in the physical education department declined the women's athletic director job, she added that to her duties. The women initially had a $5,500 budget, while the men's exceeded $1.5 million. Hill taught one class and focused on athletic administration, overseeing eight women's sports, with her $10,500 salary paid from physical education funds. As a trailblazer for women's intercollegiate sports, she chafed at the budget discrepancies for uniforms, competition, travel, and equipment. As an administrator seeking to grow her program, it seemed reasonable to survey each women's coach about what was necessary to adequately fund their programs.

"We had to drive school vans on the same routes that the men would fly. Sometimes a student-athlete had to drive. It wasn't safe. We usually only got two motel rooms for entire teams, so everybody shacked up in those two rooms together and sometimes slept on the floor. If they wanted to eat, they had to pay for their own food. It was terrible." Per diem expenses were paid only to the male athletes. Women had to purchase their own uniforms.

Staff responded with what seemed to be reasonable budgetary projections totaling over $30,000 despite nothing being included for women's athletic scholarships, which would have added another $10,000. She said that her supervisor and head of the men's physical education department, Dr. John Nettleton, thought the numbers were ridiculously high but agreed that she should take her concerns to the university president. During that meeting, the president recognized simmering resistance from the physical education department to even provide for a women's athletics budget and set up a committee to create one. According to Hill, the committee reviewed all options and suggested a budget ten times the previous amount. It included women's scholarships.

The physical education chair quietly seethed with resentment and retaliated by undermining Hill's leadership, causing her teaching contract to not be renewed. She objected, and twice, a faculty review board investigated and supported her position. Finally, her detractors demanded that she complete her doctorate within just a few months to keep her job. That request was unreasonable within that time frame and not required of males in similar positions. Initially, she attempted to comply and earned some additional doctoral-level course credits. But Hill, with limited preparation time and full-time academic duties, refused to take the required doctoral exams and was told that her contract would be dropped for the next academic year. She reacted to the discrimination and unfairness by filing a Title IX lawsuit.

Hill claimed that the nonrenewal constituted sex discrimination in employment and sued individual defendants, alleging it was retaliation for her being an aggressive advocate of Title IX in expanding women's intercollegiate athletics at Colorado State. She remained unemployed throughout the following school year as the case wound through the court system. When eventually resolved, the jury agreed with Hill and awarded her $65,000 in compensatory and punitive damages.

The judge's verdict noted that persons "in the physical education department were less than enthusiastic about developing women's sports." He added that "Hill was given the very difficult task of trying to be the leader and administrator of an emerging athletic program while assigned to a position in an academic department which did not support her efforts or goals."

In addition, the judge recognized the retaliation against her attempts to build women's college sports, a prospect potentially threatening the funding of the men's teams and the physical education department. He also cited an "apparent reluctance to accept the change in the sex stereotyped role of intercollegiate competition as a masculine domain."[10]

In the interim, Hill applied at San Diego State University and interviewed with Athletic Director Ken Karr. She found him to be more open toward women's sports, possibly, she thought, because he had daughters himself. San Diego State hired her that summer as its women's athletic director. She gained valuable experience under Karr and also Cedric Dempsey, who followed

Karr as athletic director before rising to head the NCAA in the 1990s. Eventually, San Diego State named her as its director of athletics, and Hill gained notoriety as the first woman in charge of an athletic department that included Division I football.

"I've found in my career that the men who have daughters are so much more supportive toward women's sports than men who have boys," she recalled, saying that she disclosed the ongoing Title IX litigation during the interview process. "I asked Ken Karr if he thought that was going to be an issue." She said he was unperturbed and answered that doing something like that took spunk.

"When the president [of the university] hired me, he told me he was hesitant because none of his vice presidents agreed with him. But he said it looked good on his resumé to hire a woman. Right there I should have turned him down," Hill said years later, with an edge creeping in her voice. By the summer of 1985, she said that her administration was overwhelmed by jealous whispers, backstabbing, and disloyalty. Once again, she was fired, this time never to return to intercollegiate athletic administration.

University of California, San Diego

Judy Sweet was another early trailblazer who had limited opportunities for formal athletic competition. The longtime athletic administrator at University of California, San Diego grew up with backyard sports against lots of male cousins and two older brothers in Wisconsin. The only organized outlet for her during high school was on "play days," social and athletic opportunities at Girls Athletic Association events with punch and cookies served afterward. Her alma mater, the University of Wisconsin, offered no women's intercollegiate athletics in the 1960s, but members of the Women's Recreation Association did sponsor and promote play days, with the endeavors funded by cutting and selling Christmas trees.

The UCSD campus lies a few miles north of San Diego atop the stunningly beautiful oceanside cliffs of La Jolla. Sweet had completed graduate work at the University of Arizona, working alongside Mary Roby, and had moved to San Diego in 1972, relishing the beach and climate. She taught at a local high school for a year and waited for a position to open up at UCSD, a dream job attractive to her because the school sponsored women's teams prior to Title IX when few institutions offered those opportunities. The women's teams competed locally against community colleges, small colleges like Point Loma Nazarene College and United States International University, and occasionally against San Diego State. Meanwhile, the Tritons men's teams competed in the NAIA, an organization of mostly smaller colleges that offered only men's championships in the 1970s.

Sweet noted that a four-year institution competing almost exclusively against two-year institutions with very different academic focuses didn't make sense. The athletic administration found it was much less expensive to keep women's teams in San Diego. But, according to her, it wasn't for lack of interest on the part of the students.

Primarily known for its research and development, the highly selective institution has grown from 6,000 students when Sweet arrived in 1973 to over 44,000 today. Hired initially to teach and coach, Sweet became the athletic director after two years and oversaw both men's and women's athletics, a first for intercollegiate sports. She noted that her timing was terrible as far as being an athlete, but opportune for changing the landscape of women competing in college sports. Sweet thought that she might have been a decent athlete in whatever sports she might have had coaching in, but she had zero opportunities to play on a high school team. Even more bluntly, she never could have imagined being an athletic director because there weren't any women in that position. Title IX changed all that. Failing to comply with its requirements meant facing the threat of losing federal funding.

"That [threat] got the attention of the administration; they didn't want to lose those research funds. I was able to make a case for us to compete beyond the San Diego area because of Title IX," she said. "We were able to then compete within the AIAW structure throughout Southern California."

As Sweet moved from coaching and teaching to overseeing thirty-one sports and a budget of $91,000, she instituted a policy of treating men and women equitably in terms of funds, facilities, and practice times. According to Sweet, disgruntled male coaches griped in the school newspaper about those policies as they questioned why women were playing sports and undermined the reasons for investing in women's teams.

"Some of the men's coaches felt their teams should be given priority. They didn't hesitate to speak up against the approach that I was putting into place. That was hard for some of them," Sweet acknowledged. "I did the coaches' salaries based on equity for men and women. I did the budget based on equity. Ultimately some of them went back to just teaching and gave up their coaching positions."

According to Sweet, the stated threat to research dollars was adequate to ensure compliance. After all, no institution has been penalized with the loss of funds because of Title IX. In 1981, UCSD's athletic programs gravitated to NCAA's Division III. Being under the same governance body instead of separate organizations with different rules, structures, and philosophies simplified administrative needs. The women enjoyed immediate national success, winning the first D-III national title volleyball championship. UCSD earned thirty national titles over the next few decades under Sweet's leadership.

By the early 1990s, Sweet's leadership skills led to her election as the first female president of the NCAA. At the time, some NCAA members grumbled about having a woman leading the NCAA; others questioned the relevance of a smaller D-III athletic administrator helming the organization.

"I felt fortunate to get into the governance process with the NCAA to make a case for treating our male and female athletes the same. We had to make our own opportunities. I guess I've been doing that my entire life: trying to make more opportunities."

During Sweet's tenure as NCAA president, she initiated a gender equity task force to help cement those athletic opportunities for young women. The trailblazer noted that having a woman's voice and presence in NCAA leadership was an extremely important first step.

But, she cautioned, even more important was not being the last.

Princeton University

On the East Coast in the late 1960s, Princeton University, one of the top-ten universities in the world, decided to enroll women for the first time since its founding before the Revolutionary War. There were planning groups in every facet of the university's operation, preparing for the upcoming enormous changes to traditions and culture. A handful of women arrived in the fall of 1969, but it took another year to accumulate significant enrollment. The school sought a qualified woman to lead its emerging women's physical education and athletics department and hired Merrily Dean Baker. On her first day on campus, she received a neatly typed sixty-page plan for the absorption of women into intercollegiate athletics, physical education, and intramurals. Three weeks later, she said she had checked off everything on what was intended as a five-year list.

Baker started by organizing the physical education classes, including a required swimming class and mandatory test. The test seemed easy and could be completed by either swimming a few laps or proving the ability to last ten minutes in the water. A back float was acceptable. One of her earliest students was Sonia Sotomayor, a future Supreme Court Justice.

"Most kids pass that swim test their first week at Princeton. But Sonia couldn't swim and was petrified of the water. She had grown up in the concrete jungles of New York City, in these huge buildings with apartments, no swimming pools and no money to go to the lake on vacation," recalled Baker, who worked with Sotomayor personally or assigned various staff. Finally, just weeks before graduation, Sotomayor passed the test. Baker was pleased and recounted that Sotomayor was the salutatorian of her 1976 graduating class.

"And she almost didn't graduate because she couldn't swim." Princeton kept that swimming requirement until 1990 when it was scrapped along with other physical education requirements. The changes at tradition-bound Princeton mirrored those at institutions nationwide as women sought inclusion in all facets of college life.

Baker proved to be up to the job of incorporating women into Princeton's campus life. When given a million reasons why something was impossible to get done, she would respond with a million reasons why it could. Early on, she helped resolve difficulties with another Princeton tradition dating back to post-Civil

War years called Cane Spree, an annual October intramural competition for supremacy between the freshman and sophomore classes. Baker called it an opportunity for the freshmen to pull together as a group and get to know the sophomores. For the first time, women were participating. While she helped with the planning, an older gentleman who had run the event for years ran red-faced into her office, exclaiming breathlessly that "we can't have this."

She was puzzled. What could possibly be the problem? He replied that numerous women had signed up for Cane Spree. That seemed great, she replied calmly. Troubled, he described his apprehension: The loser of the various contests had to give up their shirt to the winner. Baker thought quickly. To her, there was an easy, practical solution.

"Give the girls two shirts to wear!" she said as he looked at her, stopped in his tracks. Long-held traditions were being upended, with new traditions forthcoming.

Another early win for Baker was initiating the intercollegiate athletics program. Margie Gengler and Helen Novakova, a student from Czechoslovakia who was putting herself through school by teaching in the Slavic language department, met in Baker's office to ask her about representing the school in the eastern collegiate tennis championships. Baker looked into it and agreed. But no uniforms were available, so she bought a couple of Princeton T-shirts from the university bookstore and ironed the students' names on the back. The pair placed first and second and teamed up to win the doubles title.

"We came home with trophies in the team competition, and so we were representing the Tigers in athletics," said Baker, understandably proud. "That was just three weeks after we started." Baker realized how young women were eager for increased athletic competition when a group of passionate rowers sought her support.

She understood the urgency of implementing women's sports competition because the women who came to Princeton were only going to be there for four years. They didn't have the time to wait for athletic opportunities to emerge from some five-year plan.

Men's crew ranked among the nation's best and trained under a former Olympic rower at beautiful Lake Carnegie. The boathouse was historic, reminiscent of years of tradition and competition. Baker went to the men's coach and asked him to help get the women's team started. She was unprepared for his strong opposition as the coach stood there with his feet apart, arms crossed, and looked at her directly, stating that women would be in that boathouse over his dead body.

With her knees shaking, she thought of the young women awaiting the decision, summoned every ounce of courage in her body, and spoke quietly and firmly. She was twenty-seven and knew nothing about crew; he had the confidence and stature from success in his sport.

"Pete, I didn't come to ask for your permission," she said slowly, measuring her reply to the reluctant Pete Sparhawk. "I came to ask for your help."

Still, the intimidating Sparhawk refused to give his support. But Baker was determined. She hired a recent grad to coach the team and located some used equipment. Together, they launched the boats at six a.m. in the dark. It was the only time slot made available. The women rowers finished in third place that year in the intercollegiate national championships. The team's dedication and performance impressed the men's coach so much that an afternoon time slot was made available. The team responded by winning a national championship. Two years later, a pair of those rowers became Olympians as women's rowing was included for the first time in the 1976 Olympic Games, with Carol Brown earning a bronze medal in Montreal.

"My husband and I, along with that coach, stood on the banks of that river and cheered," recalled Baker. "And then we all cried."

Baker joined other women soon after her hiring, talking to leadership in the halls of Congress and marching on Washington. After President Richard Nixon signed the groundbreaking Title IX legislation, the Office of Civil Rights was tasked with interpreting it. Later that summer, Baker was invited to join a select committee of twelve OCR attorneys and one other athletic director, a male.

"I was young and had no idea why they selected me. But it was like getting a PhD [doctor of philosophy], an extraordinary opportunity to stretch and grow. I walked into those meetings very naive and unsure; I walked out very firm in my belief about what we had done," she recalled, emphasizing that every one of Title IX's thirty-seven words was analyzed carefully, with attorneys who would become the nation's judges haggling over nuances in interpretation and meaning.

Baker's motivation was to create better opportunities for girls and women, and she spent twelve years at Princeton before accepting athletic administration positions at Minnesota and Michigan State University and eventually with the NCAA.

"Did I always do it perfectly? I'm sure I did not. You just put one foot in front of the other. People push you and you try to get it accomplished. Princeton gave me opportunities to stretch and grow along with being put on that Title IX committee with the Office of Civil Rights. I was just very blessed to have the opportunity to grow up."

Her sensibilities and leadership on the East Coast would be important during the next few years as women's intercollegiate athletics progressed.

CHAPTER 9
Missouri's 1976 Title IX Review

1976–1978

THE STEPS TAKEN by the University of Missouri to implement the federal guidelines concerning Title IX were typical of those across the country. Just four years after its passage in 1972, the Office of Civil Rights (OCR) demanded that each institution review its women's programs and complete a lengthy self-evaluation report. Schools that failed to comply risked losing federal funds, giving Title IX regulations some legal punch.

Chancellor Herb Schooling tapped Dr. Veralee Hardin, a professor in the College of Education and a staunch supporter of gender equality, to chair a campus committee that included members such as Oklahoma football all-American Dr. Prentice Gautt, women's swimming coach David Lee Howell, Professor Hardeep Bhullar of the recreation department, and three students. The committee met throughout the 1975–76 school year and released the self-evaluation report ten days before the July 1976 national deadline.

Jean Cerra had been in her new position for six weeks and studied each line of the report, the ink barely dry. It included an introductory letter from Director of Athletics Mel Sheehan to Vice-Chancellor for Student Affairs James Banning. In it, Sheehan praised Cerra's hiring. They hoped that her employment would enhance the evaluation.

"We are pleased that we waited and feel that the report reflects the advantages of the leadership, preliminary discussions and observations she has had with members of both the men's and women's programs, and the more realistic view of where the program is currently and should be in the future," wrote Sheehan.

He described Missouri's funding and facility challenges. While many other universities helped athletic departments with staff salaries and tuition waivers, those resources were unavailable at Missouri. The men's program dated to 1890 and was self-sufficient. It received zero subsidies from campus general operations, student fees, or state appropriations. Mizzou opened an athletics complex in 1972 called the Hearnes Center, which was designed and built with state appropriations solely for men's intercollegiate competition. There were no women's locker rooms, team rooms, weight training facilities, or areas for women coaches. Sheehan wrote that the women's program was a club sports program when it was designed. Apparently, no one had envisioned the emergence in just a few years of a full-scale women's intercollegiate athletic program sponsoring eight sports, he concluded almost sarcastically.[11]

OCR required each institution to investigate ten distinct criteria, from assessing the nature and extent of both men's and women's sports programs to the funding of athletic scholarships. Suggestions for potential remedial actions in areas of inadequacies were expected.

Missouri's report acknowledged that athletics was the most visible and controversial area in the development of Title IX regulations. The men's program was self-supporting, while nearly 90 percent of the women's budget came from the chancellor's discretionary funds. Fundraising and contributions to the athletic scholarship fund were needed to close the gap, sparking concerns about the women's ability to do that.[12] That responsibility fell to Cerra. Volleyball and softball coach Debbie Duren understood the public's pushback since she had grown up in Columbia.

"Money was a big deal. It was a huge deal. There was a lot of animosity from everyone in the community about women's sports. People were aggravated," she recalled. Critics groused that funding the women's program would take money away from the football team, hindering a potential Big Eight title. Duren described a simmering, difficult and negative undercurrent promoting the idea that "you are taking away from us." The disdain grew even more when other institutions cut men's program budgets to fund the women.

"There was just that level of animosity, like 'that's not their place in the world anyway,'" Duren said. "Yes, there were people who were saying women deserve to play just like men deserve to play. But there are only so many dollars. I don't care how you slice it—there are only so many dollars to be spent. When there wasn't enough, that was not pretty. Little boys' dads were mad and all kinds of things."

But what about the parents of little girls? Hadn't that issue been determined in the New Mexico court case with golfer Nancy Lopez?

Title IX Review Criteria

Title IX impacted the following areas, which each campus was to evaluate and remedy if shortfalls were discovered.

CRITERION 1	Nature and Extent of the Sports Programs Offered
CRITERION 2	Equipment and Supplies
CRITERION 3	Scheduling of Games and Practice Times
CRITERION 4	Provision of Travel and Per Diem Allowances
CRITERION 5	Nature and Extent of the Opportunity to Receive Coaching/Academic Tutoring
CRITERION 6	Provision of Locker Rooms, Practice and Competitive Facilities
CRITERION 7	Provision of Medical and Training Supplies and Services
CRITERION 8	Provision of Housing and Dining Facilities and Services
CRITERION 9	Nature and Extent of Publicity
CRITERION 10	Scholarships

Criteria 3 and 6: Travel Differences, Scheduling Practices, Finding Lockers

The Title IX report noted that 147 women athletes competed for the Tigers, demonstrating steady growth in both participants and budgets, which grew from $15,000 out of the chancellor's discretionary moneys in the fall of 1973 to a projected budget of $160,000 as Cerra entered Missouri athletic administration.

The Title IX report speculated on possible revenue sources and questioned what was required to keep the program competitive with other schools of similar size. Travel differences between the men's and women's programs had seemingly straightforward resolutions. Female athletes could be assigned two to a room like the men instead of four women sharing a room. Incorporating more charter air and bus travel instead of having the women's coaches drive station wagons and vans was another proposal. Utilizing charter buses would help coaches work on travel and game details without having to worry about atrocious gas station bathrooms or finding restaurants. After all, travel arrangements had to be made by phone, mail, or paper maps in an era before cell phones and apps.

Coach Debbie Duren commented about the amount of work that had to be done because "you couldn't just go from having a T-shirt one day to flying on a charter jet the next." Cerra dug into her to-do list and weighed out all possibilities. There were other issues to sort out.

Only thirty-one lockers were available to the 147 female athletes. When volleyball and basketball seasons overlapped, as many as three women shared one locker. However, the 300 male athletes could choose from nearly four hundred lockers. That inequity caused a very determined Cerra to search exhaustively for satisfactory space that would impact the men's programs minimally and where possible modifications like rearranging showers and removing urinals could be made. None of the locker rooms seemed quite right.

Some men's teams, like golf and tennis, shared smaller locker rooms. The only potential space large enough for all the women athletes was assigned to the track and field team. The track team complained, but athletic department needs had to be balanced, and it was assigned another locker room. It was a small win for the women athletes, but the women's coaches were left with no separate locker space. A frustrated Cerra called it a bad situation, with athletes as well as their coaches in one locker room.

Nearly all the men's practice and competitive facilities were rated as good or excellent. Women's golf, swim, tennis, and indoor track teams shared acceptable venues with the men's program. The wrestling facility was rated only as fair, mainly because of cramped space in a fourth-floor training area. Field hockey and softball practice and competition facilities were rated as poor. Volleyball matches were played in a practice gym with no seating.

Practice times were another story. Before Cerra's hiring, female athletes had no assistance in scheduling classes around practice or games. If there was a required lab in the late after-noon during practice, student-athletes had to decide between the class or playing for the team. Cerra's help and influence brought improvements.

Men's basketball received the Hearnes Center's prime prac-tice time from 3:00 to 5:00 p.m., with every other program working around that. According to volleyball coach Debbie Duren, you could either practice in the small upstairs gym or after men's basketball coach Norm Stewart. The volleyball team chose neither and instead agreed to a two-hour practice slot before basketball, accomplished by scheduling student-athletes into early morning class times. Just that quickly, Duren said, things like that would happen.

Criteria 2, 7, 8, and 9: Equipment, Training Room, Dining Hall, and Media Services

Frequently, equipment and specialty items were shuttled between teams. The women's swim team and basketball team shared a single set of warm-ups, black jackets adorned with gold V-shaped embroidery and UMC (for the University of Missouri-Columbia), and black pants with a solitary gold stripe down the pant legs. The sizing was one-size-fits-most. During basketball season, six-foot, two-inch center Suzanne Alt struggled with pants length and a jacket with sleeves that barely reached her wrists.

"In a few pictures, I looked like the Hulk, because I'd scrunch up my shoulders and bring my arms in so my sleeves looked longer," said Alt, self-conscious at the time about being made fun of because she was tall. Players laundered their own uniforms, and she would attempt to add length by attaching a heavy cup full of coins to the bottoms of the wet pants. With limited team budgets, sets of warm-ups were shared between programs. If the swim team was still competing, the basketball team warmed up without any.

Cerra oversaw other needed improvements as women's sports settled into the Hearnes Center. The basketball team received practice gear, which would be washed, folded, and ready to be checked out from the cage the following day. Cold-weather sports like field hockey in the fall and softball in the spring were issued insulated gold parkas with hoods during the season.

Equipment challenges were ongoing since few manufacturers catered to the women's market. The season before Cerra's arrival, women's basketball played in the inaugural Big Eight Conference Championships in Manhattan, Kansas, and visited a local sporting goods store. They bought their own game shoes, popular Adidas sneakers with three black stripes generally unavailable throughout the Midwest. Most players found their sizes, but the shoes were designed for men's feet, not women's. Shorter guards or those with small feet were out of luck or forced to wear numerous pairs of socks. With their new footwear, the team defeated Kansas and Oklahoma State before losing in the championship game to the host Wildcats of Kansas State.

The provision of medical and training supplies and services was an easier area to remedy. Missouri hired Melinda Prewitt as the women's athletic trainer. The athletic training room offered space to assess injuries, access ice and moist heat, or get ankles taped before practice, or recover postpractice with a stint in the steam room. Prewitt traveled mainly with basketball while also supervising student trainers. On road trips, she drove school vans and assisted with other duties, including laundering the uniforms.

In the 1970s, there were few women serving as athletic trainers at any level. Prewitt worked alongside men's head athletic trainer Fred Wappel, who seemed skeptical at first about the women's presence. Cerra recalled that Wappel wouldn't allow any of the women athletic trainers to work on any of the men's teams, concerned that the guys would get aroused after being touched in sensitive areas.

With so many athletes and not enough women's athletic trainers, the athletes sometimes picked up scalpels to trim calluses on their feet. At first, they trimmed them too deeply, causing them to pop and bleed into shoes and socks. Quickly, they learned to moderate their efforts.

In the first few years, the women's athletic program was unable to offer dining hall options in its scholarship structure. Athletes often missed meals at the dorm because of practices. Sorority members always had cold and unappealing "late plates" that were impossible to heat up without microwave ovens. Cerra worked on adding a dining benefit during her first year at

Missouri, and by the following year, it made a difference. Alt, who finished with over a thousand points scored in her Mizzou basketball career and went on to play professionally, said the added perk her senior year was phenomenal.

"I think that [athletic dining hall] really raised our performance as a group, because a lot of people didn't have money to go buy food," she recalled. "It was fun that we could go together as a group. The dining hall helped our camaraderie."

Sharon Farrah, named to Missouri's Intercollegiate Athletics Hall of Fame in 2000, who remains sixth on Missouri's all-time scoring chart with 1,820 points, agreed wholeheartedly. After graduating, the first-round draft pick played professionally in the Women's Professional Basketball League, a forerunner to today's WNBA (Women's National Basketball Association).

"That was a huge asset for us," she said about the dining facility on Rollins Street. She encountered little pushback from the male athletes at the Lewis and Clark Dining Hall, as most were done eating by the time the women players arrived. "There was talk about that, but I didn't really care because we were so excited to be eating there. Jean was so instrumental in all of that: having our uniforms washed and practice gear laid out every day, the better travel arrangements, the scholarships, the locker room—even having a locker room."

Another teammate of Alt and Farrah's recounted what it was like for the women athletes during those transition years as travel, equipment, and educational services improved through Cerra's advocacy. Julie Maxey Ferguson was a freshman forward on the basketball team during Jean's first year at Missouri.

"Jean was fighting for us so much. We were getting opportunities to fly to New York City for games, and then out to California over the Christmas break. We could fly to Colorado, unlike my freshman year when we had a charter bus."

Today's Division I college athletes have impressive reveal parties at the beginning of each season when team members are showered with logo gear and practice equipment, shown on social media excitedly entering their locker rooms and discovering all the new items filling their custom lockers. But the women's trailblazers had none of that. Ferguson recalled writing a check using her summer job money to purchase team shoes but still expressed gratitude that the team had received not just one but two sets of uniforms along with snap-off game warm-up pants and jackets. Before she graduated, players received running shoes to help with preseason training. Notably, the dining hall privileges meant the most to her.

"It was so nice to eat at the athletic dining hall. You were there with all the athletes. You had time to shower and change and not just show up in your sweaty practice clothes," Ferguson observed. "Before, you literally had to run to the dorm to get there before the serving line closed."

"The training table was a whole different thing," said Cerra, referring to a dining hall menu designed for the football team, scoffing at claims that the women soon would look like three-hundred-pound linemen. "But I heard all the stuff that women can't be in there because they'll get fat. It's not designed for women's diets."

The Title IX report highlighted needed improvements in the key areas of media and publicity because they influenced the overall public acceptance of women's sports. Local newspapers like the *Columbia Daily Tribune* and the *Columbia Missourian*, as well as campus media such as the *Maneater* or the *Campus Digest*, typically did not cover women's events in person and depended on the respective coaches to phone in the results. Nancy Rutter Huerd, a basketball player and 2020 inductee into the

Missouri Intercollegiate Athletics Hall of Fame, recruited a South Shelby (Missouri) high school classmate enrolled in the School of Journalism, Patti Baymiller, to cover women's sports for the student newspaper. Baymiller's voluntary write-ups provided the most consistent newspaper coverage during the mid-1970s. As Cerra took charge, improvement was needed beyond the one printed brochure encompassing all sports, two schedule cards for five sports, and no posters or media guides.

Criterion 5: Coaching Experience and Compensation

Missouri's Title IX report questioned whether women's coaches received equitable compensation. Some were holdovers from physical education and worked only during the season since AIAW disavowed women's athletic scholarships and recruiting. Women's coaches were initially hired on a quarterly basis with a quarter of a full-time employment contract. Stipends averaged under $3,000. Basketball coach Joann Rutherford, who taught academic classes on campus, earned a teaching salary plus her coaching stipend. Some coaches increased their pay by assisting in other areas, like Diane Lyon (head golf coach and assistant basketball coach), Alexis Jarrett (sports information along with women's track), and Debbie Duren (head coach of both volleyball and softball).

By comparison, men's head basketball coach Norm Stewart earned $25,000 for full-time employment. As with Rutherford, this included academic responsibilities. Head football coach Al Onofrio earned $2,000 more than Stewart, according to the report.

Criterion 10: Athletic Scholarships

Athletic scholarships for men started on a very limited basis in the early 1950s and grew at a much slower pace than what is now anticipated will be the case for the women's program, stated Missouri Athletic Director Mel Sheehan in the Title IX report. There was a sizable gap between men's and women's sports in the number of and total dollars spent for scholarship aid.

"For the public to pay to watch these contests, it must be a quality program—a quality program needs talent—to get talent of the quality needed it was assumed that scholarship assistance was mandatory," concluded Sheehan in Missouri's Title IX self-evaluation report.

Sheehan addressed additional issues, including the previous influence of physical educators, and summarized physical education professional journals articulating the evils of the highly competitive men's athletic programs and the emphasis on and costs of scholarship aid. Missouri's intercollegiate athletic department weighed the choices.

"Those voices are now silent and in their place are the even louder cries for the same highly competitive athletic programs for women with athletic scholarships. After much discussion it nonetheless became evident that this element of the men's program should be included. Because of the stacking effect, the three scholarships from 1975–76 would become six so that the funds needed for scholarships more than doubles," noted Sheehan. The report questioned how this rapidly growing program would be financed.

At least 265 of Missouri's male athletes, including 125 scholarship football players, received varying amounts of financial aid in the mid-1970s, totaling nearly half a million dollars. The women's program initially allotted nothing to scholarships. In 1975–76, each sport was awarded three grants of $300 for one semester's tuition, plus a promise of another $300 that could be earned through student employment. Basketball, seen then as the only potential revenue-producing program, was allowed six scholarships. Each of the twenty-seven female scholarship athletes received at most $584, totaling nearly $16,000. It was a start.

Scholarship expenses nearly doubled the following year, as Sheehan predicted, complicated by additional costs for out-of-state tuition as recruiting cast a wider net. Student employment meant the players contributed hours of work that had to be approved by their coaches. While some jobs required more effort than others, the coaches always seemed willing to assist top players in earning the other half of their scholarships by vouching for the hours spent.

Decades later, at a reunion, the women reminisced about their work/study jobs that included taping football players' ankles before their practices, keeping the official scorebook, calling lines at intercollegiate volleyball matches, refereeing intramurals, or assisting in sports information duties on game days in the football press box. One freshman was assigned to deliver the rack of basketballs every day before practice. Basketball's leading scorer was required to supervise the automatic sprinklers on athletic department practice fields.

"I moved the sprinklers around a little bit," joked Sharon Farrah in her own defense years afterward. "But that's all it really was."

Cerra let out a hearty belly laugh when told those stories years later.

"I didn't know all that was taking place," she said and chuckled. "I was so busy getting all my own stuff done."

Fundraisers and Letter Jackets

Cerra knew significant amounts of money were needed to fill budget gaps and cover travel expenses to conference tournaments and regional and national championships, which were unfunded by AIAW. She knew they had to raise money quickly, but there were few options.

"It was impossible to budget for postseason travel. We were scrambling to find money for individuals and teams to attend championships at the end of each season instead of it being the result of success," said Cerra, who, along with Chancellor Schooling, was dissatisfied with the AIAW regulation and noted that the NCAA covered those expenses.

The athletes themselves stepped up and operated two concession stands at Saturday football games, one under the stadium and a second area in a white tent down on the cinder track. Football fans who might never have realized there were women's teams competing for Missouri were impressed by the women's work ethic and tenacity. Cerra appreciated the athletes' sacrifices and willingness to do anything to build their teams and sports, even if that meant giving up free time on a weekend to earn some bucks for their program. She commented that women student-athletes in those early days at Mizzou and other institutions across the country—because they had nothing to begin with—were more than willing to do what was needed to be able to play and compete, to move the program forward.

The Missouri women athletes reflected with gratitude and remembered those times as a bonding moment. Coaches didn't need to plan team-building exercises when shared work on chilly Saturday mornings in November provided the experience. Carrying heavy wooden soft drink trays up and down the stadium steps might be termed cross-training today while selling refreshments gained them support from thousands of potential fans. Suzanne Alt remembered walking the stadium steps with a heavy beverage tray and yelling loudly, "Cokes for a dollar."

"We thought that was a good deal to get our uniforms paid for. We never thought that working like that was below us," said Alt, who also earned academic scholarships. "We were just happy to have an avenue to pay for uniforms, because my family wasn't going to do it. You need more money? Well, go sell a few more cokes. Walk up and down those stadium steps. We were going to do anything we could to have the right to play."

Freshman Julie Maxey Ferguson took the task in stride and, with a shrug of her shoulders, said, "We were just told we had to work the coke stand. We just didn't think anything about it."

"Today I don't think you could get student-athletes to do that. My hats off to them for their attitudes," noted Cerra, dismayed that women were denied the recognition of school letter jackets, perhaps a small benefit, but a benefit nonetheless. She pursued them, with the response a decisive no; that honor was reserved just for the men. Cerra recalled no clear-cut explanation and speculated that perhaps the administration thought the women athletes fell short of the standards or were too inexperienced athletically. The women came up with their own awards, including small mementos like school binders or notepads given at an end-of-the-year banquet.

It took over thirty-five years to correct the oversight, until 2015 when Athletic Director Mack Rhoades and Assistant Director Sarah Reesman headlined a Letter Jacket Ceremony for more than three hundred women who competed for Missouri through the mid-1980s and were denied letter jackets. They were invited to campus during homecoming weekend. Enthusiastic conversations grew increasingly louder, interrupting the ceremony as the women greeted friends and teammates they hadn't seen in decades. Rhoades repeatedly encouraged the women to lower the volume so that every player could get their moment of recognition on stage, but eventually shook his head and smiled at the seemingly impossible task.

"I've been to a lot of alumni events this homecoming weekend," said Rhoades while paying tribute to the former Mizzou athletes, "but none with the energy of this room."

"It was a chapter that was incomplete," said Jean, "and I'm glad they finally completed it."

Other Institutions Award Athletic Scholarships

Institutions besides Missouri had varying methods to award scholarships. Illinois State emphasized academics, granting athletic scholarships to winners of an essay contest, according to Chris Voelz, former women's athletic director at the University of Minnesota and an Illinois State graduate. She laughed that she wasn't that good at writing so the scholarship went to a teammate. The three-sport star in volleyball, basketball and softball carved out an illustrious career in women's college sports administration, serving lengthy stints at both the University of Oregon and the University of Minnesota before joining the Women's Sports Foundation and overseeing the Collegiate Women's Sports Awards, known today as the Honda Cup. That award has been ongoing since the mid-1970s, when the Broderick Company and women leaders recognized the outstanding female college athletes in every sport, along with an overall winner. Women's sports had come a long way since the physical educators had denounced personal recognition, travel, spectators and competition.

Texas A&M University held on-campus auditions. Raised in a small town outside of College Station and the first in her family to attend college, with a high school graduating class of ninety-nine, Brenda Crim earned a volleyball half scholarship beginning in 1976. An outstanding athlete and campus leader, Crim said she turned down athletic scholarships at smaller colleges after being offered benefits that were illegal in the AIAW.

The Aggies faced the University of Houston with star players and Olympians Flo Hyman and Rita Crockett early in the season. During warm-ups, several of Crim's teammates were injured and unable to compete. Texas A&M lost a couple more during the match to ankle sprains. Crim said the coach leaned forward and looked way down toward the end of the bench to where she was sitting and ordered her into the game.

The nervous freshman jogged onto the back row. In her first appearance in uniform, on the first play, Crockett set the ball to the six-foot, five-inch Hyman, who crushed it across the net. It rocketed off Crim's forehead and back across the net. She laughed about the experience, her 1976 introduction to college volleyball.

With educational expenses mounting by her junior year, the team leader and captain had to quit playing to work and attend school full time. Crim was heartbroken as she entered athletic director Kay Don's office to resign her scholarship, telling the well-respected Don that while the athletic stipend might have paid for tuition, college costs were overwhelming with other expenses, including room and board, books, and gas for her car. Crim needed a full-time job and was unable to play, she said, still unsettled today by the disappointment. Crim later founded a ministry called Alaska Missions that works with native Alaskans.

"Those kinds of struggles reinforced why the transition away from AIAW was needed," said Cerra when she heard the story. "They were so slow to want to add scholarships, to change and give women all the benefits that the guys had." Women wanted to dedicate their time to their sports but still had to pay the bills.

The Aggies' athletic director, Kay Don, possibly may have had Crim's situation in mind when she later supported Cerra and other Division I women's athletic administrators in starting an organization to improve athletic administration skills and advocate for increased scholarships and recruiting.

The Self-Evaluation Report's Summary and Conclusions

Later in Missouri's Title IX Self-Evaluation Report, the committee recognized the enthusiasm behind Jean's hiring but cautioned that her position was not a panacea to correct the many obvious inequities in an undeveloped program. It praised Jean's already valuable input and service in her initial steps to organize, diagnose, clarify, promote and administer an effective program. There were concerns with facilities, including locker rooms, and the funding of scholarships, with no foreseeable revenue sources other than fundraising. Funding athletic scholarships was a key building block because most of the women athletes needed to work in order to fund tuition for the entire school year in addition to fulfilling team obligations. Title IX was called a proper and moral commitment to the women students on campus and throughout the state. All of the stakeholders would have to create sufficient resources for a women's intercollegiate athletic program. The report's summary concluded with idealistic watch words of persistence, discretion, faith and patience.

"Under Jean's leadership, it was all going to be ok. I can tell you that ten times and I would not have given enough credit to Jean Cerra and her hard work. It's kind of an innate thing, that she knew the right thing to do," said Coach Duren. "She represented women in the right way to administrators and worked very hard to make sure that we were being appropriately taken care of."

Jean joined other Division I leaders to ensure that that occurred.

CHAPTER 10
From the Neck Up

1976–1980

LIKE MANY YOUNG adults trying to establish themselves, Jean and high school friend Genelle Fernandez Garverick had lost touch as both settled into careers and responsibilities. Jean shopped regularly at a large regional grocery chain and, on one visit, walked past someone who seemed familiar but out of place. She thought that her high school friend Genelle was at Purdue but was surprised and delighted to discover that they both lived in Columbia. Genelle's husband, Allen, had taken a position as a professor in the University of Missouri's School of Agriculture, and Genelle mostly remained home to raise their three children. When Genelle's mother, Moochine, the coach who had recruited Jean as a youngster to play on championship city recreation teams, visited Columbia, they renewed what became lifetime bonds over dinner.

Questions Arise About AIAW Governance

Meanwhile, at the university, Cerra faced a multitude of pressing matters. Cerra frequently met with Chancellor Herb Schooling, who was highly interested in and supportive of women's athletics but asked questions that Jean was unable to answer. The chancellor was perplexed by the administrative structure of the women's organization, the Association for Intercollegiate Athletics for Women, and its rules regarding recruiting, academics, travel to championships, and athlete benefits. To him, it was nothing like the NCAA.

It reminded Jean of earlier difficulties in explaining Iowa's women's physical education grading system. She believed that Dr. Schooling and other college presidents wanted to move women's sports forward but were hampered by AIAW rules. Dr. Schooling worried about Title IX compliance at institutions that were members of two separate organizations like NCAA and AIAW. Separate but equal was unacceptable in the fight for civil rights and was a puzzling option for women's intercollegiate sports.

"Dr. Schooling was very much in favor of moving things along and he kept asking me 'why can't we do this or that?' I'd tell him, the rules won't permit us to do that. And he'd say it was holding us back," Cerra said. "Missouri could never be in full compliance with Title IX because of the women's scholarship restrictions. He told me that the presidents wanted one organization that followed all the same rules."

The men's organization had more than a seventy-five-year head start. Would being in one organization improve accountability and provide growth for women's sports? Or would women's sports suffer from neglect and slowly be choked off by an organization that, in the words of NCAA President Walter Byers in the mid-1970s, was developed by men and for men?

Conversations ratcheted up. Division I institutions wanted more competitive opportunities for women, including women athletes receiving all the same benefits, in order to reach Title IX compliance. Cutting legal benefits to men was unacceptable to those athletes, coaches, administrators, and alumni. Cerra recognized that disconnect as she developed administrative skills in a combined men's and women's athletic department.

The AIAW approach prioritized cost containment for intercollegiate sports. Growing expenses of athletic scholarships and recruiting, compliance with Title IX, gas prices, and inflation hammered athletic department budgets in the 1970s. The low-budget and volunteer-driven AIAW urged education leaders to claw back what they felt were out-of-control budgets for athletic competition. Maybe the NCAA could follow their example, they thought.

The women's organization, dominated by a majority of voting members from small colleges, reflected a physical education philosophy: Women's sports should be untainted by the excesses and commercialization seen in men's athletics. Idealistically, the leadership believed in a different foundation: that women's athletics could be built emphasizing the purity of sport. Most of the AIAW small colleges were located in the northeastern United States, where many NCAA Division II and III male athletes received limited, if any, athletic scholarships. Increasing women's scholarships might complicate funding at the smaller institutions and create inequality for their men.

In addition, strong physical education departments at the smaller state colleges and universities attracted better talent, strong athletes who were the future teachers and coaches. The smaller schools wanted to keep that competitive advantage as long as possible against the larger, better-known, and better-funded Division I universities. AIAW's one-size-fits-all philosophy frustrated the D-I institutions when they repeatedly were out-voted at delegate assemblies.

Both organizations approached legislative proposals differently. At NCAA national conventions, members voted by competitive divisions that reflected each institution's chosen level of intercollegiate athletic competition. Generally, Division I (D-I) represented schools with athletic scholarships and the biggest budgets. Division II (D-II) had some restrictions on travel and scholarships, while Division III (D-III) included smaller schools and allowed no athletic scholarships. Additionally, NCAA conventions often attracted three delegates from each institution: the faculty athletic representative, the athletics director, and frequently, the campus chancellor or president. The trio had to agree on institutional positions, with the faculty rep responsible for the actual voting.

The annual AIAW delegate assemblies drew only the senior woman administrator, who typically embraced that lofty physical education philosophy. They stepped up to coach as an extension of physical education and wrote all the rule books for women's competitive sports. But athletic scholarships and recruiting were rejected; after all, most of AIAW's voting members already had jobs teaching on the college level. They were both unfamiliar with and uneasy with full-time athletic administration, coaching, and recruiting. It was a new concept.

The D-I schools tried passing legislation that they believed to be in the best interests of women's athletics, said Cerra. They wanted to travel. They wanted to recruit. They wanted athletic scholarships. They wanted all those things but regularly were outvoted.

New Mexico's Linda Estes echoed those thoughts. Early on, she thought the AIAW was a good idea. But she repudiated the organization's limitations on athletic scholarships and recruiting.

"To me, they weren't promoting women's sports; they felt they were protecting women by denying the very things so many of us at larger schools wanted. They had this [physical education] attitude that had come down for years and they weren't going to change," the progressive leader said.

Estes bristled as she recalled the more numerous smaller schools at delegate assemblies dominating microphones and hindering the D-I schools' legislation. She claimed that the association was backward in terms of equality by wanting to control and protect women's athletics more than develop them, citing early requirements to have a woman chaperone travel with male-coached women's teams. The frustrated but powerful D-I minority soon would find a collective voice to speak its interests.

Driving Back Roads Leads to a Pilot's License

Cerra crisscrossed Missouri, promoting the women's program to alumni and sports fans. Explaining about the women's organization seemed like just another hurdle in gaining public acceptance of women's sports.

"People *knew* what the NCAA was," Jean said. "Nobody knew what the AIAW was because it was exclusively a women's organization. When I spoke to groups throughout the state, people wanted to know why we weren't in the NCAA. They didn't know anything about AIAW."

Often, Cerra drove alone and late at night on dangerous and dark two-lane asphalt highways through the hilly Ozark Mountains. They were called "Blue Highways," colored blue on popular maps of the time and described in a book with that title by University of Missouri alumnus and author William Least

Heat-Moon. Cerra decided after too many risky driving trips that flying would be a better, safer, and more efficient travel method.

Jean embarked on pilot lessons in nearby Boonville along with campus security chief Mick Deaver. She told herself with bravado that if she could learn to fly, she could do anything she set her mind to. After earning her pilot's license, she rented planes from the university's Flying Tigers Club for travel around the state. Stressful flight situations taught her about the importance of thorough preparation and quick thinking.

On the return from a Springfield, Missouri, alumni event with Deaver and his wife, Sharon Baysinger, executive director of the Mizzou Alumni Association from 1979–1981, a pre-flight checklist revealed that the landing lights were out. Nothing was open at 11:00 p.m. to purchase replacements. They would have to rely on the runway lights in Columbia. There were additional concerns about a prominent stand of trees on the south side of the runway that were hazardous even during daylight.

Deaver reassured her that when they left, the winds were coming out of the south, so they would be OK coming in from the north, avoiding the trees and flying into the wind. Jean circled the airport to check the windsock when they reached Columbia. Unfortunately, the wind had shifted and now was coming from the north. The only choice was to drop in over the trees without the benefit of landing lights.

"I'm going to fly as high as I can so that I know we are clear. As soon as I see the runway lights, I'm going to cut the engine and glide it in," she said. Steeling her nerves, Cerra guided the plane in. She laughed that it was one of her best landings ever because she was concentrating so much.

More Flying Adventures

Few women had earned pilot's licenses in the 1970s, making Jean's accomplishments even more noteworthy. Women commercial pilots were rare, with the military only just beginning to allow women to train in the cockpit. Jean pursued the skills for personal reasons and to facilitate travel throughout Missouri to represent the university.

Cerra's pilot license allowed her to fly with visual flying rules known as VFR. She rarely took passengers, usually only close friends or work associates. Returning from a holiday trip with good friend Gwen Riggs Nunes to visit Gwen's family in Lindsborg, Kansas, they were near Kansas City when a huge Midwest thunderhead arose. Jean noted the angry black clouds straight ahead and radioed the Kansas City tower, which advised her there was no direct route available to Columbia. VFR pilots are prohibited from entering cloud banks or flying in low visibility.

They were forced to veer south to avoid the storm before swinging toward St. Louis, hoping to reach Columbia from the east side. Jean thought she was way past the required ten miles of visibility needed to avoid a dangerous downdraft, but the plane suddenly fell. It dropped a few thousand feet quickly.

"The thunderheads were so big and so high that they were really sucking air from way out," she said slowly, deliberately. "They had a lot of energy. They had a lot of force. They were bad."

Disciplined training kicked in, and she executed a maneuver to recover air under the wings by slowing the plane down. It worked, but the aircraft then was just a thousand feet above the ground. Cerra had lost all of her ground reference points and had no idea where they were.

With the storm getting blacker by the minute, Jean spotted the massive Harry S. Truman Dam under construction southeast of Kansas City. She repeatedly called the small airport nearby and finally connected with the attendant, who manually turned on the runway lights.

"That was a nightmare. That's the only bad thing about flying; if the weather is not cooperating, then you're stuck."

Wheels Club and Coaching Perks

Cerra's advocacy brought increased benefits to women athletes and coaches. AIAW recruiting rules were modified intermittently, but by 1978, coaches were allowed to evaluate potential players off campus. Car dealers were encouraged to support the MU athletic department by making vehicles available to coaches, including women's coaches like Joann Rutherford and Debbie Duren. The boosters gained membership in the well-known Wheels Club, earning them prime seats in the press box, pictures in the media guide, and other social perks. Coaches drove the cars for a few months and returned them at a prearranged mileage, handing the keys to the dealer and taking a new car home for both personal and business use.

"The head women's coaches got to be part of that just like the men," Duren said. It came with an additional gas allotment card of forty dollars a month. "That doesn't sound like much but it was a big deal back then, when gas prices were fifty cents a gallon. I have to think women at other schools were receiving these perks. I'm sure everyone was trying to keep up with the Smiths. There were so few women coaches, so few who wanted to or were prepared to step into that role. I have to think those people were getting taken care of much like we were."

Staffing Hires

By the end of Cerra's first year, early Mizzou coach and administrator Alexis Jarrett left to pursue law school and later business. Jean needed to hire a sports information director and tennis coach, a specific and difficult combination. Everyone in women's athletics seemed to do more than one job. Jean attended the 1977 AIAW national basketball tournament in Minneapolis to support the Missouri women's basketball team and recalled an impromptu meeting with a prospective hire in the women's restroom while they were washing their hands at the sink.

Cerra glanced over and recognized Dru Hancock, the tournament co-chairwoman who oversaw women's sports information at the University of Minnesota. Jean knew that Hancock had completed degrees at Ohio State, serving there as a graduate assistant in tennis and sports information before Minnesota beckoned. Jean smiled, made her best pitch, and asked Hancock if she was interested in moving someplace else.

"She was already doing a good job where she was," recalled Jean. "She seemed interested and I ended up snaring her." Hancock had tired quickly of the cold winters, joking that she had gained ten pounds by just hibernating. Hancock recalled that unusual but serendipitous meeting, with Jean introducing herself as the University of Missouri's women's athletic director and mentioning they were looking for someone with a background in tennis and journalism. Hancock was intrigued by the offer, listened carefully, and later credited Jean with jump-starting her career.

Hancock stayed eight years at Missouri, working with Sports Information Director Bill Callahan and assistant John Heisler, who were true pros in the business and helped build her skills and confidence. When the tennis program was dropped briefly a few years later, Hancock transitioned to full-time sports information and worked closely with women's basketball head coach Joann Rutherford and her increasingly successful program.

Hancock credits Jean with building a respected program in those early years of women's intercollegiate competition and giving many younger women like herself life-changing opportunities. Hancock left for Tennessee as an assistant athletic director under Joan Cronan when updating press releases, stats, and pictures became routine. During Hancock's decade in Knoxville, Pat Summitt led the Lady Vols to three women's basketball national titles. In 1996, Hancock moved to the new Big 12 Conference offices in Dallas and finished her career as senior associate commissioner. During that time she was chair or cochair of four NCAA Final Fours, including the 2023 Women's Final Four basketball tournament in Dallas when Louisiana State University beat the Iowa Hawkeyes in the championship game. Women's basketball was gaining fans but confronting inequities between the men's and women's tournaments at the Final Four.

Two years prior, Oregon basketball player Sedona Prince stunned fans by posting videos on social media comparing the differences in weight training equipment provided at the women's Final Four (a couple of dumbbells and a stack of yoga mats) and the individual custom lifting stations available for the men. There were stark differences in values for player gift bags known as "swag bags." Such was the uproar that within a few months, New York civil rights attorney Roberta A. Kaplan led an NCAA review into the controversy. The resulting hundred-page gender equity report sought to correct the disparities and recommended that the trademarked exclusive branding "March Madness" be applied to the women's tournament. As Hancock finished her career, she wanted to give back to women's sports and became a mentor to others, just as Cerra had done for her.

"In the last twenty-five years of my professional life, I have really made it a point to mentor young women. It's taken a long time for women to support other women. I've had women come up to me now and say that I gave them a start. That's easily the most gratifying thing that I've done."

Nat Page Files a Reverse Discrimination Title IX Lawsuit

While women like Mary Hill, Linda Estes, and Nancy Lopez battled in court for Title IX enforcement, in a few instances, males also requested relief. Remarkably, the most significant case may have been at the University of Missouri, where reigning NCAA high jump champion Nat Page wanted to train for the 1980 Moscow Olympics. The four-time all-American was among the top ten in the world and a rival to two-time Olympic medalist Dwight Stones.

Page's grade-point average was higher than that of both of his younger sisters, who also competed on Missouri's track team, but he was academically ineligible under NCAA regulations and was about to be denied access to the school's training facilities. The NCAA had much stricter and more tightly defined academic rules, along with an enforcement arm. The AIAW operated under a much smaller budget, with regulations enforced by an unpaid representative committee. The AIAW's more lenient rules required only continual progress toward a degree.

Page filed a reverse discrimination lawsuit against Title IX, citing "differences in educational standards" and claiming that his rights had been denied. AIAW's educational model of governing women's college sports once again was challenged, this time regarding academic eligibility, similar to earlier athletic scholarship litigation. Officials at Missouri worried about additional future legal implications.

Page received a stay in court in Kansas City during the spring of 1980, delaying enforcement of the penalties. He was allowed to continue training while the issue was sorted out and earned a spot on the Olympic team when he finished second at the tryouts. Page dropped his lawsuit after qualifying for the Olympics, and the issue never was litigated, but, unfortunately for Page, the US boycotted the Moscow Games for political reasons, and he was unable to fulfill his Olympic dream. Page continued coaching after finishing his competitive career, earned a spot in the University of Missouri Intercollegiate Athletics Hall of Fame, and served as an assistant coach on the 2020 US Olympic track team.

A Promotion: From the Neck Up

By 1979, Cerra's third year at Missouri, she felt prepared for more responsibilities. Dave Hart Sr., recognized as a marketing visionary from the University of Louisville, had replaced Mel Sheehan as director of athletics. Changes were afoot. Salespeople were excited about the new market of supplying uniforms and equipment to the women's teams.

"It was everything imaginable to try and get the women up to speed. And the university said that we needed all these things. We were totally overwhelmed, with salespeople knocking on our office doors every day," Coach Debbie Duren recalled. "It was obvious that things were going to move fast."

Hart held a powerful position within the NCAA as cochair of the Division I men's basketball committee. Men's March Madness TV revenues provided invaluable funding and a huge chunk of the organization's budget. Revenues from football's postseason bowl games went mainly to the participating conferences and individual schools, not to the NCAA. Hart also needed to fill 10,500 new seats in Missouri's expanded football stadium and sought to hire an associate athletic director. His friend, Bob Hitch, was a great candidate.

That summer, Hart stopped by Cerra's desk to deliver the news that he would be going outside the department for the new hire. Out of respect for her, he wanted to inform her personally about the decision without her being surprised by the media.

Cerra, who had spent the previous three years as an assistant athletic director and director of women's athletics, asked him calmly if he would consider having two associate athletic directors. He was puzzled and asked her to clarify that.

"You've always said that I'm a very good administrator," she replied. "Why don't you have an associate athletic director for internal operations and another one for external operations?"

Hart absorbed the message and quickly realized the implications if he hired a woman to oversee men's sports. Cerra pressed on, countering the concerns he had about hiring a woman as second-in-command. She felt that she should be considered for the position equally with any candidate after building the women's program and helping incorporate it into a combined athletic department. In a moment of true inspiration, she spoke up.

"Dave, the part of my anatomy I need to do this job exists from the neck up and not from the neck down."

Cerra continued by pointing out that the university was removing gender-based roles.

"There's nothing in the university setting today that allocates responsibilities based on gender," asserted Jean. "We did away with the positions of dean of men and dean of women years ago. Why don't we in the athletic department have responsibilities that are based on qualifications and competency rather than gender?"

Hart pondered the logic in Cerra's explanation. Still, he said he was unsure and that he would have to think about it. He had always hired his friends. No other Division I college athletics department had done away with roles based on gender. This would be the nation's first.

"I understood where he was coming from. I didn't want to be pushy about it. He and I could always speak openly and honestly and we were having this conversation. It wasn't an interview. But he recognized the implications of hiring a woman," she said. "He joked that his friends were going to run him out of town or that he would be laughed out of the room at the NCAA Division I Basketball Committee meetings."

Hart did what he promised and thought about it. Cerra's management style had influenced others, but would it work this time? According to colleagues, she was careful in her communications and understood how she expected a message to be received. It was an understated strength coupled with intelligence and an ability to articulate her position clearly. Hart's perspective gradually changed. The more he thought about it, the more he realized that she was the right person for the job. A few weeks later, he returned to Jean's office to offer congratulations on her new position as associate athletic director for internal operations, overseeing most sports and operations within the athletic department, including the academic counseling unit, business office, and clerical staff. An associate athletic director for external operations handled fundraising, media relations, and alumni events, while Hart himself oversaw football and men's basketball, along with his associate AD's.

"That took a lot of courage on his part. That was going against the grain because the NCAA was still suing against Title IX. I gained a lot of respect for him." Hart reflected on that decision years later when he told her how proud he was that so many former administrative staff had gone on to successful careers as directors of athletics. He added that his decision to promote Cerra to associate athletic director was one of the proudest accomplishments of his career.

"He was a very likable guy and placed a lot of people into those positions. It took a lot of courage on his part at that time. I never viewed any of that as adversarial, even when Mel [Sheehan] said I was going to be disliked the day I walked in. I saw that as a challenge, not an obstacle, because I thought I could get along with anyone."

The men adjusted to the new reality, including the coaches and supporters of the nonrevenue sports, who realized she was also backing them as passionately as she was for women's sports. While athletic directors generally focused on the money-producing football and basketball programs, the men's nonrevenue sports had never had a proponent like Cerra. No one believed women's programs would be self-supporting, so there was no pressure to do that. Jean noted the similar status to the men's nonrevenue sports.

"Some of those coaches became my greatest advocates. Under the typical men's scenario, no one really prioritized the nonrevenue sports. But I did. That's a delicate act because you're fighting for everything you can for the women and want to keep their respect."

Pushback came from an unexpected source. Some women directors of athletics across the nation criticized her for adding administration of men's sports to her duties and, therefore, betraying the cause of women-centered intercollegiate sports. Cerra explained her resolve.

"I said that it wasn't true; that I had broadened my responsibilities and hadn't abandoned anybody. I still have responsibilities for women's sports and now also men's sports." And, she added, how did they expect women to become directors of athletics if all they ever do is oversee women's sports?

Gymnastics and the Cat Classic

With reorganization in the Missouri athletic department, the Tigers dropped field hockey and added women's gymnastics to its sports lineup. Cerra hired a proven coach in the witty Charles "Jake" Jacobson. He said that Mizzou was in a hurry to add a women's sport, and he was the guy to take a chance on it. The former Marine also coached softball and women's basketball at Grand View College but had never been a gymnast. He had watched what he called Danish gymnastics and learned the fundamentals, plus he loved the challenges of coaching. He brought his nationally competitive team from Des Moines, Iowa, and all its equipment, along with an easygoing attitude that attracted fans and supporters alike.

Now a private liberal arts university, Grand View in the 1970s was a junior college that competed against the AIAW's best since women's college sports originally had but one division. Grand View's basketball star was "Machine Gun" Molly Bolin, who averaged over fifty points a game in high school in Iowa's half-court style. After graduating from Grand View, she became teammates with Missouri's Nancy Rutter Huerd and Suzanne Alt on the Iowa Cornets of the Women's Professional Basketball League and led the women's pro league in scoring. Missouri basketball coach Joann Rutherford wanted to compete against the Midwest's best, so the Tigers played Grand View four times in those early years, with Grand View taking the first three games handily before Missouri picked up its first win. Jacobson's gymnastics squad finished seventh nationally against bigger schools like Iowa, Iowa State, Nebraska, and Minnesota, yet he downplayed his expertise.

"I just got interested in it, and pretty soon people thought I was a damn expert," he said. "Then Mizzou got a hold of me. They got a helluva deal: team, equipment and a coach." Jacobson turned down coaching offers from Iowa, Iowa State, and Memphis, following his own personal dream to start a major university gymnastics program.

Jacobson had ten athletic scholarships to award, but like most coaches, wanted a bigger budget. Cerra and Jacobson came up with an idea to ask the St. Louis-based Ralston Purina company and its Cat Chow division to sponsor a women's gymnastics event. Missouri would invite top-ranked schools with team nicknames from the feline family: Penn State's *Nittany Lions*, the Arizona *Wildcats*, the *Tigers* of Louisiana State, Auburn and Memphis, Pittsburgh's *Panthers,* plus the Brigham Young University *Cougars*, Montana State *Bobcats* and Kentucky *Wildcats*. The prestigious meet was tabbed "the Purina Cat Classic" and pitched to company executives who loved the idea at the initial meeting and quickly brought in a marketing team to develop the idea.

Within a few years, the Purina Cat Classic was drawing seven thousand spectators, enhanced by bonus exhibitions by famous gymnasts like Olympic gold medalist Mary Lou Retton and others. Soon, the Cat Classic topped the Missouri women's attendance records, attracting over ten thousand fans to the finals in 1985 and again two years later. Event sponsorship exceeded $30,000 within a dozen years, prompting athletic directors to eyeball the funds for football, thus irritating Jacobson.

"The athletic department took me out of negotiations," he recalled, prompting a personal meeting with Ralston Purina to cement the relationship. "I told them that women do the shopping and gymnastics was more of a family game where there wasn't a lot of cussing and drinking and that sort of stuff. So, they stayed with me."

The exuberant Jacobson also sold potential local sponsors with the phrase "Hey, can I interest you in a round of golf and a beer?" He promised that it would be a fun time to support the program, play some golf, and do some business. Despite the early challenges, within a generation, gymnastics became the third-highest-grossing sport at Mizzou. He laughed that it rankled the super competitive women's basketball coach to recognize that gymnastics was attracting more fans than her teams.

"The women's basketball phone budget was bigger than my recruiting budget," grumbled Jacobson. Gymnastics was the first Missouri women's sport to offer season tickets and reserved seats for women's sports, "but we brought in more revenue than women's basketball, baseball, softball and volleyball combined."

Putting Principles into Performance

Entering the 1980s and a new decade, Cerra oversaw academics and hired new personnel. One high-profile head coach expected the academic counseling unit under her direction to wake up one of his team's stars every morning and guarantee that the player got to class. To Jean, that seemed ludicrous, and she told him that she was the wrong person for that.

"That's the player's responsibility. It's my job to help them be successful, not do the job for them. College is about gaining personal responsibility."

Jean worked closely with George Walker in the academic counseling program. Together, they changed the perspective from a dreaded assignment for failing football players to an opportunity-driven one for all athletes.

"We found that students who are B students might want to become A students. For those having academic difficulties, it was like an added humiliation to be forced to go to public tutoring," recalled Walker. What they discovered was that when it was open to everyone, it made the poorer students feel less vulnerable. "We would not have been doing our job as educators unless we allowed all the student-athletes to attend."

Walker noted that Jean was one of his first mentors to emphasize that he was in the position because she trusted him to make the right decisions. She would nod in agreement when presented with a solvable problem and communicate that his solution was worth trying.

"She would say to me if you ever need something, come to me with a solution, not a problem. I realized that that prevents you from whining. It also keeps you from looking for your boss to make your decisions for you," he recalled. "She was always supportive of that and if she thought she might have some issue with it, she'd take your idea, offer a viable solution and reassure me that we could try at least part of it. Of all the leaders I've worked with since Jean Cerra, I've never had a better one."

He recalled dropping by her office at the beginning of a work day and, after saying hello, brought up things that might prove challenging. She responded with an easy laugh, helping him realize that things were going to be OK. Walker later served as executive director of the Mizzou Alumni Association from 1986 to 1992.

Meanwhile, in 1980 Deb Duren resigned coaching positions in volleyball and softball to focus on family obligations, citing the pressure and demands of increased travel and recruiting. Duren understood the battles being fought daily at Cerra's administrative level. Duren noted that there were few women who aspired to become athletic administrators and praised Cerra's ability to synthesize issues and advocate for the future of women's sports. Athletic departments were scrambling to find qualified women when there were no experienced mentors. Cerra's leadership made things look a lot smoother for those people in the trenches like herself, she said, particularly when faced with limited funds.

"I know it was certainly bumpy for her, but the next morning you never knew that. I always felt like, and I hope the student-athletes did, that she was always there for you. She was just out there doing what she thought was right for her coaches, her student-athletes, and for her institution. I can never think of a day when working for Jean Cerra didn't make me really proud. You knew there were tough times. But the kids didn't know any better. And they were so excited. The coaching staff had no idea about the things we were going to get to do. We just thought it was great."

A few years after leaving Missouri, Duren was hired at nearby Stephens, where she coached volleyball, served as the athletic director and later became vice president of student affairs. In the late 1990s, the school replaced the combination theater and gym with a new facility called Silverthorne Arena. The floor was renovated in 2013 and renamed Deb Duren Court in her honor.

As Jean became increasingly comfortable at Missouri, she gathered powerful allies like Board of Curators President Barbara Berkmeyer, a top-ranked competitive golfer with five Missouri amateur championships and four runners-up finishes. That success brought Berkmeyer inclusion into numerous halls of fame, including the University of Missouri Intercollegiate Athletics Hall of Fame in 2001.

Berkmeyer received a university scholarship to play golf in the 1960s when a wealthy alum donated money to Missouri's athletic department, hoping she could launch a professional golf career. Jean was grateful to be able to lean on another powerful woman on campus who understood what she was going through.

"Barbara was a great support person for me," recalled Jean. "If I needed something I could always talk candidly to her. She always had an interest in what was happening with the women's athletic program and wanted updates on our progress."

CHAPTER 11

Not Combative but Convincing

1971–1981

WOMEN ADJUSTED TO the new realities within college sports during the 1970s, but so did men. Cerra needed to hire a coordinator for the academic counseling office when George Walker left to work in the alumni office. Team coaches, under pressure from media, alumni, and fans to win, often dismissed the academic counseling unit because educational priorities cut into the athletes' physical training and recovery. Lower grades meant a higher possibility that an athlete faced the added burden of required postpractice tutoring and study hall. Jean realized the serious disconnect and sought the right person from outside the department to improve academic performance.

Lynn Lashbrook grew up in Kansas City, Kansas, played football at Fort Hays State University in Kansas, and coached and taught in its physical education department, earning tenure after a few years. An ad placed by Missouri in the *Chronicle of Higher Education* magazine intrigued him with the prospect of being at a Big Eight Conference institution with more than four hundred student-athletes. Fulfilling that dream would boost his career. After driving six hours for an interview, he sought to calm his nerves and socialized in the hotel bar, chatting up friendly patrons. One, Ed Scott, was a self-described "jock strap salesman" for a well-known athletic company. Unknown to Lashbrook, Scott owned the hotel and was close friends with Missouri athletic director Dave Hart, who wanted to know as much as he could about the potential hire before the formal interview. Lashbrook laughed heartily when he discovered the real connection the next morning while he was having breakfast with Hart and Scott dropped by their table.

Cerra and Hart interviewed Lashbrook separately later that morning at the Hearnes Center. Lashbrook wanted the job and showed his nervousness, knees bouncing as he sat nearby on a couch. Cerra calmly placed her hand by his leg and reassured the affable young man that everything was fine. Decades later, she surmised that his show of nerves was prompted by the novelty of his interviewing with a possible female boss. Lashbrook nuanced his recollection, citing his respect for Jean while being nearly overwhelmed by the career-changing prospect of getting hired at Mizzou. She made him feel comfortable as she lobbed difficult questions to ensure his priority was improving academics, not getting onto the Missouri football coaching staff. Lashbrook got the job.

Departmental academic concerns soon surfaced, with thirty-five football players ineligible unless they earned six credits with a B average in summer school. Implementing Cerra's vision of academic priorities was the basis of what he called "doing it right," giving him a useful foundation throughout his career. They came up with the slogan "Never miss, never fail." He wrote personal notes when players missed class. Something clicked, and by football season, all the academically deficient players had regained eligibility. Early in his time in Columbia, Cerra encouraged Lashbrook to attend a regional conference with the National Association of Academic Advisors for Athletics known as the N4A. Within a handful of years, Lashbrook returned Cerra's faith in him by becoming that organization's national president.

"That was all because of Jean, because of her vision. Everybody respected her, all the conference commissioners, everybody. I gained a lot of respect by making academics fun again, instead of making it as though I was coming in every day and tattling on players," Lashbrook said. As a former coach he understood the challenges for both athletes and coaches, and at Missouri his whole world changed. "It may have been the best five-year performance of my career, juggling the trust of the coaches with the academics, which were two very different parties."

The collaboration paid off as Missouri football led the conference in graduation rates within a few years. Lashbrook became an assistant athletic director at Missouri and later led programs at Southern Illinois-Edwardsville and the University of Alaska-Fairbanks. By the late 1990s, he had used his experience in academia and business to start his own company, Sports Management Worldwide, a broad-based agency that represented professional athletes and trained individuals through online classes to work in the sports business.

Lashbrook credits Cerra and their collegial relationship with influencing his future success as an administrator, citing her for his career's foundational building blocks. Through the process, he embraced Title IX when other men resisted, understanding it through Cerra's explanations and experiences. He also valued her thoughtful and logical approach to athletic administration, which brought balance and a skill set that he believed was needed and uniquely different.

"Title IX was a negative word for the first ten years. All the athletic directors would just complain. There were quiet whispers all the time questioning female athletes. That was all still a part of the male locker room, but I think Jean took that stigma away. We forget the courage it takes to be in the front of change. It was hard."

Lashbrook admired her reasonable intellectual approach while dismissing more aggressive women leaders.

"Jean could hold her own in any conversation without being an antagonist, even with Dave Hart. All the male coaches respected her. She didn't play the 'victim' card. She would make her point strongly but wasn't confrontational."

Lashbrook believes that Cerra boosted the growth of women's sports with her ability to express her convictions diplomatically, earning her respect at NCAA conventions. He essentially described a buddy system, a good old boys' network, prevalent at the time with males promoted in sports administration based on close relationships built through athletics, not academic degrees in administration.

"Women couldn't play the game, so it was all men. All men. Jean stuck to the blueprint and the intention of Title IX and her diplomacy helped further the cause. She was not combative; she was convincing."

Fifty years later, Lashbrook recognized the law's impact on the growth of women's sports, with improved TV coverage and the development of women's professional sports franchises. He called the progress "fun" and proclaimed that Title IX was something that government legislation got right.

"Anyone who comes into sports now thinks that women's sports opportunities have always been there. But the process took fifty years. That development never would have happened [voluntarily] with a bunch of white male athletic directors. Title IX wasn't just legislation." Lashbrook went on to compare Jean to a tennis legend who fought for women's professional sports opportunities, calling her the Billie Jean King of college sports. "There's no way they would have ever done anything. I'm motivated every day to make my company a success, and it's built upon the principles I learned working closely with Jean at Missouri."

NCAA Responds to Membership

The NCAA, founded in 1906, was a small operation initially headquartered in a Chicago hotel. It offered a single competitive division for its first fifty years of existence, then split into separate university and college divisions during Dwight Eisenhower's presidency. In August 1973, just a year after Title IX passed, the University Division was renamed Division I (D-I) as the College Division split into Division II (D-II) and Division III (D-III). The D-II schools granted limited athletic scholarships, and D-III allowed none. Five years later, Division I split into two divisions for football: DI-A and DI-AA, which consisted of smaller revenue programs.

Walter Byers, a Kansas City native and sportswriter with little personal college athletic experience, became NCAA executive director at the age of twenty-nine and moved the offices to downtown Kansas City in the mid-1950s. The NCAA prospered with commercial endeavors, sponsorships, and television revenues and added personnel. It moved twice to gleaming modern buildings in suburban Kansas and finally relocated to Indianapolis, where the national headquarters remain today with over five hundred employees.

NCAA records show that the organization initially reached out to women's sports programs during the 1960s but was rebuffed by the physical educators and their philosophy. The physical educators wanted only a limited and noble type of athletic competition run solely by women and for women, seemingly content with play days and shared post-game refreshments. The NCAA dismissed that as true sports competition. The stage was set for future conflict.

With the developments of Title IX and the increasing social acceptance of women's sports, by 1975 the NCAA explored what legally was required of their all-male association. The NCAA Council, the organization's twenty-member leadership team, prompted by the organization's attorneys, needed to determine whether it was legally necessary to sponsor a pilot program for women's championships and prepared a comprehensive report that was shared at the annual convention. The NCAA move threatened AIAW representatives who were meeting at the same time in a different city. Alarmed by the foray, they called their counterparts repeatedly to protest. The initiative failed as NCAA delegates realized that women, who were not included in the NCAA debate but were affected by it, should be involved in discussions.

However, the matter remained unresolved. A follow-up resolution utilized the same exact wording, with requirements for input and recommendations from both men's and women's organizations. It passed. As reviewed in the November 30, 1980, *NCAA News*, this new proposal sought a much more inclusive and open investigative process and required that the special committee distribute the findings to all NCAA and AIAW members. Through the process, the NCAA Council realized that member institutions would have to drive structural change, not the leadership or NCAA Council.[13] The governance issues popped up repeatedly like annoying and determined mosquitoes as NCAA D-II and D-III schools proposed but failed to pass resolutions to add women's championships over the next several years.

AIAW Balances Competition and a Physical Education Philosophy

Both the NCAA and AIAW adjusted and reorganized through-out the 1970s to better support membership goals. All AIAW institutions, from junior colleges to large universities, competed initially in a single division, similar to the NCAA's early years. Progress and growth within five years prompted the women's organization to divide into small (female enrollment under three thousand) and large college sections. By the end of the decade, AIAW adopted the NCAA structure as it conducted separate championships for Division II and Division III.

At AIAW delegate assemblies, all schools voted on proposed rules *en masse* together, which was believed to be both democratic and inclusive as leadership insisted that issues facing smaller schools ultimately would affect the larger schools. Voting in one legislative body bonded all institutions and AIAW supporters in a sisterhood of strength to grow their programs and fight for Title IX while voting in divisions like the NCAA might encourage the development of narrow self-interests geared toward the wealthy or dominant institutions.

The small colleges and their philosophical allies were the primary beneficiaries of AIAW's educational model and voting setup, unaware of or perhaps unwilling to recognize the impending damage. Their issue was fairness and the need for unity to build women's college sports in the face of the powerful and more established men's programs. But fairness was treated as what was fair for the smaller schools to compete equitably alongside and against the larger schools. Early delegate assembly policy discussions frequently extended well past midnight as member institutions stressed developing a different model of governing intercollegiate sports, one controlled by professional physical educators.

As the 1970s closed, athletic administrators at larger schools grew frustrated over being unable to promote favorable legislation that allowed them to comply with Title IX.

During this era, many women's programs at larger institutions migrated out of physical education departments and began operating alongside men's programs that were regulated by the NCAA. Missouri brought both programs into a single department of intercollegiate athletics in 1976. Merging the departments aligned athlete services, avoided duplication, and brought greater name recognition and support services for the women's programs. Missouri and other institutions like USC, UCLA, Arizona, Stanford, and Ohio State wanted increased athletic and competitive opportunities for women that were on par with men's programs, a true varsity-level competition.

"The opportunities for men had to be the standard to achieve Title IX compliance. Women's program opportunities had to be compared to the men's opportunity levels at each institution," Cerra said. She pointed out that her prior institution, Stephens College, enrolled no men, so compliance with Title IX was simpler. "The big schools had a bigger gap that was harder to close. The bar was much higher."

Differences in Athlete Benefits Emphasized

During Judie Holland's year as AIAW president in 1977–78, UCLA women's teams performed impressively and collected AIAW national titles in basketball and softball. The Bruins hosted the women's basketball Final Four at Pauley Pavilion and beat Maryland for the national championship, the first time D I schools faced off in an AIAW championship. Softball battled to a Women's College World Series national title a few months later in Omaha. Recruiting and financial aid were becoming issues that affected families of daughters, including Dave and Ann Meyers, a renowned basketball-playing brother-sister duo from Orange County, California, who both starred at UCLA. Ann Meyers, a couple of years younger than her brother, experienced decidedly different recruiting and athlete benefits because of AIAW rules.

AIAW philosophy emphasized that female students should be free to choose a school based on academic offerings, not the size or focus of the athletic department, unhindered by recruiting pressures from coaches. Rules prohibited coaches and institutional representatives from being paid for or excused from teaching duties to recruit. Students were encouraged to visit campuses at their own expense for evaluations, even though it was illegal for high schoolers to try out against current college players. Cerra and others perceived that policy as being discriminatory against lower-income prospects who couldn't afford campus visits. AIAW leaders believed that the policy protected female athletes from potentially unwanted home visits and saved the coaches the time and expense of travel. Why wouldn't coaches and fans support a system that rejected the exhaustive and degrading process of wooing a seventeen-year-old?

Instead, staff time and effort could be devoted to all athletes and a total program rather than recruiting individuals for their athletic abilities. This reflected AIAW's ideal of equitable competition carefully controlled by professional physical educators. Accordingly, many of the women coaches during the 1970s focused on their paid university teaching positions and often coached more than one sport. Visits that were a regular part of the institutions' admission process were the only ones approved. The overarching intent was to avoid being like the NCAA and prevent recruiting from being underwritten by universities and colleges in women's programs.

"When Dave and Ann Meyers were at UCLA, the brother could get fees, tutoring, room and board, additional coaching, per diem expenses, equipment, better travel and accommodations, books, laundry and so many benefits, while Annie initially could only get tuition and fees," Holland said. She bemoaned AIAW voting procedures. "There were more of the smaller schools than there were of us. We just couldn't get anything done."

Although Holland recognized that the NCAA was imperfect, she cited the benefits of making and applying rules that would affect both genders equitably while simultaneously concerned that AIAW would never be able to modify its approach.

Dave Meyers won a pair of national championship rings playing for Coach John Wooden, alongside notables like Bill Walton, Marques Johnson, and Jamaal Wilkes, earned all-American honors, and played professionally for four years. Ann, who graduated in 1978, was the first woman to receive a four-year athletic scholarship to UCLA. Her leadership as a senior earned her the Broderick Cup as the nation's outstanding female athlete, and she became a four-time all-American as she led UCLA to a national title.

Despite some advances, questions persisted about the differences in permissible benefits between the men's and women's programs. As women's athletics programs relocated into combined athletic departments, the growing spotlight revealed deeper contrasts. One former president of the national physical education alliance questioned Holland about the growth and direction of women's college sports, perplexed about why a girl from Florida would want to go to UCLA.

"Why shouldn't she go to UCLA? That woman thought everybody should stay home and go to school," Holland said.

"That's not the real world. To her and the other physical educators no one was supposed to recruit or go out of state."

D-I women athletic administrators like Holland chafed under the predicament of trying to comply with Title IX while limiting women's athletic scholarships and balancing the numerous national regulations that differed from the men's system. Cerra grew frustrated in trying to explain to Chancellor Schooling that solutions to issues that he proposed were actually illegal under AIAW regulations.

Men's and women's college sports operated under distinct differences in eligibility and transfer rules, with women athletes able to change schools with few, if any, restrictions and gain immediate eligibility. Male athletes faced the consequences of sitting out for a year or two under conference rules that discouraged transferring. AIAW insisted that its flexibility supported a student's autonomy in pursuing her education since she or her parents generally were funding it. AIAW's academic rules required only that female athletes be full-time students making progress toward a degree; seemingly simple, but there was very little budgeted for enforcement. Each institution was responsible for overseeing academic eligibility.

Frustrations with AIAW Arise

Cerra wrote in March 1978 to Chancellor Schooling and expressed misgivings and frustrations with AIAW governance. Both agreed about supporting a move to the NCAA in the near future, but the current timing was unsatisfactory. Jean detailed the difficulties in combined departments of administering athletics programs that followed conflicting rules systems.

"Some legal questions have been raised because of advantages or disadvantages in one set of rules over the other which favor one sex against the other," Cerra wrote to her campus chief. She mentioned that registrars and financial aid officers at many institutions were confused about differences in eligibility and athletic scholarship rules and how to accurately interpret them. Not only were their jobs made harder, but also there was always the risk of failing to implement them accurately and incurring penalties from either governance organization.

Cerra evaluated the additional costs to women's budgets to send teams to postseason competition because the AIAW provided no reimbursement for expenses, unlike the NCAA. The Missouri women's budget was forced annually to set aside an additional $20,000 to prepare for those, she said, as each institution assumed the financial responsibility to compete in championships. There were other risks as well, as host schools for postseason championships absorbed any losses for the event, while the AIAW or regional body potentially took 50 percent of any profits, according to the 1974 AIAW handbook.

"There is currently much dissatisfaction with the [AIAW] organization because they are understaffed," Cerra observed, aware that all of the officers and ethics and eligibility personnel were operating as volunteers while holding full-time positions with their institutions. She said that was absurd when AIAW totaled more members than the NCAA. "Record keeping is poor and institutions cannot contact individuals for decisions when they are needed. There is a considerable time delay in obtaining answers to key eligibility questions. Institutions have to wait until the week or month that a committee convenes because the committee members are spread out throughout the country."

Cerra further explained to Dr. Schooling that women's athletic directors at most Big Eight, Big Ten, and Southeastern

Conference institutions were concerned about AIAW insistence that its championships be conducted in regions different from their men's conferences. The NCAA had built its fan base through a well-known conference system featuring rivalries that energized alumni, media, and fans. AIAW's geographical and regional emphases were being challenged by the rise of women's conference championships similar to the men's.

Seven Midwestern states comprised AIAW Region VI: Missouri, Kansas, Iowa, Nebraska, Minnesota, North Dakota, and South Dakota. Big Eight members Oklahoma, Oklahoma State, and Colorado competed in two other AIAW regions.

Cerra foresaw that unfamiliar AIAW competition would hinder the development of the women's fan base, impacting attendance at home games and decreasing potential media attention, making her job that much harder. School rivalries like Missouri versus Kansas would be ditched in favor of state and then regional competition arranged through AIAW. The Missouri women's teams typically drove, whether in vans or buses. Getting to regular-season competition in North Dakota was more complicated and more expensive than traveling to Boulder and the University of Colorado, ordinarily Missouri's longest conference road trip.

Cerra's carefully worded letter to Dr. Schooling highlighted two items: the importance of institutional freedom of choice and competition between businesses and organizations. AIAW was the only organization offering national competition for women and brought together programs of varying sizes, intensities, and emphases, whereas the NAIA and NCAA presented institutions with choices for men's sports.

"Holding a monopoly on women's athletics is neither good for the membership nor the AIAW. Every year, however, it seems like we (AIAW members) are appearing more and more like the men's programs," said Cerra. She agreed initially that women needed independence during a developmental period. That seemed to have passed. She had learned while working with men at Missouri to value their decades of experience in athletic administration.[14]

NCAA governance promised potential benefits. Votes were organized by divisions and D-I institutions were more fully represented on numerous committees. The larger schools were guaranteed voting power on committees by being allocated at least one more member than those of Division II and Division III combined. That prevented the D-I schools from being outvoted by the smaller schools, she said. In contrast, AIAW was developing into three competitive divisions but offered only a single legislative division. AIAW schools could choose any of those divisions in most activities by sport, not a divisional assignment program-wide like the NCAA. AIAW voting processes virtually guaranteed that Division I members would be unable to pass needed legislation.

Frustrations mounted. Differences in athletic governance, including eligibility, recruiting, scholarships, tutoring, postseason championships qualification, transfer rules, and administration became increasingly apparent in combined athletics departments. The NCAA D-I schools had bigger budgets to provide athlete benefits, support hard-working coaches, and cover travel expenses. But AIAW demanded that its members follow only its values and rules.

AIAW leadership claimed that enforcing rules through an honors system reflected a belief in the integrity of the vast majority of people. An all-volunteer national enforcement committee had minimal penalty options for compliance. Issues were frequently resolved with a phone call since the women's college sports scene was so small that leaders often knew each other.

According to Cerra, even tutoring was problematic. Academic assistance was helpful, but women athletes were limited to regular on-campus sessions outside of the athletic department that were available to all students. Unfortunately, many of those times conflicted with practices, travel, or games. The women's organization also suspected that tutors hired by an athletics department might have incentives to do the actual classwork or take tests for the athletes. Although few occurrences were investigated, suspicions of unfair practices and illegal tutoring arose against UCLA and Judie Holland, its women's athletic director. She explained the controversy years later, describing how she had found a campus-wide academic assistance program to help freshmen entering with lower study skills, which was free and available to all students. The head of AIAW's academic committee needed clarification and called Holland.

"AIAW believed that tutoring was wrong and should not be given to any athlete, including the men. For them it was an example of why the NCAA was so bad. Men already had approved it [just a few years prior] and were going to keep on offering it," Holland said, noting UCLA's rigorous academic reputation. "Withholding tutoring from the women didn't create a fair situation for the women. I got our women athletes into those programs so they could get help. I thought they deserved it. But certainly, it was misunderstood."

Holland, ensconced in a highly competitive intercollegiate athletic department, responded with her own criticisms and questions. She complained about the inadequacy of a volunteer committee that was unable to pursue complaints with limited funding. A threatening, forceful phone call might be the only penalty. AIAW rules were far less stringent than NCAA rules, with no minimum required course load, no requirements for transferring students to sit out, and no minimum grade-point average for entering freshmen. Key issues slipped through the cracks, Holland said.

"They didn't have the resources to investigate schools. The committee was just there and people were expected to follow the rules," said Holland. To her, it was inconceivable that AIAW nullified direct financial aid for books but OK'ed a loan system as long as no funds were given to individuals. "That money could not go directly to the student. AIAW was all about an educational model but they weren't all about education. They were all about power. That's what runs the world and they wanted to have their way."

Athletic scholarship regulations sparked passions that resulted in frequent modifications as smaller schools attempted to compete equitably with the big-budget schools. The smaller schools passed legislation in 1977 to revert to previous athletic scholarship rules that allowed only tuition and fees. Holland called that a backward step and an attempt to stay competitive with the bigger schools like UCLA and USC.

"Why would you want to limit women to just tuition and fees when men could get everything else? That didn't make any sense to me. And to me it was terribly unfair to women!" Holland dismissed the opposition as misunderstanding the situation. "They weren't going to stay up with us anyway. We had more resources and were going to be able to attract more of the top athletes. Passing that rule told me that they were going to keep on doing things like that to try and stay competitive with us."

A one-year waiting period allowed Holland and the D-I schools time to overturn it at the 1978 Delegate Assembly, which she presided over as AIAW president. Fearing that female athletes would begin filing sex-discrimination lawsuits against the AIAW, the women's group voted 275–145 to return to full athletic scholarships. It also agreed to allow academic tutoring paid for by the athletic department. Holland remarked that the votes would have failed in previous conventions because of the prevailing opinion that women should forge a different path beyond the men's course. But at the same delegate assembly, AIAW rejected 230–212 a proposal to allow colleges to pay for "talent assessment" trips to high schools and junior colleges. Any recruiting would be paid for out of the coaches' pockets and on their own time. The issues surrounding the voting process signaled a future that troubled Holland immensely.[15]

AIAW's voting structure was impacting UCLA's women athletes unfairly as smaller schools rallied behind physical education-focused regulations. Holland and others dreamed of a different process that represented the bigger schools more equitably and pondered what that might be.

Men's and Women's Athletic Departments Are Combined

Division I athletic departments generally combined men's and women's programs during the mid-1970s in order to lower budget costs and avoid duplicating services. Women sometimes lost jobs in the process, no longer had autonomy over their own programs, or became assistant or associate athletic directors. Some women were uncomfortable with highly competitive athletic competition and moved solely into teaching and academics. Meanwhile, the NCAA mounted legal battles against Title IX, trying to water down its mandates while attempting to exclude revenue-producing sports. According to Cerra, the NCAA pursued those lawsuits over concerns from its membership about funding and resources while trying to clarify the intentions of the Office of Civil Rights.

"[Missouri Athletic Director] Mel Sheehan was trying to warn me that it was a whole different world that I was coming into," recalled Cerra, noting that she was beginning to understand through her administrative work how men's programs were funded. Working in a combined department brought her face-to-face with what she called AIAW's antiquated policies.

"Two different management philosophies were colliding. We were coming out of women's physical education into highly competitive athletic departments. Women had to adjust or make a choice."

By the end of the 1970s, Title IX had turbocharged the growth of women's college sports programs. Women in administrative leadership roles disagreed on how far and how fast they should develop those competitive opportunities. At many smaller schools, athletic competition was seen as an important part of a well-rounded education process, not as entertainment for alumni, to establish a successful school image, or as an "arms race" to obtain the best athletes.

Philosophies clashed, and the chasm loomed increasingly larger for Division I institutions facing a threat of losing research dollars and federal funding if they failed to comply with Title IX deadlines. Cutting benefits for male athletes in order to replicate what the physical educators found acceptable was unreasonable.

Would women's intercollegiate sports blossom within a carefully controlled physical education-based philosophy typified then by the University of Iowa and others? According to Cerra, young women had gotten a taste of athletic competition and wanted more. They were no longer content with play days, limited athletic scholarships, and no off-campus recruiting.

"Women weren't going to be satisfied under the old physical education model. Opening up that door [for athletic scholarships] through the Kellmeyer case was the beginning of more opportunities for women," Cerra said. In retrospect, she added, offering athletic scholarships may have marked the beginning of the end for the organization as it began operating in the NCAA's cultural reality.

"The AIAW lost the high ground of moral purity for sports after years of strong resistance the minute they accepted scholarships. It was something that had to be done because of Title IX and equal opportunity. I don't think anyone saw that at the time."

Cerra described an unforeseen disconnect between what the physical educators wanted and expected for women's athletics and the desires of many of the athletes they were supposed to be serving. The young women yearned for more.

So did the women athletic administrators at the Division I schools.

CHAPTER 12
Eleven Leaders Seek Solutions

1979–1981

CERRA KNEW FROM Missouri Chancellor Herb Schooling that several college presidents were concerned about Title IX compliance when dealing with two separate organizations having such contrasting philosophies. Cerra understood all aspects of the issues from her personal experiences at the University of Iowa as well as five years spent at Stephens College, plus her current position at a highly competitive Division I university. It had become clear that women administrators from large schools were frustrated with the disparity in voting power within AIAW. Others at AIAW delegate assemblies shared her views. An organizational structure was needed to advocate for the larger schools.

UCLA's Judie Holland recognized that the voting method was beneficial for most of the AIAW. In her experience, many campus administrators had a hands-off approach toward women's issues and allowed them to work out governance problems independently. That caused Holland to question whether AIAW representatives even met with their school presidents before casting votes at delegate assemblies. The challenges were persistent, perplexing, and perpetual.

Cerra also wondered if those without faculty status cast votes that reflected upon the school but were without the carefully reasoned safeguards gained from consulting the school president, faculty athletic representative, and athletic director, like the NCAA. Instead, many AIAW representatives voted for their personal beliefs, which generally reflected physical education doctrines.

Cerra valued that consensus required by the NCAA. Both Cerra and Holland understood that, in order for women to become directors of athletics, they needed experience overseeing men's sports as well as women's programs. UCLA men's and women's athletics were combined in 1980, but they had worked closely together prior to that. For Holland, Cerra, and others, that meant understanding and embracing an NCAA philosophy that AIAW loathed. AIAW defended its governance—it had built women's intercollegiate competition independently and felt it was the only organization needed for women's sports.

The University of Southern California's Barbara Hedges shared those frustrations and brainstormed with Holland how to best support their student-athletes. They agreed that a new D-I administrative structure was needed to overcome the smaller schools' powerful voting bloc that overrode any meaningful change.

"The college presidents and faculty reps at our schools were frustrated; they wanted one set of uniform rules for their men's and women's programs to compete under. It wasn't going to be the AIAW. No one had heard of it," Hedges said bluntly. AIAW's programs and principles were difficult for her to explain to administrators and donors. "They knew and understood the NCAA but not the AIAW."

Hedges phoned Holland after a very frustrating AIAW delegate assembly in early 1979 to discuss potential solutions, and together, they built a list of prominent institutions possibly interested in overcoming the roadblocks developing in women's college athletics. Because the group needed to build cohesiveness and identity, it strategically offered invitations, generally overlooking the EAIAW, the Eastern Association for Intercollegiate Athletics for Women, a region with numerous smaller schools seen as a strong AIAW affiliate area uninterested in discussing NCAA involvement. The leaders realized that starting a spin-off organization might be controversial and planned carefully in order to avoid provoking unnecessary backlash.

The eleven-member working group of women, tentatively known as the Council of Collegiate Women Athletic Administrators (CCWAA) met in August 1979 in Palo Alto, California. Stanford's Pam Strathairn hosted the small group of Division I universities, with only Ohio State University and Pennsylvania State University located east of the Mississippi River. Hedges praised Stanford's prominence both as an academic institution and for its outstanding pursuit of women's sports.

"It just made sense for us to meet there," noted Hedges, adamant about the purpose of the group. "We had to have a voice or we were going to be stuck with never being able to do what we thought was best for our female student-athletes, like scholarships, travel and recruiting."

While Hedges and Holland represented deep-seated rival schools ten miles apart in Los Angeles, they became the complementary forces, the yin and yang, of the CCWAA. Hedges was the more visible spokesperson, while Holland felt more comfortable working behind the scenes to organize and complete the council's necessary filings and paperwork. Following up on the hand-picked group's initial enthusiasm, Holland created and sent out framework proposals, later inserting modifications as requested. She developed the group's constitution and bylaws, with the organization open to anyone who wanted to join and pay the annual twenty-five dollars dues.

Preliminary work was completed by mail, and a fall forum was planned for Denver the following year. Jean Cerra led efforts to recruit others. That November 1980 forum attracted two hundred women and provided a springboard for proposals at an upcoming NCAA convention. The NCAA voting structure was attractive, while AIAW seemed to ignore increasing tensions.

"At the time we formed the CCWAA, we wanted to bring women together to discuss ideals and direction, women who believed we needed to move forward for our women athletes," Hedges recalled. "We were so harmonious and so thoughtful about the direction that we should go." The eleven founders of the CCWAA committed to network together, support each other in addressing shared issues, and build administrative skills. They realized the clock was ticking for their athletes' competitive college sports careers. Bonded by a sense of urgency, the CCWAA focused on achieving Title IX compliance while acknowledging that AIAW limitations on athletic scholarships, recruiting, and athlete benefits hindered the Division I schools' progress.

The CCWAA founders represented six of the major athletic conferences of the day: four representatives from the Pacific Ten Conference, two each from the Western Athletic Conference and Big Eight Conference, and one representative each from the Southwest Conference, Atlantic Ten Conference, and Big Ten Conference. Cerra took part, along with Mary Roby from the University of Arizona, Sue Garrison (University of Houston), Linda Estes (University of New Mexico), Phyllis Bailey (Ohio State), June Davis (Nebraska), Della Durant (Penn State), Mary

Hill (San Diego State), Pam Strathairn (Stanford), Holland from UCLA and Hedges from USC, while the University of Tennessee was marked as unable to attend.

The extensive agenda reflected ongoing and unresolved issues over Division I needs, election processes, administration, leadership, headquarters location, evaluation of legal counsel, television contracts, and more. Planned discussions seemed both complex and personal.

With the 1984 Olympics on the horizon, three appointees to the prestigious organizing committee were from one institution east of the Mississippi River, while none were from Los Angeles institutions directly involved in the Olympic Games. Officer elections for AIAW's top positions were questioned when nominations for some Division I leaders were either lost or overlooked. Attendees wondered if AIAW was a political group so opposed to men's organizations that it affected the organization's operation, including decisions about potential relocation and the immense expense of ongoing legal advice.

A Beaumont, Texas, citizens group had offered land and support for a new national office in the city of one hundred thousand east of Houston. AIAW's East Coast location presented challenges for those on the West Coast, and the group wanted more information about that possibility.

By the mid-1970s, the association had $180,000 in income but spent only $15,000 conducting championships, compared to legal expenses exceeding $43,000.[16] The disparity between outlays for legal counsel versus spending on championships grew even more over the next few years. AIAW had promised but neglected to evaluate attorney Margo Polivy's performance at the executive board meeting, with questions left unanswered about whether the organization needed a general counsel or just a lawyer to answer legal questions.

Other issues arose in the initial CCWAA meeting. The large schools wanted to pursue their own TV contracts, but AIAW claimed sole authority for negotiations. Missouri and Penn State sought a vote in the full delegate assembly to set minimum academic standards for all AIAW athletes, but an AIAW committee rejected that. Those incidents and others raised uncertainties that AIAW leaders were responsive to the views of the entire membership.[17]

The disconnect bothered Cerra, who had served for five years at an all-women's school with no men's programs to compare with or budgets to share. She pointed out that, at the small school level, men's and women's programs split limited institutional funds.

"The smaller schools didn't have that pressing need that we had with our female athletes, coaches and university administrators who were pushing us to give them the greatest competitive opportunities. They couldn't relate to and couldn't understand what the larger schools were experiencing," said Cerra. "Our athletes were biting at the bit for every opportunity possible in the four short years they were eligible to compete."

Cerra yearned to expand women's athletics at Missouri. Intercollegiate athletic competition was the highest achievement possible for most women athletes. Career and professional opportunities might be available in women's tennis and golf, but there were few women's team sports available after college. Cerra, Holland, and Hedges were supported by campus chancellors like University of Missouri's Herb Schooling and Barbara Uehling; Chancellor Charles Young and athletic director Pete Dalis at UCLA; and USC athletic directors like Dick Perry and John McKay, a former USC football coach. Together, they envisioned greater opportunities for women than AIAW wanted to provide.

"In the Pac-10 the majority quickly supported their women's programs going into the NCAA because they saw greater opportunity and it made sense. That really was the split," said USC's Hedges, noting that some regions of the country were slow to embrace women's athletics. West Coast universities seemed to reflect a pioneer spirit handed down from families who undertook journeys in covered wagons, women who pitched in to build the family farm or business, and immigrants seeking a better life. "I felt very fortunate to be in the Pacific Ten Conference because it was very forward-looking."

Working with men in combined athletics departments helped the CCWAA founding members learn new business, organizational, and fundraising methods. The founders were intrigued by an NCAA governance structure that had developed over decades and emphasized institutional control, unlike an AIAW system in its infancy that was unwilling to shake its physical education roots. The CCWAA also focused on preparing young women to enter the sports administration profession since there was no college degree in that field, particularly for women.

"You were just thrown in, baptism by fire basically. That career option had never been available to women," recalled Cerra. As an educator, she was concerned with the lack of training to prepare women in sports administration. "We formed the CCWAA to be able to mentor young women who were being hired into administrative or leadership positions with little experience, who could be helped with a seminar or convention once a year."

The NCAA governing model emphasized institutional control, requiring a faculty athletic representative who worked closely with the athletic director and held oversight powers on everything pertaining to athletics, including eligibility and academic concerns and compliance with the NCAA regulations. This leadership team reached consensus in contrast to decisions made by a single individual. To Cerra, that seemed like a much truer academic and competitive model than AIAW's. Hedges agreed.

"We were focused totally and completely on providing our athletes the greatest opportunities that we could. It made no sense to continue to be miserable within the AIAW structure. The AIAW looked at the NCAA as an evil organization and rejected that model of governance," said Hedges. "AIAW didn't realize that we would become stronger and provide greater opportunities [to female athletes] and seemed unable to break out of that old-school physical education philosophy." She added that AIAW was unable to fund its championships adequately and grumbled that AIAW spent far greater amounts on legal services.

Cerra suggested that most of the Denver fall forum attendees were curious about and open to potential NCAA governance. Additional leaders included Phyllis Howlett of Kansas University and later with the Big Ten Conference, Sondra Norrell-Thomas of Howard University, Mona Plummer of Arizona State, and Kay Don of Texas A&M. Attendees approved a constitution and bylaws and elected the outgoing and engaging Hedges as its first president. The CCWAA Fall Forum attracted significant numbers weeks before an NCAA vote on initiating Women's Division I championships. The impact was soon evident.

Jean and the other CCWAA members had developed leadership skills through AIAW positions all over the country and rightfully were proud of their contributions. They chose to organize carefully and covertly to avoid backlash. They anticipated that close friends, peers, and colleagues might disagree with their positions. Facing outward animosity was difficult.

"We wanted another alternative. We had learned in our programs to work with the men and doing that presented us with one big philosophical difference," Cerra emphasized. She disagreed with AIAW's rejection of NCAA standards. "I always have gotten along with the guys because I understood where they were coming from; I didn't think of them as 'chauvinist pigs.' I realized that their background and their life experiences were without women in sport."

The Ivy League universities presented a quandary by being Division I schools that did not award athletic scholarships. The highly academic and historic institutions like Princeton, Yale, Brown University, and Dartmouth became coeducational during the decade and quickly supported women's athletics and promoted women's Ivy League Championships. But Cerra noted the philosophical differences between the Ivies and the Midwestern, football-oriented programs she dealt with regularly in the Big Eight Conference.

"The Ivy League was a whole different world than what we were dealing with in our institutions. The men we were dealing with had been fighting Title IX," Cerra observed.

Other conferences, like the Southeastern Conference, refused to certify the women's SEC championships, allowing them to be branded only as invitational championships. Ann Marie Rogers, the first women's athletic director at Alabama before moving to the University of Florida, described the difficulties she faced in gaining that recognition.

"When we started having invitational championships in the 1970s the SEC would not allow us to call them SEC championships," said Rogers. She quietly noted the initial women's tournaments in basketball, volleyball, golf, and tennis were called invitationals and not SEC championships, seemingly because they were not in the NCAA. "I don't think they really understood the AIAW. We were not operating under the same rules and they hadn't approved it. We were informed they were invitational championships, not SEC championships." Eventually, she put hundreds of miles on her car driving to the league offices in Birmingham to work on proposals for inclusion.

Despite the challenges, Hedges said at least one Ivy League institution, Brown University in Rhode Island, sent a representative to the first fall forum. But others in the Eastern AIAW affiliate area, like Princeton's Merrily Dean Baker, missed out on the invitation. Baker, who was elected as AIAW's final president, recalled rumors about a group forming on the West Coast, but she was uncertain about its purpose without getting an invitation.

Other women painted the CCWAA in starker terms as a phantom group out of California, West Coast renegades who were forming a secret society. Some detractors labeled them turncoats or traitors to the cause of women's sports. Many were surprised to discover Cerra's connection.

Overcoming Bumpy Roads

AIAW leadership, including Iowa's Christine Grant, opposed the women who were open to working with the NCAA. Cerra's former grad school colleague called her several times to question her support of NCAA governance. Grant expressed a physical education viewpoint that increasing women's athletic competition to mirror the NCAA was too big a leap and brought too much pressure to the women, coaches, and teams. Grant fought eloquently and passionately for those values. Cerra responded calmly. After all, they were friends. They had taken classes together. They had known each other for years.

Cerra described a totally different experience from Grant and others who remained in independent and separated athletic departments. Tempered by loyalty and positive experiences with AIAW, Cerra recounted the broader benefits and experience she had gained following her promotion to oversee both men's and women's sports. Being involved with both men's and women's athletics brought an understanding and experience that fostered insightful comparisons. She worked daily with men's athletic administrators; they did not. Cerra speculated that those women might have thought men had a lot, but by being involved with both men's and women's programs, she understood where men had adjusted to accommodate the women's programs.

The influential Iowa philosophy embodied by Grant was the beating heart that sustained AIAW and gave it life, said Cerra. She respected Grant's determination through the frequently fierce conversations and Grant's allegiance to the physical education approach. Jean requested the same considerations.

"You're not going to refute the fact that we both want what's best for women's sports. We just disagree on how to get there and how fast to get there," clarified Cerra while emphasizing the word *fast*. "And fast was the train that we were on. You could call it the Express Train."

She said that Missouri and other major schools wanted to jump on that train. NCAA governance gave Division I women athletes the greatest possible growth potential. It seemed a paradox that competitive athletic frameworks and athlete benefits at the D-I schools were light years ahead organizationally from those at smaller schools but were dominated by the smaller schools because of the voting structure. AIAW ignored issues faced by the CCWAA founders.

Although much has been written about the history and development of the AIAW, there are few details about why Division I institutions were so dissatisfied that they sought a change in governance. Cerra called it a historical void about why the D-I leaders like herself supported women's full intercollegiate competition by aligning with the NCAA.

"The history of that whole internal challenge that was dividing women has never been told or explained in detail; the motivation of why several women wanted to move into the NCAA and away from AIAW. They've missed the boat in terms of recognizing the eleven CCWAA founders that really were the effective ones in bringing the women into the NCAA. The whole battle—I don't mean a physical one—was tough on us especially when we were opposed by friends of ours. We had to go against all the other women in the country."

The small contingent of Division I administrators seemed to be confronted by all the pioneers of women's college sports. Cerra speculated that administrators and CCWAA founders like Phyllis Bailey at Ohio State and Della Durant of Penn State faced the most backlash because of their proximity to the Eastern AIAW.

"We weren't threatened; my life wasn't in danger," Cerra said. "It was more like we were harassed or belittled. They pressured us a lot to not support the NCAA. They wanted us to conform. Eleven women, with all the other women in the room having the viewpoint of 'let's stand up for ourselves, let's promote the AIAW, women's rights, women power.' And our eleven are coun tering that by saying we're going to be better off joining with the NCAA. It was a brave move."

Cerra was a real outlier, according to Barbara Hedges, be-cause many people felt that she never would gravitate toward supporting the NCAA. Pro-AIAW supporters worked tirelessly to persuade Cerra to reconsider.

"But Jean was very logical," said Hedges. That level-headedness allowed Cerra to carefully examine all sides of the issues before she determined a position.

In Judie Holland's recollection, some people joined the CCWAA and some people didn't because they recognized that the group was trying to make some bold changes. She colorful-ly dismissed the opposition as self-proclaimed feminists more interested in burning bras than working toward putting on great championships.

"Funding championships didn't seem to be high in their thinking," she surmised. "Change wasn't on the agenda for a lot of people."

Joe Crowley, former University of Nevada president, chronicled the NCAA's history in his 2006 book entitled *In the Arena: The NCAA's First Century.* The book described hot-button issues of the previous quarter century, including governmental legislation, more participation by women and minorities, repeated litigation, particularly over Title IX, and rules enforcement. Crowley acknowledged that the university presidents were against a separate but equal kind of philosophy for men's and women's athletic competition and that change was needed. The events leading to the historic NCAA votes to initiate women's championships were challenging to describe, so he settled on a single phrase: Some women were dissatisfied.[18] But the transition from AIAW to NCAA required reconciling two very different philosophies.

AIAW had no reason to preserve anything that countered its own history and failed to recognize the reasons for CCWAA's development. At the same time, the NCAA overlooked the women who worked and organized to bring about that change. It disregarded the history of CCWAA's formation, which occurred prior to its involvement. But the courage and conviction of the eleven CCWAA founders deserve recognition.

Decades later, resentments remained. Early women's intercollegiate athletics trailblazers like Cerra were invited to contribute historical documents pertaining to that era. When she offered to donate items about the formation of the CCWAA and the deeper reasons for the move to the NCAA, her gesture was dismissed with a "thanks but no thanks, we don't want or need that history." While today much of the history is digitized and online, a big gap remains in terms of why some women wanted to work with the NCAA, she said.

"Back then unless you kept papers and records, there was no documentation," she noted. "And the history [of women's college sports] has been presented in a certain way that fails to recognize the efforts of the CCWAA founders."

Joe Crowley's extensive NCAA research overlooked the pivotal role of the eleven CCWAA founders. Instead, Crowley recognized the CCWAA's 1990s rebranding when the organization was renamed the National Association of College Women's Athletic Administrators (NACWAA). Currently, the same organization has grown to six thousand members and is known as Women Leaders in Sports with headquarters in Kansas City. It encompasses a broad cross section of women working on many levels of sports administration, including both college and professional levels. The group continues the original goals of utilizing an annual fall conference for networking and training.

Cerra's allies recalled other difficulties in developing a governance structure that supported the needs of the Division I minority. New Mexico firebrand Linda Estes today makes no apologies for her strong advocacy, an approach that infuriated many contemporaries. Estes recognized her own personal limitations in attracting allies and gaining consensus. She proclaimed a deep gratitude for the legitimacy that the CCWAA brought to their collective efforts. Estes, the most outspoken progressive leader for change, credited Cerra's networking skills as accomplishing more than people realized.

"She wasn't looking to get credit. She was looking to get things accomplished," recalled Estes. "When it was me out there it was like I was this one rebel. The CCWAA included people like Jean who were admired for their accomplishments and that gave it a lot more credibility than I ever had by myself in trying to get things changed."

Estes recalled how she often was a solitary figure initially in publicly opposing many AIAW policies. The University of New Mexico administrator cast a single courageous yet dissenting vote at a 1980 Delegate Assembly supporting the NCAA and NAIA proposals to initiate women's championships while the majority prevailed 339–1. Estes's brazenness rallied CCWAA allies, who recognized Estes's fervency and willingness to speak passionately in promoting their cause.

"She would go berserk and we loved her," recalled Barbara Hedges. "We told her to keep going, that she was doing a great job, that we didn't care what she said."

Women athletic administrators at Division I universities grew bolder as the decade closed.

Athletic Organizations Implement Women's Championships

AIAW faced existential threats not only from the NCAA but also from two-year colleges and small colleges governed by the NAIA that sought to implement women's sports. Confusion over rules led Judie Holland, as AIAW president-elect in 1976, to investigate the national athletic governance systems of four college organizations: NAIA, NCAA, NJCAA, and AIAW. Her extensive research compared all areas of governance, including academic eligibility, transfer rules, recruiting, financial aid and amateur status for student-athletes, and charted each organization's approach.[19]

The NJCAA, the National Junior College Athletic Association, incorporated women's championships beginning in

1975. Even though that impacted AIAW membership numbers, within three years, the NJCAA assumed control of all women's junior college championships with little interference. NJCAA Executive Director George Killian highlighted one key area: a voting structure that guaranteed women identical powers in decision-making.[20]

The NAIA also evaluated Title IX governance issues and wanted to add women's sports. The organization of smaller schools was founded in 1937 with a hundred members and expanded quickly. It had headquarters in Kansas City, like the NCAA. By the 1950s, it nearly matched the number of NCAA-affiliated colleges and challenged the NCAA for leadership in governing intercollegiate athletics. The NCAA responded to the threat by separating larger and smaller institutions into university and college competitive divisions.

In 1978, NAIA sought to develop common rules and guidelines for both genders in sports competition, guarantee equitable and proportionate representation, and provide district and national competitions for women beginning in the 1979–1980 school year. The exploratory report alarmed AIAW leadership.[21]

President Charlotte West expressed her organization's shock and disappointment in an October 1978 letter to AIAW voting representatives, directors of women's athletics, and presidents of AIAW member institutions. West proclaimed there was no need for further governance bodies since AIAW was already meeting the needs of small colleges. She praised the representation of small colleges on the AIAW Executive Board.

She wrote that "AIAW's short seven-year history has proven that educationally-focused women's organization serves the needs of female student-athletes. Women involved in intercollegiate athletics have overwhelmingly indicated that it is their preference that AIAW remains the governing organization for women's intercollegiate athletics. AIAW views this as a mandate and while cooperation with other collegiate sports governing bodies will continue to be actively pursued…a merger is not foreseeably in the best interests of the growth of a strong, independent women's athletic program."

West feared that women would be forced to enter an established governing structure that included men's athletic conferences, detracting from the existing AIAW regional setup. The Southern Illinois women's athletic director added that, in order to meet the needs of some AIAW members, the 1979 Delegate Assembly would consider a new class of membership for athletic conferences and provide voting privileges. She reminded AIAW members that small institutions received special AIAW considerations in the form of lower dues and that competitive divisions were allowed on a sport-by-sport basis, giving each institution the flexibility to tailor AIAW's program to its particular needs. Plus, small colleges were promised financial benefits due to increased revenue from sponsorships and television contracts.[22]

AIAW wanted to retain and control all women's programs despite being largely unknown to most sports fans. Regardless of West's objections, NAIA moved forward with its deliberations. Essentially, with the NAIA action, women were being presented with similar opportunities as the men, explained Cerra.

The NCAA Division I schools also sought to provide alternatives and held intermittent discussions with AIAW. Judie Holland said that those meetings failed to enact meaningful changes, with few areas of mutual understanding.

"Everybody had their own positions and nobody was going to change," observed Holland. "I was not part of that group that met with the NCAA. I figured those meetings weren't going to go anywhere and they didn't. But it was worth a try in my opinion."

Courage and Conviction

Ann Marie Rogers, the Alabama and Florida women's athletic director, agreed that the group of eleven largely was overlooked, with little written about them.

"The women of the AIAW were upset with them for advocating for change. Then later, the men in the NCAA had to address the concerns of those who were the most against joining it. It was kind of like this group that had made such a large impact has largely been forgotten," Rogers said with a sigh.

"People like Jean, Judie, Barbara, Mary Roby, Pam Strathairn, Linda Estes and Mary Hill and all the women of the CCWAA were courageous women who stepped forward. It was not popular at the time to support that change. Those women haven't been recognized for the courage it took to bring about change. The history that we see today is not right in that aspect," said Rogers, adding that women who were the least supportive of athletic scholarships, recruiting, and increased travel and benefits were honored in very public ways at NCAA headquarters.

"The women of that time who were mostly against that progress and what we wanted have been acknowledged for their contributions instead of the CCWAA trailblazers."

With a quiet determination, Cerra acknowledged her deep respect for AIAW and its leadership while emphasizing how numerous D-I institutions wanted to move along at a faster pace via NCAA governance. AIAW laid the foundation for organizing women's sports and created opportunities for women's championships when none existed. And yet, for Cerra and the CCWAA Founders, taking a stance for their institutions while opposing other women was necessary but personally difficult.

Linda Estes also elaborated on the divisive issues. While she supported the move to the NCAA, she questioned its resistance to Title IX in numerous blistering letters.

"The NCAA did everything they could to stop Title IX and get athletics exempted from it. They were going to lose because it was the law. It was a legal matter, not moral or philosophical. I liked just about everything else they did but not that."

Christine Grant summed up the differing philosophies as either educational sport or athletic business.

"[It's] much more than a financial difference, it's a philosophical difference. I believe that we can help guide the men out of a system that has become uncontrollable and into a system that makes good educational and fiscal sense."[23]

The business of college sports would be reckoned with as the intangible and idealistic values of the AIAW collided with the commercial model of NCAA college sports. With no agreements and two very different approaches to intercollegiate athletics, the January 1980 NCAA convention in New Orleans provided the first salvo. NCAA Division II and Division III voted overwhelmingly to offer championships in five women's sports beginning in the 1981–82 school year. Bigger turmoil was coming at the next NCAA convention in Miami when Division I considered women's championships.

CHAPTER 13
NCAA Conventions Vote for Change

1979–1982

THE YEAR BEFORE Jean arrived at Missouri, Cheryl Lightfoot Levick competed on the Tigers' synchronized swim team called the Mo-Maids. Levick missed out on intercollegiate sports competition as Missouri funded its pilot program during her senior year. After briefly teaching high school, she enrolled at Indiana University to complete a master's degree and serve as a graduate assistant in gymnastics. Levick's coaching and administrative career barely had started when she attended that momentous 1981 NCAA Convention. Levick realized that men's and women's college athletic programs needed to be combined under one system. She said she had additional concerns about limited paths to leadership and response times from the mostly volunteer committees.

"Jean and I agreed on that. We were in the minority but we both saw the bigger picture. I was frustrated because AIAW had become very insulated. I knew that it was inevitable for college sports to get anywhere that they needed to be integrated, not segregated. And we needed to make sure that Title IX worked within the integrated model." Memories of the 1981 NCAA Convention remain vivid.

"I was a young pup watching this debate on organizational structure, sitting there in disbelief next to my athletic director and watching this whole thing come down, with all the strong pros and cons. All those in favor would raise their paddles, and row counters would come along with clickers." Eventually, votes were conducted electronically by pushing yes or no on a handheld device, with each institution guaranteed one vote.

"It was a very difficult convention to chair and have some kind of decorum, with a thousand or more people in the room. There were standing microphones in the aisles and at the sides of the room. You would get in line and when it was your turn you would say your name and your school and then give your opinion. It was masterful." Levick called Christine Grant's passionate speeches articulate and impressive.

Career advancements later led Levick to work for a few years at NCAA headquarters, then for the Pacific Ten Conference. Levick rose to become Stanford's senior associate director of athletics and senior women's administrator during her twelve years on the Farm in the 1990s. She spent the next ten years serving as a director of athletics at three different Division I institutions. Today, she runs her own consulting business focused on executive coaching and educational workshops, including Title IX.

CCWAA Supports Women Administrators

The Council of Collegiate Women Athletic Administrators gathered support for NCAA governance behind the scenes. The women athletic directors of the Division I schools had grown increasingly frustrated with AIAW's indifference toward their ongoing concerns. They collaborated with Ruth Berkey, hired by the NCAA to direct women's championships, and NCAA leaders like John Toner and James Frank to lay the groundwork for full inclusion into the NCAA.

"The pressure was coming from college presidents: We've got men's and women's athletics in the same department; why can't we have one set of rules?" recalled Cerra. Chancellor Herb Schooling questioned how institutions would meet federal mandates with conflicting rules for men and women. It seemed impossible. Cerra disputed AIAW accusations that the NCAA envied the increasing AIAW sponsorships and TV contracts and instituted women's championships out of greed. She continued.

"My sense was that it wasn't about the revenue. I don't think pro-AIAW people have any factual basis for claiming that. The arenas were more than half empty for women's basketball. The real money in women's sports came *after* the women went into the NCAA. I don't think it ever would have materialized to that extent, in that short of time, if they had stayed in the AIAW. Nobody knew what the AIAW was. I'm telling you: The sports fans and alumni didn't *know* what the AIAW was."

Smaller schools had their own concerns. At the 1979 AIAW Delegate Assembly in Los Angeles, members argued about establishing three new competitive divisions and approved legislation that mirrored the NCAA's setup. The assembly limited Division III to institutions where athletes received no financial aid based on athletic ability.

Later, some Division III institutions brought the resolutions up for reconsideration. They wanted to award female athletes up to 10 percent of the maximum aid allowed by AIAW for athletes in particular sports. The assembly reversed its earlier action and agreed to let institutions legally compete in AIAW D-III while awarding fractional scholarships.[24] Controversy ensued within

AIAW as its organizational style was growing more similar to the NCAA despite its best efforts "to remain pure."[25]

That delegate assembly also modified overall recruiting rules. Previous restrictions had proven untenable. Coaches were able to engage a prospect or her parents only by phone or mail. The coach was instructed under AIAW guidelines to use the cold shoulder technique, with face-to-face contact only on the coach's campus. However, the cost of visiting a campus fell to the recruit and her family since AIAW members were prohibited from paying recruits' transportation costs. Cerra defined the dilemma in comments to *Columbia Missourian* writer Pete Wunsch in a March 4, 1979, article entitled "Title IX Threat to Women's Athletic Group."

"The AIAW feels it is helping women with these rules by eliminating all the so-called evils associated with men's athletics. We either comply with Title IX and violate the AIAW regulations, or we comply with AIAW regulations and violate the Title IX mandate in terms of recruiting."[26]

The 1979 AIAW Delegate Assembly agreed to let members pick up prospects at airports, bus stations, or train stations and pay for room and board expenses during a visit. But the student-athlete still had to pay transportation costs to the campus.

The cracks in AIAW's philosophy were becoming more exposed. Modifying AIAW philosophy to allow the larger schools to comply with Title IX seemed to be the answer. But for Cerra and the D-I women administrators, it appeared to be too slow.

Challenges in Merging Men's and Women's Sports

After the mid-1970s, many NCAA Division I schools, including Missouri and the majority of the Big Eight Conference, combined both men's and women's programs into one athletic administration. They faced the monumental task of resolving issues for both genders through wildly different governance rules. Big Eight members had held women's Big Eight championships since 1975, but involvement was voluntary, paid for by each participating school, and organized outside the conference offices. It was now time to consider fully funding the women's championships.

Iowa State University's Dr. Ruth Lauver, Chairperson of the Directors of Women's Intercollegiate Athletics at Big Eight Institutions, wrote in a September 1978 letter to Big Eight Commissioner Charles "Chuck" Neinas that the merger of nearly all men's and women's athletic programs in the conference revealed the need for discussing common problems in a more formal setting. Lauver requested a meeting that included four men's and four women's athletics directors representing each conference school, which she hoped would result in a Big Eight Conference for Women.[27]

Two months later, University of Missouri Chancellor Barbara Uehling, who had succeeded Dr. Schooling and was the only female campus chief executive officer in the conference and the first woman to lead a land grant university, echoed that sentiment in another letter to Neinas. Dr. Uehling proposed a task force of faculty representatives, athletic directors, and persons designated to speak for the women's programs. They would determine if the Big Eight Conference women's championships would be conducted under a separate, stand-alone organization with the Big Eight name or if those would be brought into the conference athletic system completely.

"I believe that eventually men's and women's rules will become much more uniform," predicted Dr. Uehling, "but I do not believe that differences in existing rules should impede the discussions that I have suggested."[28] All task force members were apprehensive about differences in men's and women's rules relating to eligibility, financial aid, recruiting, and other matters, differences that arose because the men's programs were administered under NCAA and Big Eight rules, while AIAW governed women's programs.

The Big Eight Conference extended over three different AIAW regions, but under AIAW, it would be a regional champion, not a conference champion like men's sports, that earned a guaranteed spot in postseason play. Conceivably, three Big Eight women's teams could represent the three different regions as an automatic designee, or perhaps none would. The work of combining men's and women's athletic departments was being done on Big Eight campuses. That now would be taken to the conference level, with the intense analysis needed on finances, promotions and publicity, statistical records, awards, costs for postseason travel, and the differing dues structures between AIAW and NCAA. Building identity and pride from representing one of the nation's most competitive athletic conferences brought advantages to the women's programs.

Cerra noted some risks to Missouri and other conference teams if they ran afoul of AIAW regulations. After all, AIAW completely controlled women's intercollegiate competition.

"Does the Big 8 Conference think that women could be incorporated into the Big Eight and still maintain their governance under the AIAW?" Cerra wrote to her campus chief executive in late January 1979. "How?"

Jean speculated about when the NCAA might institute women's championships, an idea frequently bandied about. Big Eight women's directors of athletics had conducted a straw vote that indicated four institutions at the time in favor of supporting NCAA championships for women. Two schools voted no and two voted as undecided.

"Including women fully in the Big 8 Conference could be a catalyst to a nationwide approach for resolving differences among men and women in athletics. Hopefully our national governing bodies can follow suit," Cerra remarked. Full inclusion into the Big 8 Conference could increase public interest and fan support, bring additional gate receipts, and drive fundraising since potential donors would begin to view the department as "one and the same." To her, it was advantageous to pursue the formation of a Big Eight Conference for women even if the AIAW denied recognizing the Big Eight tournament champion as a guaranteed representative for postseason play.

"What we all need to realize is that getting the conference started is the main thing! All of our problems are not going to be resolved in order to create a perfect situation for forming a Big Eight Conference for Women. If we wait that long, it will never be realized. But once the structure is available, the mechanism should allow for problems to be tackled as they present themselves. There would be a 'family unity concept' since most Big Eight athletic programs are now in one department, or moving in that direction. Conference affiliation should also be aligned in that way."[29]

Meanwhile, the MAIAW, Missouri's state association of AIAW members, voted to limit the number of women's basketball games to twenty-five per season, with home and away games required with each school. Missouri, a national power, was restricted in the number of games it could play against competition from around the country. The state schools insisted that the rule prevented richer schools from playing more games.

"I think the needs of our programs are vastly different from those of the small schools," Cerra said to the *Columbia Missourian*. Notably, the women's budget had grown to $500,000 that year. "It's very possible that when we are in full compliance at our institution, our women's program may have more money than the smaller schools' men's programs."[30]

By May 1979, the Task Force on Women's Athletics in the Big Eight Conference, with strong support from Missouri Chancellor Uehling, asserted its national leadership and approved the integration of women's competition and championships. Commissioner Chuck Neinas explained in a memo to campus leaders that in order to facilitate and inspire the development of women's athletics, the Big Eight Conference unanimously agreed to fully sponsor ten championship events during the 1979–80 school year.[31]

The developments sparked national interest. University of New Mexico women's athletic director Linda Estes praised Dr. Uehling for her stance and thanked her for her leadership and initiative. Estes had attended a national meeting of collegiate athletic directors a month after the Big Eight announcement, and those involved in women's sports administration enthusiastically embraced the league's efforts in instituting conference play and championships for the upcoming school year.

"In my opinion, the Big Eight plan is the most progressive thing that has happened in women's athletics since the AIAW was sued and forced to drop their prohibition on athletic scholarships for women," Estes declared to Missouri's chancellor. She wished her own school was part of the Big Eight. "What has happened in your conference will soon spread to other conferences and we will all eventually benefit from what you have done."[32]

During this time, Cerra's promotion to associate athletic director and her proposal to remove gender-based job descriptions cemented Missouri's determination to align men's and women's programs. The athletic department also sought to standardize regulations and enforce the more stringent of some vastly different NCAA and AIAW rules. One glaring area concerned grades and eligibility. Nat Page's Title IX lawsuit over academic regulations tied to eligibility forced Missouri to implement similar grade standards for both genders. The AIAW responded by warning Cerra about straying from AIAW rules, which seemed nebulous, required only progress toward a degree, and carried minimal penalties. The criticism seemed incomprehensible to Cerra since the more rigorous NCAA standards set higher academic accountability for the women. The AIAW complaint forced Missouri to carefully word its academic and eligibility requirements in order to meet both organizations' regulations.

Two vastly different systems of intercollegiate athletic governance faced off. College presidents wanted solutions for the frustrating and never-ending threat of losing federal funds for failing to comply with Title IX mandates. The NCAA moved decisively and formed a Special Committee on NCAA Governance, Organization, and Services in the fall of 1979. NCAA Secretary-Treasurer James Frank, president of Lincoln University in Jefferson City, Missouri, chaired the committee of college presidents, faculty athletic representatives, athletic directors, and one conference commissioner. The group's gravitas and firepower might help resolve the ongoing and critical issues.

The NCAA Approves Initial Women's Championships in 1980

NCAA's annual conventions voted on hundreds of proposals, some dealt with by the entire assemblage but most addressed within specific divisions. NCAA surveys showed that nearly 20 percent of D-II institutions and over 25 percent of D-III schools were unaffiliated with the AIAW and needed to establish women's sports competitions to satisfy Title IX. Proponents of the NCAA plan believed that an organizational choice should be available for women's competition.

Multiple D-II and D-III schools proposed that the NCAA establish women's championships in five specific sports: volleyball, field hockey, basketball, swimming, and tennis. The 1980 resolution was approved by a wide margin. Division I institutions observed the process. Competition would start in the 1981–82 school year after a lengthy 18-month preparation process. Unforeseen difficulties would be hammered out at the next national convention.

AIAW leadership was stunned, hurt, and angry following the NCAA proceedings. It rightfully questioned the sincerity of an organization that had fought Title IX's principles for nearly a decade but now wanted to develop women's intercollegiate sports. Boycotts of NCAA sponsors, letter-writing campaigns, and threats to file antitrust lawsuits were planned, along with lobbying of college presidents, alumni, and Congress. Cerra recalled the organized response as ineffective compared to the intensity after the Division I vote the following year. For the first time, the vast majority of AIAW's nine-hundred-plus members, potentially six hundred or more D-II and D-III institutions, had a choice in governance.

The Special Committee on NCAA Governance, Organization,

and Services surveyed members afterward about women's athletics. There were still more questions than answers, as only 100 of 725 surveys were returned, the lowest response in NCAA history.[33] The uncertainty indicated that most NCAA members needed reassurance about fulfilling Title IX obligations, with numerous questions about developing women's programs.

The survey intensified AIAW's alarm bells. In a letter to college presidents and chancellors, President Christine Grant and former president Carole Mushier castigated their NCAA counterparts for creating "an atmosphere unconducive to cooperative exploration of future alternatives." The women's organization wanted complete independence during any discussions with the NCAA and NAIA over governance and demanded that the NCAA rescind its actions at its next convention. To them, women's athletics needed and deserved an organization dedicated solely to women athletes. Grant feared that a switch to NCAA governance would result in diminished opportunities for women and called for a five-year moratorium in order to allow AIAW to assess the effects of its own policies.[34]

Grant's letter applauded the women's governance approach on a number of issues. Their "full participation television plan" gave revenues from a three-year million-dollar television contract to all members regardless of competitive division. The income distribution plan favored the smaller budget schools at the expense of the Division I schools that had invested in earning it.

Grant extolled AIAW's voting process, which combined all members regardless of competitive level or size. To her, that ensured equal "say" for women in determining direction and policy for the common good. Finally, AIAW needed additional time to establish an economical, highly competitive, and student-oriented women's program, assailing the NCAA for failing to resolve its ongoing financial difficulties.[35]

Grant compared both organization's approaches. Women's teams selected competitive divisions for each sport, not program-wide designations like the NCAA. Under AIAW, a women's basketball team like West Chester University of Pennsylvania, the 1972 AIAW champion, might classify as Division I, but all other teams were allowed to play at other levels based on budget, resources, and priorities. AIAW warned that NCAA requirements to place all of an institution's athletic teams in the same competitive division potentially would increase costs. Instituting NCAA's paid campus visits for athletes would also do that. AIAW granted four years of eligibility whenever an athlete chose to attend, unlike the NCAA restrictions at the time, which stated that four years of eligibility must be completed in a five-year time span. While NCAA and athletic conference rules provided penalties to male athletes who transferred schools, women could transfer indiscriminately, with the only risk being the potential loss of athletic aid.[36]

Progress and Pushback

Weeks after the January 1980 NCAA convention, a pair of CCWAA founders and vocal AIAW critics visited NCAA headquarters in suburban Kansas City. On an extremely cold winter day, New Mexico's Linda Estes and San Diego State's Mary Hill explained that there were women administrators organizing as the CCWAA who were frustrated with AIAW leadership. They sought alternatives to the women's group and were positive about the NCAA.

They needed more information, they said, as they urged the NCAA to contact dozens of Division I women's athletic administrators whose views frequently were overlooked or dismissed.

NCAA staff later spoke with about fifteen, who documented the dissension within AIAW as positions taken by AIAW leadership often did not reflect all the AIAW members, with no avenue for resolution.

"Our emphasis was that the women athletes *want* this to happen," recalled Hill, stressing the word want. "Some women administrators want it to happen. And this is what we think you need to do." They suggested potential nominees for NCAA committee positions other than themselves who were perhaps less vocal or strident.

Hill said that NCAA Executive Director Walter Byers listened closely as he sought to understand the women's goals. Byers brought in his top lieutenants for discussions about unresolved and sticky issues in finance, eligibility, championships, enforcement, and bringing women into the NCAA. Byers was struck by the women's boldness and, following his retirement, noted in a memoir about how impressed he was by that clandestine meeting in the NCAA offices. The NCAA was discovering committed allies among the CCWAA as back channels opened up.

The NCAA Special Committee on Governance, Organization, and Services met at the Indianapolis Hilton Hotel in March 1980 to discuss women's intercollegiate athletics. The post-meeting minutes defined two distinct groups operating within AIAW: one oriented toward physical education and another segment interested in establishing a true competitive varsity intercollegiate structure. The strongest enthusiasm for NCAA governance appeared to come from the Big Eight Conference, California, and the Southeast region. Indeed, the report concluded that there was little animosity toward the NCAA from the group of women's athletic administrators who were surveyed, but it noted that the women were concerned about the depth of potential NCAA involvement.

In other items, committee chairperson James Frank insisted that decisions regarding the governance of intercollegiate athletics must be made by the institutions themselves and cannot be "brokered" by national organizations. USC Athletic Director Richard Perry mentioned that the Pacific Ten Conference supported the work of the committee in resolving the issues of women's governance. It was imperative, he said, that each school consider the value of having one organization for men's and women's athletics and the potential financial relief from eliminating confusing and duplicated services or administration.[37]

Throughout the fall of 1980, NCAA officers James Frank and William Flynn reminded faculty athletic representatives and athletic directors that the NCAA intended to provide an option to member schools and denied that it was a merger or takeover of women's sports. They emphasized the choices now available because of the decisive actions taken at the 1980 NCAA convention.

Before the 1980 school year began, Judie Holland of UCLA disagreed with the acrimonious tone of an AIAW Presidents' resolution that called the NCAA actions to initiate women's championships destructive. The document vociferously opposed the NCAA, and Holland asked that her name be removed from it.[38] She questioned AIAW's path of isolation and inability to work together with the NCAA. Holland repeated those concerns and more a few months later in a letter to college presidents asking them to carefully and objectively consider the NCAA proposals at the upcoming convention.

"No member institution is required to place its women's program in the NCAA or utilize the various opportunities projected for women. However, many women in collegiate athletics feel this is a propitious time for NCAA resources to be available to women. Providing this opportunity does not mandate a course of action for every institution. It simply provides a choice… It is important to remember that all of us have a major goal, that of providing the optimum opportunity for our student-athletes within a framework that best serves our institutions. We must carefully analyze all national organizations to select the forum which provides an environment of excellence for our student-athletes."[39]

Holland countered questions about her loyalty, emphasizing that it was to the institution paying her salary, not the AIAW.

"Universities should be able to choose a governance system that works best for them," said Holland. "Those of us at major schools seemed to gravitate toward each other and we decided to get some changes made."

AIAW dug in. Grant called the NCAA plan unwarranted and a prescription for chaos as she prepared a voting guide for AIAW representatives. The proposed four-year transition period created confusion over championship planning. It increased costs and lacked flexibility for competitive divisions on a sport-by-sport basis. Women were given too few slots on NCAA committees. The NCAA lacked an emphasis on student representation in governance and placed too much pressure on the student-athlete as an investment property.

Two days before the 1981 NCAA Convention began, the women rejected NCAA governance by a vote of 280–40.[40]

NCAA Prepares Carefully for a Contentious 1981 Vote

Several weeks before its annual conventions, the NCAA national office mailed out the convention agenda in a booklet known as the "Official Notice." Within it were summaries of the intent and implications of legislation proposed either by schools or through steering committees. NCAA actions reflected the consensus of each campus's leadership team—the college president, athletic director, and faculty athletic representative responsible for the school's vote.

With Division II and Division III beginning women's championships the next school year and a looming Division I vote on it, the 1981 gathering was truly historic, with a senior woman administrator or women's athletic director now included in the official party. Together, the quartet shaped an institution's positions on voting matters. The NCAA stressed "one institution, one vote," according to Cerra. Wide-ranging and deeply held opinions for women's governance for all divisions presented a potential dogfight dominating the agenda.

CCWAA founders Judie Holland and Barbara Hedges officially represented UCLA and USC, respectively, in Miami. Both women previously had attended NCAA conventions when they met in the same cities as AIAW delegate assemblies, including Atlanta (1978) and New Orleans (1980). They laughed that they were observers watching the convention floor activities from afar, unable to vote on or impact any legislation. But that knowledge and experience helped prepare them for the 1981 Diamond Anniversary Convention commemorating NCAA's seventy-five years of existence. Cerra attended alongside the Missouri delegation, with other members of the Council of Collegiate Women Athletic Administrators representing their universities.

Division I institutions considered proposals for women's championships that stressed a four-year phase-in period, kind of like a test drive to try it and see if you want to buy it, with no final decisions necessary until 1985. The organization vowed to add women to governing committees, like the executive committees, the steering committees, and the councils; only a few to start, but with more promised. The NCAA also stressed that the women's programs could be accommodated initially without increasing membership dues.

Every school determined its institutional approach differently, said Cerra. She valued the faculty athletics representatives, sometimes referred to as the FAR, prestigious academics typically appointed by the campus president or chancellor. Missouri's FAR was the well-respected Henry Lowe, a law professor and an influential member of numerous NCAA and Big Eight Conference committees. Lowe feared that different participation rules for men and women would increase legal challenges to the university. Essentially, male athletes competed under a highly regulated system of checks and balances, with penalties for transferring or failing to maintain an adequate grade-point average. Strong enforcement with penalties applied through the national office ensured compliance. Eligibility was confirmed each semester by the school's official registrar.

Women under AIAW jurisdiction did not face those restrictions, enforcements, or penalties. To Lowe, the law professor, male athletes could sue for equal protection under the law, with the federal court's ruling that men and women had to be treated alike by applying the more lenient AIAW transfer and eligibility rules to male students. Missouri had already faced that scenario with track star Nat Page, but more lawsuits might be expected since both the Big Eight Conference and NCAA rules on eligibility were more restrictive than AIAW rules.

"If there were such a ruling, basic participation rules for men in the Big 8 Conference would be effectively abrogated and conditions bordering on chaos would ensue," Lowe warned in 1979. "Conference institutions could recruit one another's male athletes with no loss of eligibility." The basic right to participate in a school-sponsored activity should be the same for men and women, he said, while recognizing that such an action by the Big 8 Conference would have immediate and unpredictable ramifications with the AIAW, which claimed exclusivity for enforcing rules on women's programs.[41]

Cerra appreciated the Convention Book's insightful analyses, which helped delegates consider the pros and cons of impending legislation. According to her, AIAW offered nothing comparable to assist its delegates. Most just voted their own viewpoints since consulting with the faculty athletics rep or campus president seemed to be voluntary. While some termed the 1981 NCAA Convention as a battle between the sexes, it more accurately could be described as a clash between two opposing philosophies at very different stages of historical development. Dan Kelly described that in a lead article featuring Jean Cerra, Christine Grant, and James Frank for the *Columbia Daily Tribune* at the beginning of the 1980–81 school year.

In the article, Grant questioned why a system designed to serve men's athletic programs should be forcibly imposed upon women. Athletic departments faced increasing travel expenses because of inflation and rising gasoline costs, plus funding Title IX compliance. To her, it was the right time to limit ballooning athletic department budgets by curtailing the two major drains of scholarships and recruiting. Familiar with the Canadian style of college sports, Grant idealistically claimed that the quality of play for men's sports would be unaffected if they followed the women's approach. She appealed to college presidents, requesting arbitration through an eminent education organization. The low-budget, volunteer-dependent, and education-focused AIAW, which had only seven full-time staff members, supported that.[42]

Frank pictured the conflict quite differently and pushed back. It was a misnomer to claim that the NCAA makes the decisions about governance. He insisted that institutions that make up the NCAA were caught in a bind and had to decide which direction to go.

"The AIAW is a relatively new organization. They push for women's sports, which is good. The NCAA has been the men's organization and they (the women) say we haven't wanted any part of women's athletics. Well, the women wanted it that way. The women didn't want to get involved in sports on the same level the men were. Their emphasis was less competitive," Frank concluded.

"Well, now they've changed. They are more competitive. And now they're talking about merging 50–50. Well, it's not 50–50. Not in terms of money, not in terms of people, not in terms of anything."[43]

Cerra recognized that many friends felt a strong allegiance to AIAW and a deep distrust of the NCAA. She recalled that leadership questioned why their organization had to adapt its more student-centered and student-empowered system of governance led by physical education professionals to the men's model. National education leaders should be changing the system to get the men to do what they had done, particularly in cost containment. Having dealt with the NCAA in Missouri's merged department, Cerra realized that many men felt they had operated successfully for decades and were against changing. But AIAW's stubborn approach concerned her more.

"The AIAW doesn't think it's a problem. They don't feel there is anything wrong with having different rules." To her, at least the NCAA was striving to find solutions.

While the national governing bodies waged the war, administrators like Cerra were fighting the daily battles. Women seemed to be hampering the advancement of women at the highly competitive levels by rejecting athletic scholarships, recruiting, and more.

Missouri's Board of Curators had standardized eligibility rules for men and women by designating the stricter of the two rules in each instance as the norm. It increased Jean's frustrations as Missouri's athletic department faced one set of rules for both men and women in some areas, along with another set of rules in other areas. Sometimes, there was a third set of rules for men only in various areas and a fourth set of rules for women only in those same areas.[44]

For AIAW supporters, further review and potential delay over NCAA implementation of women's championships was a victory. A roundtable discussion held before the 1981 convention foreshadowed the NCAA's dogged determination to conduct a decisive up-or-down vote on Proposal 72, initiating Women's Division I championships. The controversy had roiled member schools for nearly a decade. The roundtable's resulting resolution rang loud and clear.

"The [NCAA] Council firmly believes this Association is completely capable, both financially and administratively, of providing programs, services and representation for women's intercollegiate athletics on an equitable and comparable basis with existing men's programs.

"It is apparent that a large number of member institutions want the NCAA to do that. The Council is pleased that the plan would serve the interest of those institutions without requiring any other institution to affiliate its women's programs with the NCAA. The Council believes this is the best approach to serving the expressed needs and wishes of the NCAA membership."[45]

The governance crisis had reached a final breaking point. The CCWAA leaders concluded that AIAW emphases constrained women's college sports. A small cadre of D-I women athletic administrators broke from their colleagues' views and impacted that change. Their schools never could reach compliance with Title IX unless women received all the same benefits as male athletes.

CHAPTER 14

Chilly Conditions in Miami

1981

MOST YEARS, THE NCAA's winter meetings, hosted annually at warm weather resorts in early January, might have gaps in the schedule that allowed delegates to enjoy a round of golf, hit the beach, or whack some tennis balls. But the 1981 convention promised a packed house with deep-seated passions igniting fireworks from competing proposals, plus atypical weather that promised to keep delegates inside and engaged in the topics at hand.

Miami's average January daily temps in the midseventies generally earned the envy of the entire country. Jean Cerra, a Florida native and today a longtime South Florida resident, recalled only a few times when the temperatures might be in the low thirties for more than a couple of days and remarked that a lot of homes and hotels didn't have central heat.

"It doesn't stay cold long. I grew up in Florida and during that convention it was really cold, bitterly cold. You could see your breath inside the Fontainebleau Hotel. That's how cold it was," she laughed. "I don't know if it was just because it was a really, really cold day and the heating system couldn't handle it or if they didn't have heating. It was a really cold day in more ways than one—and not in terms of just room temperature."

Facing Controversy

James Frank presided over the consequential 1981 NCAA Convention and began a two-year presidential term following its conclusion. As the first African American elected as NCAA president, he, of all the people in the room, knew personally that "separate but equal did not lead to equality," as noted by the United States Supreme Court in a 1950s' landmark case *Brown versus the Board of Education.*

Frank, as secretary-treasurer of the NCAA and head of the Special Committee on NCAA Governance, Organization, and Services, wrote to faculty athletics representatives and directors of athletics as the school year began: "The enclosed plan is not intended to effect a merger or takeover… It is an attempt to provide an option—an integrated option to compare with the separatist women's programs offered by the Association for Intercollegiate Athletics for Women. We assume that effective leadership and the attraction of the basic philosophy of the AIAW to many institutions will assure the success of that organization, and we note that the new program of women's championships to be offered by the National Association of Intercollegiate Athletics will provide yet another option."[46]

He went on to claim that the NCAA plan to vote on women's championships resulted from the committee's work and was impressed by the decisive votes of Divisions II and III at the previous NCAA convention.

Later that fall, Frank addressed some of the concerns in a

letter to the president of the University of Georgia and numerous others. He wrote that "it is likely that the infusion of women's athletics in the NCAA will create a common rules-making forum in which the overall issues of intercollegiate athletics can be treated. Intercollegiate athletics in all of its phases is the mission of the NCAA and its members. Many institutions... believe such a forum may be the only answer to the problem of compliance with the proportionality and equivalency requirements of Title IX."[47]

Institutions themselves debated the issues on their respective campuses. Cerra and other women noted the benefits of being in merged athletics departments. Ann Marie Rogers said Alabama's Athletic Committee Chairman Charley Scott had helped to improve her professional skills and mentored her after Alabama combined its men's and women's athletic departments. Rogers valued Scott's national leadership as a member of the NCAA Executive Committee and the NCAA Council and as an NCAA vice president. She supported the move to the NCAA and noted that when the departments merged, the funding for the women's program and the men's nonrevenue sports came primarily from football and men's basketball. Clearly, she said, it didn't make a lot of sense to remain under AIAW governance when it was so opposed to scholarships and recruiting. She recounted that most of the SEC women directors or assistant directors, including Liz Murphey at Georgia and Ruth Alexander at Florida, agreed, also stymied by AIAW's slow march toward progress.

AIAW's scholarships and recruiting rules had been modified continually during the late 1970s. Division III schools griped that AIAW had placed them in a competitive quandary after the 1979 Delegate Assembly had approved partial financial athletic aid at their level.[48] One convention attendee noted that his college didn't allow athletic scholarships for men or women, and its women's teams now would have to compete against schools that were both recruiting and offering scholarships. In retrospect, AIAW's dilemma was apparent: eliminate scholarships and recruiting to keep the small schools happy—unacceptable with the legal implications of Title IX—or increase athletic scholarships and recruiting to satisfy the Division I schools. AIAW regulations were unraveling with criticism from both large and small schools.

Debate Rages on Governance Proposals

Proposal 51, to include at least two women representatives on all NCAA committees, including the prestigious NCAA Council, executive, and steering committees, passed easily with the necessary two-thirds majority. Proposal 72, for Women's Division I championships, required but a simple majority, intensifying the already inflamed passions. The vote of every institution mattered. An AIAW organizational philosophy that satisfied Division III institutions seemed inadequate for the Division I institutions. Faculty athletic representatives at the convention might overrule all the strong pro-AIAW women and vote in favor of women's NCAA championships since it was an NCAA convention. Or a pro-AIAW position was possible. There were myriad factors under consideration, some of which school presidents agreed to defer to the women's position and reject NCAA governance.

"The NCAA proposal permitted choices for each institution—not the NCAA—to make," said Cerra. "That's the quandary a lot of women found themselves in, especially the women who really wanted to stay with the AIAW, who wanted their school to vote no on that proposal."

In other situations, the college's president might conclude that it's in the institution's best interest to have one organization and, therefore, support the move to NCAA governance. The University of California, Berkeley mirrored that turmoil, where the senior woman administrator at the West Coast school, Luella Lilly, was staunchly pro-AIAW, while the faculty representative, Robert Steidel, welcomed more clarity on the issues affecting women. Convention business forged ahead.

Representatives of the women's organization strategically scattered at various microphone stands throughout the ballroom and appealed strongly to the assemblage, prompting USC's Barbara Hedges to think there was a lot of opposition before recognizing the game plan. When they realized what was happening, she and the CCWAA leadership countered that by waiting repeatedly in long lines to press their own points, prodded by the experienced NCAA delegates. Passions and emotions erupted. Neither side budged. The group seated with the Alabama delegation released some of the tension with a wisecrack by Charley Scott, the faculty athletic representative.

Donna Lopiano, staunch AIAW supporter and AIAW's president-elect, was seated at the same table and had knocked a bunch of papers on the floor, fumbling desperately to pick them up from under the table. According to Rogers, Scott cracked a joke that he had always been supportive of and had gotten along with women and quipped that there was one by his leg right then.

"It cracked everybody up. We needed a little bit of humor at that time because things were pretty tight," chuckled Rogers, who then lamented over an unfortunate interaction with an AIAW representative who smacked her in the head and uttered a warning as she walked by Rogers's table. "It was pretty funny, but she hit me pretty hard! And she made some kind of comment that 'you can put a gun to your head, but you don't have to pull the trigger.' That really made me mad."

The battle of opinions raged back and forth. Delegates were divided. Debate ceased. The vote was called for. The tie vote of 124–124 meant that the measure had failed. A recount was requested, and Proposal 72 fell short again, 128–127. Pro-NCAA delegates asked for a roll call to evaluate where institutions had voted, but conference attendees could stomach no more discussion, and the roll call request lost by a wide margin. Seemingly, they had heard enough and signaled a readiness to undertake remaining business. The NCAA's pursuit of initiating women's D-I championships seemed dead for the near future.

AIAW leaders listened to James Frank tally the vote and cheered. They rushed gleefully off the convention floor to deal with the press outside and celebrate their victory, however narrow, confident that they would continue governing women's college sports. After a break, convention business resumed with discussions about the D-II and D-III championships that were approved the year before.

Parliamentary Procedures: A Request for Reconsideration

"When the vote went down, we did not give up. We all came together, a core of us, and talked about how we were going to change that vote. CCWAA members from every athletic conference worked the room to influence the faculty reps, the athletic directors and college presidents and it had an incredible effect," said Hedges earnestly. "We just wanted another chance. We really felt it was the right thing. I deeply appreciate all the things that AIAW did for women, but it came to a breaking point."

The only solution was to find someone on the prevailing side to ask for a vote of reconsideration. As the fervor died down and the convention resumed, Hedges looked around for the AIAW leadership team, unsure if they all had made it back in. Many were in the hallways outside, speaking with the press and exulting over their victory. The CCWAA women and their allies were unwilling to accept the outcome and pivoted to another strategy. Hedges praised Arizona's Mary Roby and UCLA's Holland for leading the effort to work the room and change the vote.

"Of course we were not going to give up that easily," she concluded, citing Roby for being what she called "a little tiger that day." Roby engaged the University of California, Berkeley's faculty athletic rep, Robert Steidel, in a heart-to-heart discussion after his campus's senior woman administrator had left the room. The senior woman administrator opposed NCAA governance and had influenced her faculty rep to vote to support the AIAW views. But she had exited the room, and Roby and the CCWAA leaders saw an opportunity, presenting meaningful points that hit the mark. As the convention resumed after a break, Steidel knew of one available option and carefully pondered the possibility.

Amid the continued buzz, convention delegates returned to their seats. Other proposals about women's governance remained. The D-II and D-III delegates ignored AIAW objections and passed Proposal 73 to expand the number of women's championships approved previously, adding cross-country, softball, and outdoor track. The AIAW continued to oppose all NCAA governance measures and tried to advance Proposal 74, sponsored by the University of Iowa and others, which called for dropping the D-II and D-III championships *in toto*, undoing everything that the NCAA had just passed. Convention delegates quickly and overwhelmingly voted down the measure, refusing requests for roll call counts and moving to cease debate. Convention delegates needed to move on, seemingly tired of the all-consuming controversy. But jaw-dropping surprises loomed ahead.

Roby's forceful persuasion impressed Steidel, a prominent parliamentarian who sought to do the right thing, and convinced him to get the attention of Frank, who remained busy with ongoing convention matters. Steidel announced that he had voted on the prevailing side and asked the chair for reconsideration, a parliamentary procedure utilized when a party on the winning side wanted to revisit an issue. Robert's Rules of Order were about to get a workout.

"All those women who had been intimidated about supporting the movement of the women's programs into the NCAA started talking, standing up at the microphones around the room and advocating about why this was best for women's athletics and why this was the time to make the change," remarked Hedges, adding that her own efforts paled in comparison to Roby's, who captured university presidents by clearly enunciating the mission and the message. "I was devastated as I really thought we had the votes to win the first time."

Remarkably, the tide in the room had shifted as debate reopened. Roby spoke first, followed by Cerra, Linda Dempsey from the University of California-Irvine, and James Jarrett of Old Dominion University, among others.

"Since Division II and Division III have reaffirmed their interest in continuing [NCAA] championships, I urge the assembly to vote for the Division I championships, to give those women the same opportunity," said Roby.[49]

Cerra stressed that AIAW Division I institutions with men's teams in NCAA Divisions II and III would compete in NCAA Division II or III championships instead of at the Division I level. Her support of reconsideration emphasized the importance of choice for organizations in terms of governance.[50]

"The services and the quality of the championships would be of tremendous value for many programs," said Dempsey, one of the nation's first women athletics directors to oversee both men and women, aware of the financial benefits of travel and per diem. "I think the benefits for our women's programs are tremendous."[51]

Old Dominion's Jarrett also cited financial reimbursements to support the move, noting they were reimbursed only $4,000 of the $46,000 spent participating in AIAW Championships. But, to him, there was more.

"I think it's a real shame if this convention votes against these Division I championships and does not allow the good female talent in this country to do more than be relegated to simply working in the AIAW for women because the men need these women, too."[52]

Alarmed AIAW representatives rushed back in and requested a recess until the next morning. It was defeated. The panic built as delegates broadly approved a motion to reconsider. A delegate moved to cease debate, and it was quickly passed. Steidel stressed the importance of voting on the parliamentary procedure question that evening so there were no surprises in the morning.

Finally, there was a revote on Proposal 72. This time, the majority gave its approval by a twenty-vote margin, 137–117. AIAW proponents were shocked. There were no parliamentary procedures available to overturn it, so the vote would stand.[53]

"Enough people changed their minds and it passed. Nobody on the prevailing side was going to make a motion to reconsider that decision. The AIAW people weren't on the prevailing side, so they couldn't do it," recalled Hedges. "The other side was absolutely stunned. They thought they had won. From there on, history was made. If AIAW thought they had the better idea for governing athletics, and I didn't think they did, but if they really believed it they never would have given up."

Notably, Cal Berkeley's Lilly, believing the issue was over, apparently never made it back into the ballroom and only found out about the revote the next day. She, of course, was shocked.

"When I talked to Bob [Steidel] he said he never dreamed that what happened would happen and that was never his intention," said Lilly years later about her colleague. She added that Steidel actually voted against the proposal and was surprised with the outcome of the new vote. "Bob understood our position as a university—that we were in full support of the AIAW. From what I understood, Bob felt that if there was a second vote and the proposal was confirmed as defeated, it couldn't be brought up for a year under the NCAA convention rules."[54]

The tense session was punctuated by an uncomfortable elevator ride afterward when Cerra found herself packed in with the AIAW leadership.

"It was tough to get in there, right in the middle of all of them. I pretty much was by myself at that point. I was always very friendly. I didn't take anything personally even though they might have. It's like I said to Christine all along: We both want what's best for women's sports. We just disagree on how to get there. I respect her position and I respect everything the AIAW did for women's sports because they were the catalysts that got things going. I will forever be thankful for that.

"But we were moving into a different time. People wanted things to happen and time was of the essence. If you were a senior, you had only one year to enjoy whatever benefits were going to be reaped. Freshmen might have four years. But nobody wanted to say, oh, let's have a five-year plan," Cerra said. She added with an easy laugh that going into the NCAA was pretty much a ready-made deal. "You didn't have to reinvent the wheel. The rules and organizational structure were in place."

A Football Coach Brings a Blistering Response

Hall of Fame football coach and Arkansas athletic director Frank Broyles offered some of the most candid comments during the process. His clear, booming voice was perfect for his side gig commentating on televised college football games alongside ABC's Keith Jackson. The University of Missouri once hired Broyles after coaching legend Don Faurot retired in the mid-1950s. He stayed a single season before getting a better offer from the Razorbacks and moved to Fayetteville. Broyles's departure led to the hiring of Dan Devine, who was instrumental in one of Mizzou football's winningest decades ever during the 1960s.

Broyles grabbed the attention of everyone in the room when he called the NCAA takeover "a power play, the likes of which he wished that he had when he was coaching football and a blitzkrieg against a group of people who have worked hard to develop their own organization. My women are happy in the AIAW. You are asking the women to join a method of recruiting [going into homes] that is forcing people out of this profession."[55]

"He had an impressive voice when he took the microphone because he didn't do it that often," said Cerra, who recalled that speech, noting Broyles's infrequent appearances at the microphone. Other football coaches were far more likely to crave attention. "I remember thinking there's more behind that statement because he really wasn't that supportive of women's sports. Those big football guys were perfectly happy to keep the women in the AIAW and weren't eager to have the women in the NCAA. They were under the assumption that it was going to take money from football and basketball. There's a lot more there than him simply supporting the AIAW."

Grant, too, realized that Broyles probably feared the drain on his own budget, not because he was a fervent supporter of women's sports. While Broyles may not have been voicing his strong opinion for the right reasons, nevertheless, AIAW supporters appreciated his remarks and joked that they adopted him at that convention.[56]

"On face value, it sounds great; like Broyles was a big proponent of the AIAW. Does it raise suspicions for me and some who know the history of them wanting to fight Title IX and women coming into their departments? Yes, because you really have to know where he is coming from. He didn't want anything to do with women's athletics and would have been content to have the women governed by their own organization. Certainly, he felt like the women were going to come in and take funds and scholarships from his program," asserted Cerra, adding that Broyles and the football coaches' national organization were very much opposed to Title IX, first trying to get athletics exempted from it, before trying to get football excluded. "They were protecting their own skin. Some men spoke [during the debate], but for the most part they sat back and let the women go at it at the microphones, to fight their own battles."

The outspoken Linda Estes recalled her own interactions and experiences with Broyles during that time. She described being the first woman nominated for what was then known as the NCAA Postseason Football Committee, which included Broyles and a group of what she called "good ol' boys." According to her, the NCAA had proposed a postseason bowl game to be held in Japan to the consternation of Broyles, who howled in opposition because of what he said was Japan's World War II animosities. After the meeting, Nebraska football coach Bob Devaney pulled Estes aside to explain Broyles's protests in terms of business competition. Devaney reasoned that Broyles had a Chevrolet dealership, and the Japanese auto manufacturers were eating his lunch. Thus, Broyles was unwilling to support any football games in Japan. The NCAA overlooked Broyles's objections and scheduled season-ending games there until 1993, as well as a college football all-star game called the Japan Bowl.

AIAW Faces an Existential Threat

The NCAA vote rattled AIAW leaders, who lambasted the decision during the next few weeks and claimed in the media that the 1981 NCAA Convention was hostile and antagonistic toward those opposed to the NCAA plan for women.

Donna Lopiano, University of Texas women's athletic director and AIAW president, complained on cable television and in the media that AIAW delegates were perceived as outsiders with vested interests. From her perspective, the conflict concerned educational issues, which men and women in athletics should be able to discuss without hostilities.[57]

"This NCAA attempt is ill-conceived and poorly planned. If this is how the NCAA intends to look after women's athletics, the fox will be guarding the hen house."[58]

The NCAA insisted that its actions were in response to members' requests and allowed flexibility with its phase-in period. The AIAW called it flawed, creating panic and chaos with women's championships and eligibility allowed under multiple rules systems during that span, either NCAA rules or any formalized, published rules used before August 1981.

Institutions faced the messy situation and evaluated their options. Games needed to be scheduled for the upcoming season, and colleges and universities did not know if traditional rivals would adopt NCAA, NAIA, or AIAW rules. Lopiano feared schools gaining quick advantages by adopting NCAA recruiting methods illegal under AIAW, like subsidized campus and in-home visits for prospective student-athletes. Lopiano urged AIAW members to continue to support AIAW but warned them to follow AIAW rules in all sports if they wanted to compete in both AIAW and NCAA. Breaking those rules in one sport rendered an AIAW institution's entire program ineligible for national championships.[59]

James Frank disagreed with Lopiano's assertion that panic and chaos now reigned in the sports world, called her comments inflammatory and said he was not optimistic about progress in February 1981 correspondence with her. The official letterhead now included the names of four women serving on the 1981 NCAA Council: Judie Holland of UCLA; Elizabeth Kruczek, Fitchburg State College; Gwendolyn Norrell, Michigan State University; and Laverne Sweat, Hampton Institute. The letterhead also listed women on the NCAA Executive Committee: Linda Estes (University of New Mexico) and Mary Zimmerman (University of South Dakota), plus men like the University of Missouri's Henry Lowe. Frank responded directly to Lopiano.

"I saw the January 26th USA Network show and I'm very concerned about the general tone of your remarks. I am referring to your repeated charge that the NCAA is attempting to gain greater power in the Olympic organization, your negative references to Walter Byers, your characterization of the NCAA Convention as hostile and antagonistic, and your description that panic and chaos reigns throughout the collegiate sports world as a result of proposals passed in January. As long as you continue to make such inflammatory statements, I am not optimistic that we can make any real progress in reaching an agreement as to what is best for all athletes, especially women athletes."[60]

Cerra's NCAA Leadership Positions

Cerra was named to the Division I Steering Committee, which added six other women among the twenty members, including fellow CCWAA founders Mary Hill, associate director of athletics at San Diego State, and Judie Holland, UCLA's senior associate director of athletics. Cerra later served on the NCAA Council.

AIAW's budget paled in comparison to the NCAA juggernaut. NCAA revenues topped more than $15 million at the time, with expenses of nearly $14 million. More than half of its income came from the men's Division I basketball championships known as March Madness, with over $6 million spent on costs for those. AIAW's solitary television contract paid over multiple years was minimal, comparatively.

"Certainly, the NCAA had money," said Holland. But incorporating women into the NCAA would be challenging. "The NCAA also had a lot of guys who despised the women because, in their words, we took away resources that should have gone to the men. But we're in the NCAA now and it's not just about money. It's about women's voices being heard and still fighting for things."

When Title IX passed in 1972, no existing men's organization was interested in developing women's college sports. Ten years later, three organizations splintered off different segments of AIAW membership: the NJCAA, NAIA, and NCAA. The move to NCAA governance draws the most animosity today. Those who remember the AIAW days affectionately call the NCAA decisions a "hostile takeover" without recognition of AIAW actions—or lack thereof—that led to its own demise. Most of the resentment and blame focused on AIAW's loss of its television contract, despite the fact that there were women, including the newly formed CCWAA, who were catalysts for the move to the NCAA.

As the public embraced burgeoning collegiate sports during the late 1970s, AIAW snagged a million-dollar multi-year television contract with NBC. The amount was to be distributed to all AIAW members over three years in a revenue-sharing plan. Its leadership felt the approach provided greater long-term financial advantages for all programs, not just the handful of winners that made it to the national championships.

The D-I schools grumbled about being forced to share revenues with programs that rejected similar investments while they paid for hiring coaches, travel expenses, scholarships, and competition. The additional income potential seemed an afterthought to UCLA's Holland.

"The contract wasn't that good. It was not worth very much," said Holland. "It's not until just recently that people have begun to think that the women's basketball championship was really worth something. They never really knew what women's basketball was worth because it wasn't sold separately." The NCAA, for years, has bundled and sold all other sports, but the increasing popularity of women's team sports like volleyball, basketball, and softball will change that.

Springtime 1981 Brings Litigation

The renewed AIAW focus on its television contract, which featured the best D-I basketball teams and players, mystified Cerra. It was too little, too late; ineffective, insincere and irritating to the larger institutions, which questioned why AIAW leadership prioritized it *now* when they previously discounted D-I legislative matters or ruled them out of order. That frustration provided reasons for the larger schools to seek alternatives.

"I just find it interesting that they said they folded because of the D-I schools, and yet the D-I schools were ignored by everybody in the leadership of the AIAW when we tried to present legislation," Cerra said. "Our needs were unique but were completely ignored. They [AIAW leadership] valued that basketball contract so much, but in my opinion, they should have paid a little more attention to us when we tried to pass legislation. Or perhaps been more willing to meet the diverse needs of their membership and not just paint everybody with the same brush. We had giant steps to take to comply with Title IX in order to overcome any and all disparities between the men's and women's athletic programs. Our ability to meet compliance was left in the hands of the smaller institutions that were the voting majority."

Barbara Hedges agreed and listed numerous targets necessary to align the Division I women with what male athletes received: improved coaching, increased coaching staffs and support personnel, media coverage, athletic dining tables, recruiting, paid campus visits, paid travel to championships, tutoring, and covering per diem expenses to start. Hedges agreed that the D-I administrators' needs got shoved aside and overlooked.

"Those were big issues to us," Hedges said, disappointed that AIAW's membership seemed unable to change and recalling an ally's unsuccessful campaign to become AIAW president as the controversy peaked. "That was the straw that broke the camel's back. Finally, we said, that's it. Our needs aren't being met, we keep trying to do things through the normal structure to adopt new rules and we couldn't get anything going. We didn't have the votes."

Throughout the spring of 1981, institutions assessed potential options while AIAW and NCAA bickered. Letters from schools across the country declining membership poured into AIAW offices before the May 1 deadline. The threats regarding potential litigation backfired, according to some administrators.

"Recent postures of the AIAW Executive Board have forced us into a position which we had never anticipated, that of questioning the value of AIAW membership. The AIAW has been placed in a very awkward situation because of recent decisions by the NCAA... Many of us wonder, however, whether the Executive Board is now devoting more attention to political maneuvers than to the welfare of student-athletes. The decision to force member institutions to choose between AIAW or NCAA women's championships at such an early date, and to make at this time a formal declaration of this choice, appears to us a pressuring tactic which does not serve the best interests of the student-athletes," wrote University of California Santa Barbara Chancellor Robert Huttenback.

"The AIAW has threatened legal action against the NCAA and others acting in concert with the NCAA. Institutions such as our own have been members of the NCAA for years and therefore have 'acted in concert with it.' Surely, we cannot reasonably be expected to commit ourselves to AIAW membership for the coming year when our membership money may be used for litigation with which we do not agree.

"At this very critical point in the history of AIAW the threatening posture appears designed not to encourage member institutions but to alienate them, not to strengthen or restore the Association, but rather to ensure its demise. Pressure politics, secrecy and vague threats have certainly made us hesitant about renewing our membership."

University of North Carolina Greensboro Athletic Director Tony Ladd acknowledged his school's historic leadership role in the development of the AIAW, but they, too, were leaving. The majority of institutions in North Carolina with which they competed had chosen NCAA Division III, he said, forcing their athletic programs to follow.

A similar situation occurred on the West Coast when all seven Golden State Conference members chose the NCAA, causing California State University, Hayward, which initially had placed its programs with AIAW, to revise its "Declaration of Intent Not to Participate" in AIAW basketball championships the upcoming season.

"We feel that it would be inappropriate for Hayward to be the only conference school participating in the AIAW Championships," said athletics director Al Mathews. He included payment of a fifty-dollar administrative fee with his letter.

The University of Hawaii, a powerhouse in volleyball under coach Dave Shoji, stressed that it was committed to AIAW's principles, standards, and philosophies but was moving that sport to NCAA jurisdiction.

"Because the majority of high-caliber competitors have aligned with NCAA, and because we must provide the best competitive experience possible for our women athletes, we feel at this time we must join them as well," wrote Dr. Donnis Thompson, the women's athletic director.[61]

Women's sports leaders, including those within AIAW, were deeply divided. AIAW regulations placed female athletes at a disadvantage. Different sets of rules meant that women athletes would never get their fair share. Battle lines evolved as AIAW assessed its losses and considered legal recourse.

Setbacks for AIAW

AIAW suffered a series of cascading setbacks after the NCAA vote, including a loss in enthusiasm, with only ninety-five of over seven hundred members indicating they would send representatives to the next AIAW Delegates Assembly.[62] By late autumn,

AIAW retaliated with an antitrust lawsuit filed in Washington, DC, alleging that the NCAA was a monopoly, which had forced it out of business. Within a year of the NCAA vote, AIAW lost half its D-I members and one-third of its membership overall, along with hundreds of thousands of dollars in revenue. That, coupled with overwhelming legal fees incurred to challenge the NCAA, blew enormous holes in the AIAW budget.

AIAW's claims that the NCAA was a monopoly that wanted to put the women's organization out of business made no sense to Cerra. After all, men had three different options for affiliation. Women were gaining more governance opportunities with the NAIA and NJCAA. But the NCAA was the villain, the organization it opposed in court.

CHAPTER 15
A New Path for Women's College Sports

1981–1985

AIAW'S "SEPARATE BUT equal" approach to athletic governance faced titanic pressures as the NCAA scheduled women's championships for all levels in the fall of 1981 under the direction of Ruth Berkey, former athletic director at Occidental College in Los Angeles. Multiple organizations—NJCAA, NAIA, NCAA, and AIAW—now promoted women's championships. National sponsors like Broderick and Eastman-Kodak faced important decisions as well. The companies funded two of the major awards in women's intercollegiate sports: the Broderick Cup for the outstanding college woman athlete and the AIAW/Kodak All-American basketball team.

By September 4, Broderick Company attorneys emphasized that the primary purpose of its awards program would be thwarted if participation was limited exclusively to one women's sanctioning organization. It asked to modify the existing arrangement and proposed a committee that included two representatives from AIAW, two from NCAA, and three from the company to determine the honorees.

Meanwhile, Kodak, which had provided nearly $1 million to AIAW through sponsorship of its all-American women's basketball team, had two years left on its contract. Kodak representatives noted that many of the best players would not be attending AIAW Championships in 1982. Old Dominion, California State University Long Beach, Louisiana Tech, Tennessee, and South Carolina had been among the top programs the previous two years and had selected NCAA championships. Old Dominion featured all-American Nancy Lieberman and was hosting the 1982 NCAA women's basketball championships, scheduled for the same weekend as the AIAW Championships in Philadelphia. Kodak's solution was to impanel coaches from around the country without regard to AIAW or NCAA affiliation and use the contract guarantees to support AIAW in other ways, like hosting a banquet at an AIAW delegate assembly. Despite the impediments, AIAW reassured Kodak that it understood the problems in an all-American selection process which utilized only AIAW championship-eligible teams.

Impressions as Men Adjust and Work with Leaders Like Cerra

Longtime University of Oklahoma athletics director Joe Castiglione was just two years into his career in the brand-new area of sports marketing when hired by the University of Missouri in October of 1981 as its first full-time promotions director. Castiglione, AD at Oklahoma since 1998, remembered how those experiences at Missouri influenced his development as an administrator.

"I was a one-person show back then; I would beg for volunteer help because we were trying to do a lot with a little," Castiglione said. One volunteer assistant on the student athletic board was

Sarah Reesman, who later earned a law degree and returned to her alma mater as an associate athletic director and senior woman administrator eight years after Cerra departed in 1985, her legal background influential with compliance issues.

When Castiglione entered college athletic administration at Missouri a decade after Title IX became law, no one unpacked the grievances between AIAW and NCAA for him. He understood it as a turf war between the old-school and new-school approaches. He felt no personal bias in protecting one side while denying the other side the same opportunities. To him, organizing championships was gender neutral and needed to evolve through whichever group could better organize them. The move to NCAA governance, he added, started to create more equitable experiences for those championships for women.

"I'm not discounting at all that both sides could have had very noble positions that deserve merit," Castiglione said. He was aghast at stories that he heard. When Castiglione arrived at Oklahoma in 1998, Marita Hynes had been the senior woman administrator for twenty years and also coached softball. He recalled her stories about outfitting the women's teams with the men's hand-me-down uniforms and with minimal equipment. "But as a young man I didn't have the historical perspective about the AIAW and no one stepped in to explain it to me."

As women's sports grew, experienced women head coaches frequently served in dual capacities as senior women administrators. Women's basketball head coach and SWA Joann Rutherford was sometimes unable to attend Big 8 Conference meetings because of basketball duties, so Castiglione stepped in. His attendance helped him understand the women's concerns as he often was the only male present at the women's conference meetings. After a handful of years, Rutherford felt the administrative position was a full-time job and that it interfered with her coaching and recruiting. Castiglione accepted the role for a few months until Sarah Reesman became Missouri's assistant athletic director and senior woman administrator.

Throughout the 1980s and beyond, Castiglione recalled moments in national college athletics meetings when he thought people were still stuck in the old thinking. Some of the problems with inequity were related to those on the committees that resisted evolving, remnants of the fight between AIAW and NCAA, he said.

"I served on a lot of NCAA committees and came away with some head-scratching moments that made me ask why there was so much resistance," Castiglione said. "Fortunately, there were many more people in positions to push for continued growth. But it seemed like there was an internal fight, with differences in philosophy."

In the decade after the NCAA had initiated women's championships, his concerns were less about gender and more about attitudinal challenges from those who nitpicked men's budgets and focused specifically on what the men got versus what the women got. Instead, he called for creative solutions that helped women's sports grow. He was puzzled by the limited thinking that he heard and called the lack of creativity stunning.

"I just never understood that. It might be more! It might be different! It might be a whole different angle to try. But if that was the best way to grow a sport, why wouldn't people talk about it?"

Castiglione recognized that even though he was supportive of women's sports, others had negative biases. He remembered how Cerra overcame difficult challenges.

"She knew what she was doing. She was very smart. She never gave up and handled frustrations the right way. Like any good administrator, coaches and athletes were her number one priority as she explored how to put them in the best position to succeed." He called Cerra a pioneer.

"I'll guarantee you that the coaches who reported to her definitely knew that she was always fighting for their highest possible good. As an administrator you look for people who know the right path and are committed to forging it—but bringing along a bunch of friends and converts as they go, in spite of adversity or resistance. They do it in such a way that they teach, they educate, and they open people's eyes. That's Jean."

He continued that good leaders are patient through difficult processes, especially when dealing with opposition. Sometimes, people can't even tell you why they are resistant, but for whatever reason, they are.

"The right kind of leaders bring people along and do things they didn't think were possible."

AIAW Sues the NCAA

Division I institutions, as Missouri Chancellor Herb Schooling had predicted, welcomed the consistency of one governing organization and joined the NCAA. The big schools broadly saw the increased opportunities and directed their dollars and enthusiasm that way.

AIAW lost championship sites, sponsorships, and television revenues, as well as 20 percent of overall membership. Half of Division I schools departed, including nine of the top-ten volleyball teams, eighteen of the top-twenty basketball programs, 60 percent of cross-country championship teams, 70 percent in gymnastics, 80 percent in swimming and diving, and 70 percent in track and field.

An AIAW committee toiled through long summer days scrambling to assess the damage from what they termed a hostile takeover. The loss of revenues from sponsors, membership dues, and a television contract threatened AIAW's existence and drove their determination to fight. AIAW counsel Margo Polivy filed a 1,500-page antitrust lawsuit in October 1981, in Washington, DC, accusing the NCAA of being a monopoly that had run it out of business.

The spotlight was on the television contract, which was essential for funding AIAW activities. NBC had telecast nine AIAW Championships in the 1980–81 school year but now guaranteed only five and required AIAW to provide the same quantity and quality of teams. Unless AIAW could attract the best teams, the company claimed that the television contract was significantly less than what had been promised and marketed to them. By December, NBC pulled back even further. It would televise no AIAW events and withhold all moneys for the remaining two years of the contract—nearly $500,000. AIAW argued that the revenues provided the NCAA with an economic incentive to destroy AIAW.

Generally, antitrust litigation is resolved over years, not months, but this case demanded answers. While AIAW had hoped to delay the court battle with legal maneuvers that would allow it to survive, presiding judge Thomas P. Jackson realized that urgency and expedited the case. AIAW quickly trimmed $200,000 from its budget in order to fund the lawsuit and complete the scheduled championships. Resolute AIAW President Donna Lopiano warned a national delegate assembly in January of 1982 about losing the independence of women's intercollegiate athletics. She questioned the NCAA's math: inducements of nearly $3 million for women's championships despite those generating less than $500,000 in revenues.

Leaders like Cerra and other CCWAA founders envisioned working with men, not against them, in building intercollegiate athletics. They observed that AIAW leadership had become isolated within independent women's departments as they attempted to implement a more limited version of women's college sports. Cerra noted that athletics seemed to be the only remaining place on campus where women were expected to govern women only.

With the lawsuit continuing through the spring of 1982, a select group of former AIAW presidents who disdained any association with the NCAA name or logo dreamed up plans to create an entirely new and separate organization called the Alliance Council for Collegiate Athletics. Perhaps a new organization with a name change might evolve differently. This merger proposal was created without NCAA input or collaboration.

Supported by Christine Grant and a host of former AIAW presidents, including Carole Mushier, Charlotte West, Peg Burke, and Leotus Morrison, and current president Donna Lopiano, the ACCA prioritized AIAW's educational values and its financially reasonable approach to college athletic budgets. It was to be overseen closely by college presidents and chancellors. Despite an astronomical disparity in revenues, recognition, and prestige, AIAW contended that it was a counterbalance to the NCAA. The organization advanced a wish list that included guarantees for its sport-by-sport divisional classifications, the retention of AIAW qualifying routes to national championships, a student-athlete Bill of Rights, and voting as one legislative body. A new independent Women's Division in a combined organization seemed reasonable to them and allowed AIAW ideals to survive. In their experience, men's athletics leaders were uninterested in women's athletics but wanted control with only cosmetic changes.

There were six key areas of disagreement: financial aid limits, recruiting rules, transfer rules, eligibility requirements, championship opportunities, and enforcement procedures.[63] The proposal encapsulated AIAW's singular ideals but remained tone deaf to the impending tidal wave of other forces.

Jean Cerra and allies like Barbara Hedges, Judie Holland, Mary Hill, Linda Estes, and many others had created the Council of Collegiate Women Athletic Administrators to resolve those very issues for Division I. That small but determined minority of women had taken their leadership skills into combined programs and the NCAA. AIAW felt that the loss of those leaders was balanced by attracting allies from men who rejected equal spending for men's and women's athletics. Perhaps gender was becoming less important than philosophy.

Cerra Questioned About Missouri's Support of the NCAA

Litigation proceeded, and each side called eight witnesses, with depositions undertaken throughout the summer of 1982. Among those representing NCAA interests were Executive Director Walter Byers; Ruth Berkey, NCAA assistant executive director; Judie Holland from UCLA; Barbara Hedges from USC; and Missouri's Jean Cerra. AIAW countered with Donna Lopiano, AIAW President-elect Merrily Dean Baker, AIAW Executive Director Ann Uhlir, and AIAW Officer and Lock Haven Athletic Director Sharon Taylor, among others.

While Cerra's AIAW friends questioned her support of the NCAA when the organization continually challenged Title IX, Cerra, in turn, doubted the lawsuit's merits. She felt it would be easier to influence change from within the NCAA versus being an outsider.

"How do you sue the NCAA for antitrust when the men have

so many choices? And women have only one? It seems to me that the issue of antitrust would be the countersuit from the NCAA to the AIAW, because they were the ones with the monopoly. I don't think any of the eleven women founders of the CCWAA [Council of Collegiate Women Athletic Administrators] went into it with the idea that NCAA governance would bring about the demise of the AIAW," Cerra said. Most of the D-I schools would make that move, but she really thought smaller schools would remain. Campus presidents who wanted their men's and women's programs in the same organization might be satisfied with the AIAW philosophy for their men's programs, too.

"I really felt that was a possible option or outcome. Never in my wildest dreams did I think the AIAW would dissolve. They had so many members and hundreds of schools."

The NCAA wanted to show that the issue was more than men versus women and that many women like Cerra wanted an alternative to AIAW. Throughout her deposition and in-court testimony, she described a consistent and well-reasoned approach, expressing gratitude for AIAW's groundwork. She began with her own academic and employment history, her current pursuit of a doctorate degree in educational administration, and her work as a regional AIAW officer. She had been nominated for the AIAW presidency in January 1980, but Christine Grant won. Within months of that, Cerra was appointed to the first of numerous NCAA committees. In a confident, calm, and reassuring voice, Cerra outlined Missouri's positions.

"Missouri voted in favor of NCAA governance because the university believed that it was necessary to develop comparable rules for male and female student-athletes. The governance plan would provide that opportunity. Like many other institutions, Missouri is concerned that applying two different sets of rules can lead to inequitable differences in the treatment of male and female student-athletes. In addition, working with two different complex rule systems causes unnecessary administrative problems."

She was asked if the rules differences had ever created legal problems for her institution. Yes, she said and cited the Nat Page lawsuit accusing Missouri of a Title IX infraction for applying differing rules of academic eligibility to men and women student-athletes. The women's rules generally were less restrictive than the men's rules, with fewer penalties. She summarized how the NCAA plan helped by formulating comparable men's and women's rules within a single legislative forum. NCAA resources and services would also bring the women's program greater public recognition, she added.

She testified that Missouri, Penn State, and other large universities were disturbed by the controversial Nat Page lawsuit and had proposed more restrictive academic rules for AIAW to consider. A strong majority voted in favor. But bylaws gave each of the twenty-six members of the AIAW Executive Board an additional vote, which it utilized to defeat the legislation by a mere two votes.

"Missouri and other schools were very upset because the measure would have provided the flexibility needed to minimize rules conflicts. For two straight years some political 'jockeying' prevented it from happening. Missouri voted to establish the NCAA Division I women's championships for that reason and because it believed that these championships would provide increased competitive opportunities and public exposure for female student-athletes at Missouri and at other institutions."

Cerra added that Missouri favored NCAA recruiting rules, which provided coaches with greater opportunities to get to know potential athletes. Under AIAW rules, coaches were allowed few student-athlete contacts unless an individual could afford to travel to a campus.

Attorneys asked if Cerra was misled, coerced, or induced by NCAA leadership at the 1981 Convention to vote for the NCAA governance plan or NCAA women's championships.

"No," she replied.

They inquired if, to her knowledge, there were other NCAA institutions so misled, coerced, or induced.

Again, she answered with a resounding no. The vote reflected Missouri's objective to do what was best for the University and its female student-athletes without consideration for the effect of those votes on AIAW, she concluded. The AIAW could continue to appeal to some schools. The NCAA was the best place for Missouri, but many institutions' intercollegiate athletic programs were better suited to AIAW, especially those that wanted to conduct their various women's programs at different competitive levels. That way, a smaller college might sponsor a number of sports without having to make the investment necessary to make all sports competitive at the highest level, Cerra reasoned.

She then was asked if she and other members of the legislative committee engaged in a conspiracy to destroy the AIAW so that the NCAA could monopolize women's athletics.

"No," Cerra replied.

Was there any anticompetitive or unlawful purpose behind that?

"No," she repeated. "They had never sought to harm the AIAW. The University of Missouri and many other institutions wanted an integrated system of rules with provisions appropriate for female student-athletes and an opportunity for women to contribute to the development of athletics rules and regulations affecting *both* men's and women's programs."

One last question addressed the four-year transition period between 1981 and 1985. AIAW claimed that it was planned anarchy that resulted in confusion and chaos.

"The committee wanted to give member institutions the greatest possible flexibility with regard to rules and championships. The four-year transition period made the governance plan the voluntary alternative it was intended to be."

To her, the NCAA's involvement was positive and beneficial. She had worked hard for the AIAW and was proud of her efforts on its behalf. With those memories, she wished AIAW well but asserted that the NCAA women's program provided the best alternative for the University of Missouri.

AIAW Loses the Fight

By midsummer 1982, with heavy legal expenses and diminished revenue from membership fees and sponsorships, AIAW called it quits and declared bankruptcy. It suspended its programs and services and awaited the outcome of the antitrust action. Later that fall, the verdict arrived: NCAA had prevailed. But AIAW battled on. It appealed the ruling and lost. It asked for mediation, unsuccessfully. It spent far more on litigation costs ($569,000) over its last three years of operation than organizing championships over ten years ($315,000).[64]

Cerra praised today's highly competitive levels of women's sports, acceptance by the media, and the overwhelming support resulting from the move to the NCAA when compliance with Title IX surprisingly meant seeking out the NCAA to govern women's college sports.

"Every time I turn on the TV the newscast carries something about women's sports. It's the exclamation point of everything we envisioned," Cerra said. "The wins didn't come easy." She's adamant about the foundation for that.

"That success never would have happened if we had stayed in

the AIAW. That's the part that has never been written. Anyone reading this [book] can understand that all this didn't come easy. You have to be willing to follow your convictions in the right way, which will lead to more positive outcomes. Sometimes that means taking a different or courageous stance, like opposing the majority of women in college athletics, several of whom were longtime friends. They were calling and harassing us. In this case it wasn't the men who were objecting, it was the women."

Barbara Hedges cited the courage of Pennsylvania State University's Della Durant and Phyllis Bailey of Ohio State, women who faced an onslaught of criticism because their schools were located nearer to the pro-AIAW Eastern area.

"Most of us in the Pac-10 conference wanted to move forward now, not in ten years. The CCWAA helped women who knew their student-athletes needed more opportunities but were unsure how to go about it. Phyllis and Della had tremendous pressure from others in the Big Ten Conference. It was time for change and AIAW's moment had passed."

Raw feelings and resentments simmer on both sides. Cerra asserted that NCAA adversaries projected themselves as the great saviors of women's sports when they had initially opposed full athletic scholarships and recruiting. AIAW leaders resisted efforts that gave women the opportunity to compete at a higher, more equal level. The irony is painfully clear to Cerra and other CCWAA founders.

"The very people who opposed the transition to the NCAA are being credited for the current successes of women's sports today, although they staunchly opposed the NCAA and highly competitive athletics," Cerra said. She added that AIAW philosophy slowed down women's sports.

"The people who worked behind the scenes have never been given the credit for that growth. The ones that took the credit were the ones who were fighting the NCAA all the way. They kept ignoring us and ignoring us; we were being held back when we were in the AIAW. We could never get our proposals through because we could never get the votes. We were outnumbered. The peer pressure was immense. We took a lot of criticism and were called renegades. We tried everything possible for years within the system to make change and just kept hitting road-blocks, getting voted down and denied. And yet, they saw it as a betrayal. Out of frustration we said, 'to heck with this, we have to find another route.'"

That avenue was the CCWAA and working quietly with Ruth Berkey at NCAA headquarters to ensure appropriate women's representation on NCAA committees and to initiate champion-ships. The CCWAA founders were targeted as sell-outs, traitors, and turncoats. Some leaders were shunned. Many former AIAW leaders blamed the powerful NCAA for crushing a dedicated and resourceful group and remembered wistfully what to them had been a Camelot period, with hopes of bringing it back. They villainized the NCAA, incensed that a system designed for men had been forced upon women.

"AIAW didn't have the coffers that the NCAA did because they were just beginning to get TV revenue. They spent money on litigation that they didn't have to begin with. It wasn't a matter of deciding to put AIAW out of business. That had never really crossed anyone's mind and was not the intent. There were so many women, hundreds at the D-II and D-III schools, who wanted to stay in the AIAW."

Cerra surmised that in the years after AIAW decided to disband, the NCAA attempted to mend bridges with the AIAW leaders and appointed them to NCAA committees. Nevertheless, the results would be unchanged. Many D-I schools jumped to the NCAA, but numerous smaller institutions that were the core of AIAW membership also chose governance through NCAA D-II or D-III or the NAIA. Having spent its limited resources on litigation, AIAW ceased operations, and women's athletic programs were administered through the NCAA or NAIA.

Christine Grant continued to address women's issues throughout her career. In a 1984 speech about Gender Equity in Athletics, she reminded AIAW enthusiasts to look forward because AIAW was not just an organization; it was an idea built by a dedicated group of individuals who brought those dreams into reality. In the speech, Grant recalled going home after the 1981 NCAA Convention to console herself privately and writing about her feelings of sheer rage and bitter despondency in a letter to Carole Oglesby, AIAW's first president.

"I silently wept for our thousands of students and hundreds of strong women and men in AIAW. It was first the sheer injustice of the action that permitted the NCAA to put AIAW out of business and second, that organization's total disregard for and disinterest in the values that were operative in the women's organization. It is like a death with which I have not dealt."[65]

Rage and despair like Grant's divided many of those early trailblazers, including former Iowa grad school students. Cerra said that Iowa's Christine Grant took the change the hardest and twenty years passed before Grant relented, and the two could discuss their different paths and Grant's lingering pain over that.

"She fought like hell to *not* go into the NCAA. It tore her up. Her life blood was the AIAW. No doubt the leadership in AIAW was not happy with the eleven of us. They were terribly hurt and disappointed. They didn't want to have anything to do with those of us who had succeeded in making that transition. They always looked at it like it was the demise of the AIAW. They thought we had betrayed them."

Personal Challenges and Professional Opportunities

After testifying in Washington, DC, Cerra returned to Columbia to continue building Missouri's intercollegiate athletics program while also pursuing a doctoral degree, her personal life changed by a brief marriage and subsequent divorce from Columbia insurance executive Bob Decker. During that time, she would be known as Jean Cerra-Decker.

In the late 1970s and early 1980s, it was unheard of for women to lead entire athletics departments, particularly at Division I schools with football. But Cerra's experience in a combined department as an associate athletic director for internal operations overseeing most of the sixteen men's and women's sports intrigued Illinois State, which had fired its athletic director. Women in the physical education and intercollegiate athletics departments there, like Laurie Mabry, AIAW president in 1975–76, basketball coach Jill Hutchinson, and volleyball coach Linda Hermann, were elated to have a woman finalist.

During the hiring process, Cerra met with the entire coaching staff, including men's basketball head coach Bob Donewald, an assistant under the fiery Bobby Knight in the 1970s, including Indiana's undefeated 1976 national championship team. Everything went exceptionally well except with Donewald. They were sitting together, and he condescendingly said that if she became the athletic director, she would be unable to ride on the bus to any of the away games with the men's team.

Cerra, always unflappable, took the comment in stride and asked why.

Donewald shrugged his shoulders and replied that women, including wives and girlfriends, were banned from traveling on the team bus.

"He was putting me in the same category as wives and girl-friends," Cerra retorted, feeling the indignity when she would be his boss. "So, I said, 'Let me just put it this way: If I'm the Athletic Director here, you won't have a choice.'"

Cerra had gotten to know a number of athletic directors through serving on the NCAA Steering Committee, including Indiana athletic director Ralph Floyd. She needed to understand more about the basketball coach, so she called her friend to tell him about the interview at Illinois State and inquire about Donewald. Floyd answered the call and asked Cerra if he could help. When Cerra mentioned the name of Bobby Knight's basketball assistant, Floyd said that Knight was right there in his office and suggested that they talk as he handed over the phone. They spoke for a moment, and Knight said Donewald would do a wonderful job for her. Cerra tried to absorb details that seemed out of place with the coach's stance during her on-campus interviews.

After Knight left the office, Cerra called back to discuss that and some additional concerns about reporting directly to the campus president. Unfortunately, the school president planned to retire within a year, which could leave her uncertain of support on campus, she said.

Floyd responded that sometimes the first job is not the right job and encouraged her that there would be other offers in the future because people respected her. He said to really think about it. After a second visit to Illinois State to discuss the chain of command, she realized that she would be unable to accept it. Cerra turned down its offer to become athletic director, which would have made her one of the first women nationally to hold such a position.

"If things were going to blow up, I needed to have the ear of the president. I didn't need somebody between me and the president," Cerra said. "That was extremely important. I actually got a call from the governor of Illinois, trying to get me to reconsider."

Hiccups with NCAA Governance

By the January 1983 NCAA convention, AIAW had folded but the NCAA, which wanted to incorporate women's programs over four years, had set up only limited enforcement powers until 1985. AIAW's demise accelerated that timeline, and the NCAA needed additional penalty options since the only applicable punishment was being declared ineligible for national championships. Coaches whose programs were too weak to compete for a national championship thought it was worth the risk to break the rules when the only deterrence seemed like a slap on the wrist. The public seemed unaware of that cheating because the women's programs were less visible. Cerra explained her views to Steve Richardson in the January 11, 1983, *Kansas City Star*.

"That is a bunch of baloney. People are doing things out there," Cerra warned in an article about the cheating and rules-breaking. "These rules need to go in now." Missouri, Penn State, North Dakota State, and the University of California, San Diego sponsored legislation boosting penalties beginning the next school year. The legislation passed.

A few months after the 1983 NCAA convention, Cerra and the Missouri administration faced additional concerns with NCAA governance. Gate profits influenced the selection of NCAA playing sites for the women's basketball championships, which initially were hosted on college campuses and not at neutral venues. Bolstered by strong play from Lorraine Ferret and Joni Davis, the Tigers, 24–5, had won three straight Big Eight tournament games on consecutive days to earn the Big Eight championship. Missouri beat Kansas State for the second time that season in the title game, but the Saturday matchup was held too late to be considered by the selection committee. The Wildcats were awarded a higher seed in the Midwest Regional and a home game.

Instead of receiving the benefits from winning a conference championship, the Tigers were seeded number four in the South Regional and were sent to number five Auburn, mostly because of profit potential since Auburn's bid offered $1,400 more. Cerra protested unsuccessfully over Kansas State receiving a higher seeding and Missouri going on the road to Auburn. To add to Missouri's woes, its application to host, sent via US Mail and by fax, never arrived before the deadline. Nora Lynn Finch, head of the selection committee, said that even if it had, the determining factor in selecting host sites was profit potential. Missouri, the only team in the entire tournament forced to play a lower-seeded team on the road, ended up losing to Auburn.

By the third year of NCAA tournament play, Missouri had been ranked as high as seventh nationally and dreamed of the Final Four, but Louisiana Tech, the 1981 AIAW champion and 1982 NCAA champion, was hosting the Tigers' regional at home in Ruston, Louisiana. Once again, Cerra complained that playing a powerhouse team in front of a partisan home crowd was unfair and suggested that perhaps the women were ready to move to neutral, off-campus sites for postseason competition.

By the spring of 1985, Cerra, who was not yet forty years old, was finishing a doctorate in higher education administration, intending to pursue a path to become a university president or chancellor. She had been one of two finalists for the athletic director position at Washington State University while she weighed out career advancements. The landscape of intercollegiate athletics was changing, and she thought that she could be more influential as a president or chancellor than as an athletic director. She discussed her future with Missouri Chancellor Barbara Uehling.

Dr. Uehling advised her that most women lacked fundraising experience and that Missouri's director of development position was open temporarily. If Cerra intended to become a school president with its increased revenue responsibilities, she needed to cleanse her resumé of athletics and work on fundraising. Cerra was afforded a six-month leave from the athletic department, with an option to return to the athletic department. Through all of this, the North Star remained the lofty goal of becoming a college or university president.

CHAPTER 16
Business Success

1985-1991

UNDERCURRENTS OF CHANGE rumbled through Cerra's personal life as she approached age forty, with many sleepless nights spent on her office floor trying to rest while working full time and writing her dissertation. Two decades after graduating from Our Lady of Perpetual Help Academy, Cerra achieved a doctorate in education administration from the University of Missouri. Moochine Fernandez, her youth coach from Tampa and her friend Genelle's mother, gifted Jean the symbolic doctoral hood. Jean was as surprised as anyone about what came next.

Circumstances intervened that shocked the educational and athletic community as the *Columbia Daily Tribune* headline blared, "Cerra leaving Missouri to Try Her Hand Selling Frozen Yogurt."

Cerra's friend, Gwen Riggs Nunes, had been teaching in Columbia public schools after graduating from Stephens College. Teachers and colleagues had discovered a tasty product called frozen yogurt and frequently invited Riggs to join them on yogurt runs. Many had bought stock in a company called TCBY—This

Can't Be Yogurt—started in 1981 by a former junior high principal in Little Rock, Arkansas. Later, it was rebranded as "The Country's Best Yogurt." Froyo was touted as a healthier version of soft-serve ice cream because it had less milk fat with fewer ingredients and live probiotic cultures.

One cold winter day, Riggs drove through downtown Columbia and saw students in a crowded line down Ninth Street, enthusiastic about the nation's latest health fad. Gwen was captivated. The Froyo boom was exploding across the country, and Riggs pondered the possibility of developing what might be a fun business. Excitedly, she described the scene for Cerra and, despite Cerra's reservations, encouraged her skeptical friend to taste it.

"Jeannie," Riggs said to Cerra, "it's *frozen* yogurt and you've got to taste it."

Through the early months of 1985, Riggs researched the endeavor and found that she needed $50,000 to open a single store and reached out to family instead of a bank. Regulations at the time might require a male relative to cosign as a guarantor. She said she had no clue about the amount of work it would take to run a business.

Women business entrepreneurs at the time had limited protections in financial areas. Banks and credit card companies routinely discriminated on the basis of sex or marital status until Congress passed the Equal Credit Opportunity Act in 1974 and the Women's Business Ownership Act in 1988. Perhaps that would have helped fund this business opportunity, but it was 1985, when female ownership of something like a yogurt franchise was unusual.

Riggs asked Cerra, who was skilled with numbers but busy with a new job and a dissertation that spring, to help write a business plan. Riggs needed co-investors and reached out to her mom, who was skeptical about her daughter investing in a yogurt business. To her, it was an unnecessary gamble when her daughter already had a job with a paycheck. Cerra hesitated as well when asked, citing limited savings after two decades in education. She could chip in only a fraction of that amount. Plus, she had higher aspirations beyond becoming a national yogurt chain franchisee. Riggs persisted and secured the investment stake from family in Arizona.

While Riggs's enthusiasm for the business grew, Cerra studied the business plan's projections, which showed that her friend would be overwhelmed without additional support. During this process, the steady and capable administrator discovered that she knew the local franchisee, a Missouri intercollegiate athletics donor and trusted childhood friend of the TCBY founder. The University of Missouri alum had left his own prosperous insurance business in Columbia to develop the first franchise that was not corporate-owned. Cerra wanted the very determined Riggs to succeed and agreed to accompany her to a final interview that might bolster that application. TCBY's president had researched the prospective franchisees and challenged Cerra to embrace this opportunity to make some money.

Riggs hoped for a location in Tucson, Arizona, near extended family, but the company said no because of supply chain problems for a store that far west. Instead, TCBY offered the Ft. Lauderdale, Florida, metropolitan area but with a wrinkle: It required investment in not one but four stores within eighteen months. Cerra was familiar with that area, so she asked her brother, Emilio, to research its business potential. Soon, she was getting more and more involved. Emilio, an architect who drew plans for shopping centers and multiunit storage places, felt it was a good opportunity and subsequently came on board. Cerra contemplated TCBY's challenge.

"I thought if I'm going to do it, I better do it now," Cerra said. "That opportunity in Broward County would be lost. Opening four stores in a year and a half would be too much for one person to handle, plus the additional financing required. If I'd had more time to think about it, I probably would have said no. But it was one of those things; the decision had to be made."

Cerra's colleagues at Missouri and many others throughout the NCAA were surprised at the abrupt change in life direction. Athletic director Dave Hart valued Cerra's skills and service. He called Cerra a pillar within the athletic department and described her as an excellent administrator with great insight and the ability to make good decisions and judgments. Would this be one of those?

The final boost may have come from Missouri Chancellor Barbara Uehling, who reassured Cerra that there would always be a job for her at Mizzou if she needed to come back. Cerra had been in the academic world for twenty years and was at a crossroads. She approached her mother, who was confused by and uncertain about the scheme.

"She asked me 'why in the world would you want to go sell yogurt after just finishing your doctorate?'" recalled Jean, who agreed that, yes, it sounded kind of crazy. Jean's mom considered the proposal. The loan might take her entire life savings, guaranteed by a promise to be repaid with interest as quickly as possible. Cerra appreciated hearing the supportive words that she always had a good head on her shoulders as her mother trusted that this was the right decision and agreed to help.

"How I had the nerve to ask her, I don't know. I remember telling my mother that each of us had to find a backer since we didn't have the money to do four stores. There was no way I could accept failure because I assumed it was a big chunk of her life savings. I had no desire to go into business; it was never on my list of things to do. It worked out great in the end, but it was touch and go in the beginning. One bad decision might have caused everything to crumble. We were very close sometimes to failing, completely failing."

A Business Partnership Expands Cerra's Life Experience

A week-long training at Yogurt University in Little Rock was required to learn the business. Each partner brought different strengths. Cerra's brother, Emilio, prioritized site development and building out the stores. Riggs taught the menu items to employees and created the weekly work schedules.

Cerra's role in the partnership was bookkeeping and marketing. Customers needed to taste the unfamiliar product, so the trio handed out samples at corporate events or a few doors down at the Winn-Dixie supermarket. Local elementary school students earned free waffle cones for reading a certain number of books. The owners stressed weighing each customer's purchase precisely to prevent profits from walking out the door. Everyone laughed over early attempts to dip the cones in chocolate without dropping the treat into the hot melted mixture.

Cerra also worked hard at recruiting top-notch students as employees. The owners regularly heard compliments about the quality of their staff.

"They're high school students whose priorities are everything except your business," recalled Cerra with a hearty laugh. Getting a car and gas for it and buying new clothes topped their list. Cerra tapped into her educational background and experiences with recruiting. "Those students couldn't care less if your business thrived or whether the bathrooms were clean. You really had to work hard on getting them to do the dishes and mop the floors." The students' parents certainly appreciated the life lessons and praised the business owners.

As each new store opened, Cerra called high schools nearby and talked to the National Honor Society sponsor or the student government sponsor and explained about the kind of teenagers they were seeking. Recruiting good people and building them into a team reflected Cerra's life experiences on a college campus. After a year or so, those students attracted their friends and school community as both customers and potential employees. She called those young employees their front line because they were the ones interacting with the customers. The local Chamber of Commerce noted the company's work with high schoolers and asked Cerra to speak on the topic of "Hiring for Success" since they had drawn so many good students.

Cerra quickly learned that retail was a total commitment extremely different from academic life. TCBY, as the franchisor, got a big chunk of a small ticket item, taking 7 percent off the gross income, not the amount that was left after expenses were paid, called the net. The rookie owners sacrificed everything while they developed a customer base, paying themselves only living expenses out of interest earned on the certificates of deposit that backed their business loans. They were confident that the product would catch on eventually, but their first store initially hemorrhaged money as expenses outran income, a typical occurrence with new businesses.

"I think our average ticket sale was $2.15. When your rent is $1,500 a month and the average sale is $2.15, you have to sell a helluva lot of yogurt. If you sell a product that's a higher ticket item, you don't have to do so much volume," said Cerra. She calculated the exact number of cups needed to be sold daily in order to pay the light bill. "It was a real education for me because, as an owner, you only got paid if there was money left over. I'd always worked for a paycheck, and in business, everyone else always gets paid first."

The three owners worked seven days a week from 9:00 a.m. until midnight. There was tremendous pressure to be successful, and all three partners were driven by fears of losing their family's money. Instead of grocery shopping, they were eating yogurt every day—for breakfast, lunch, and dinner practically, sometimes adding fruit, berries, or nuts. There were other challenges: The product arrived in frozen blocks, and they had to learn to anticipate business rushes by thawing an ample amount in preparation. The frozen yogurt had to be consistent every day and measured carefully.

Cerra recalled the intense devotion to building the business and making it successful. The company stressed the importance of getting the product in people's mouths because nobody knew at the time that it tasted like ice cream, so she offered it as a complimentary dessert for local service club meetings. It was a huge investment to give away an expensive product, but that had to be done instead of using printed advertising in magazines and newspapers. She chuckled that most people will say yes to anything that's free, especially the area's many retirees.

The venture truly became an extended family business. Jean and Emilio's mom whipped out waffle cones at grand openings like a seasoned professional. Together, they learned from the experiences. Their first and second stores became two of the top revenue-producing locations in the country. Eventually, all of the stores did extremely well, earning them distinction on the TCBY President's Council as a Top Ten Franchise. The trio recognized increased competition from additional frozen yogurt and ice cream businesses and sold the stores after three years. All personal loans were repaid with interest.

"I was happy. Everybody was happy. It turned out to be successful. We did very well in our sale," Cerra said. With receipts proving their business acumen, the trio had sold at the right time. The experience deepened Cerra's appreciation for retail sales.

"I can tell you: It's not easy. You're the last person to get paid. It was a struggle and there wasn't any money left for the first year or two because we put any profits into opening new stores. It worked out well in the end—thank God."

Selling yogurt and working continuously for three years took its toll. Cerra put some money in the bank and enjoyed her respite by playing golf once again. A return to campus and education seemed to be in her future, especially with a PhD behind her name.

While playing golf with a friend who was an assistant provost at Florida International University, she mentioned that she was getting bored and needed a job to give her some purpose. That friend remarked that FIU was opening an adult education program on its Ft. Lauderdale campus, which would be perfect for Cerra to re-enter academic administration: Cerra could play golf all day and work nights. Cerra went through the formal application and interview process and got the job. But FIU was waiting on a funding grant that might take four to six months.

CHAPTER 17
Barry University Beckons

1991-2008

STEVE HATCHELL GOT to know Cerra when he served as associate commissioner of the Big Eight Conference. He always held his interactions with Cerra in high regard and talked about that in a January 1984 issue of *Missouri Alumnus Magazine,* saying that, early on, a lot of the women's approach to organized athletics was that they were owed something.

"Jean would have none of that. She was always rational, not emotional. She would step back and say, 'Here are the options.' That has allowed her to accomplish what she has and to get to where she is now."[66]

As part of his duties, he helped arrange on-campus football workouts at Barry University for the Big 8 Conference's Orange Bowl representative. The beautiful five-thousand-student private school was located in Miami Shores, Florida, midway between Ft. Lauderdale and Miami. Later, Hatchell parlayed those experiences as an intermediary into becoming executive director of the Orange Bowl and maintained close ties with Barry. The university's president, Sister Jeanne O'Laughlin, was on the

Orange Bowl executive committee, along with Ben Benjamin, an assistant to the president, and Gene Autry, vice president for development.

In 1991, Hatchell called Cerra and wanted to catch up. At lunch, he asked if she was interested in returning to athletics, and she said absolutely not. Shortly afterward, he called again to let her know that he had recommended her to Barry University, which was looking for a director of athletics. She responded in alarm and questioned why he did that when she had just told him that she was not interested. Cerra hoped her doctorate in higher education administration might lead to an administrative position at a college or university.

Cerra was familiar with Barry University since many of her high school classmates enrolled there. Hatchell explained that reticence to Barry University administrators, who, undeterred, requested that she apply and submit a resumé. She reluctantly agreed, influenced by what she called her habits of blind obedience from her background in Catholic school. Otherwise, she said, she would have expressed a firm *no*. Finally, she accepted a personal on-campus meeting, hoping to deter Barry University's interest.

Sister Jeanne, the president of Barry University, had arrived at the all-female college ten years before after a previous stop at St. Louis University. She envisioned Barry as a coed institution and already had implemented that change. Developing intercollegiate athletics was an important part of attracting men. Entering Sister Jeanne's office, Cerra knew she was in big trouble when she walked in. Sister Jeanne clasped her hands in prayer and commented on how God had answered her supplications.

Cerra recalled her utter shock when Sister Jeanne suggested that she accompany her to the conference room to meet her entire cabinet. During that meeting, Cerra explained her reservations about the position and that she had set her sights on other things. Selling a successful business had made her a little more comfortable financially. Intercollegiate athletics required a lot of time and effort, which she honestly was unwilling to give.

Sister Jeanne asked if perhaps something less pressure-filled would be attractive to her. She thought the position was simpler and easier than Division I Missouri. Cerra disagreed.

"It was worse because you're a one-person show. You have to do everything yourself."

Despite Cerra's misgivings, Sister Jeanne remained adamant about hiring her. Cerra immediately thought of Hatchell dropping her name to Barry and wondered how in the world a lunch with a friend had gotten her into this dilemma. Cerra threw up one final excuse: She had accepted a job at Florida International University and was awaiting a grant to fund her position.

Sister Jeanne urged Cerra to call her contact there and explain that she was unable to come. Cerra recoiled at the thought, said there was no way she could do that, and thanked Sister Jeanne for her time and the offer.

"Thank you for thinking so highly of me and that you have offered me this job. I'm sure you're going to find the right person for it. I just don't think I'm the right person at this time."

Weeks later, Ben Benjamin called to invite her to play golf with fellow Barry board member Gene Autry at a prestigious country club, La Gorce. While Cerra was deciding whether or not to accept the invitation, she joked that it was too expensive for her budget and asked if Benjamin's goal was to repeat the job offer. Benjamin downplayed that possibility and reassured her that they had just enjoyed meeting her and thought she would like to go out and play. She agreed, enticed by golfing at one of the most magnificent private clubs in the area. But by the eighth or ninth hole, they asked what it would take to get her to Barry.

"I said zero, nada, nothing. He said, 'c'mon, everybody has their price.' I said seriously, I'm not interested. I don't take a job simply for the money or title. I've got to feel something for a place."

A few more weeks passed, and Benjamin called once again, emphasizing that Sister Jeanne wanted to see her and talk with her one last time for just an hour or two. Cerra said that, once again, her Catholic upbringing was her downfall. She listened and agreed to one final meeting. This time, she revealed her true reservations, stressing that very few athletics programs were serious about treating athletes as students first and as athletes second.

Sister Jeanne understood from prior interactions that Cerra really valued academics. Decisively, in two hours, Sister Jeanne laid out a plan to restructure the university. Athletics would be taken out of the student services area. It would be placed in the academic affairs division and combined with sports sciences and sport-related disciplines.

Sister Jeanne was adamant about putting the program together and said that Cerra needed to have an academic title like dean to have the necessary clout when they put athletics into the academic affairs division. Those huge changes were unheard of in intercollegiate athletics nationally. Cerra could make all the academic rules necessary because she was going to be the person in charge. It would be Cerra's program.

Cerra was stunned. She wanted no part of either role. She thought she had made that clear. Her head spun, and she called for a pause. Things were moving too quickly. She had turned down the athletic director's job, and now they were asking her to take *two* jobs as athletic director *and* dean. It was a lot to process.

Sister Jeanne knew all the right buttons to push and stressed that Cerra would have the authority to make decisions about building the program. The job offer was tantalizing, allowing

Cerra an opportunity to prove something that she always believed in but never could do.

"I had always dreamed of being able to build a very successful athletics program with good students, students who were committed to their education and graduating and weren't there just to get drafted and play pro." She weighed her commitment to Florida International University.

Sister Jeanne wanted Cerra to say yes and encouraged her again to call her friend and explain that she was going to come to Barry. This time, Cerra made the phone call. Cerra's friend advised her to take it because that job was perfect and everything that she believed in. There were others who could fill a night school position. Cerra swallowed hard and, with a nod of her head, accepted Barry's offer.

Implementing Academics for Student-Athletes

On Cerra's first day at Barry, Sister Jeanne handed her computer sheets stacked two or three inches thick, printouts of the student-athlete accounts totaling hundreds of thousands of dollars in arrears. Cerra absorbed this surprising and unexpected news.

Barry was Division II with only a few full-ride athletic scholarships. Students owed money for tuition and room and board, and Cerra knew immediately that all accounts would need to be paid up by the end of the year. Cerra teamed up with the school cashier, made phone calls to parents, and worked countless late nights

"I had my people at registration. If athletes didn't pay or weren't in good standing with a university payment plan, they weren't going to register for the next semester," Cerra said. "That didn't make me popular, by any means. They didn't like that at all, obviously. That leverage was the only way to get those bills paid, if their eligibility was in jeopardy."

By the end of the year, the policy proved effective, with fewer nonpayments and most of the enormous debt recovered.

As Cerra returned to her academic roots, she followed personal convictions established twenty years before at Stephens College. Her demands that students be punctual to that early morning kinesiology class for a quiz might have been tough, but it was nothing compared to implementing Barry's new academic requirements. Cerra hoped to derail potential surprises about her expectations and designed a handbook for incoming fall student-athletes, who were required to sign the policy sheets.

Soccer was just coming into many intercollegiate athletics programs, and Barry had a dynamite women's team that had earned the school's first national title before Cerra arrived. Barry played and sometimes beat North Carolina, known for its powerhouse program. Despite the team's success, Cerra was unimpressed that athletes sauntered across campus and showed up tardy for team buses to away matches. The display of entitlement was unacceptable, and she vowed to turn that around.

The soccer players were told to be in front of the Health and Sports Center at three o'clock sharp for an away game. Barry's athletic director was there to enforce team expectations. The bus departed on time. Fifteen minutes later, a bunch of the players, including starters, showed up, asked where the bus was, and wailed about the predicament. They were starters, and what would the team do without them? Cerra repeated that three o'clock was the bus departure time, and, yes, it could and did leave without them.

"I put in place rules, like if you're an athlete and miss two classes, you're suspended from the next competitive event," Cerra said. "If a student-athlete missed four of the same class, then they were kicked off the team and lost their athletic scholarship." The first person to test the system had starred on a national championship team. Cerra showed her commitment to academics—the player was dismissed from the team for missing too many classes.

There were other academic deficiencies. At the time only about one-third of student-athletes achieved a grade-point average of 3.0 or above. Cerra wanted improvements and instituted tougher policies. The high expectations antagonized the student-athletes. Faculty doubted Cerra's overtures, skeptical that the university truly would risk losing athletes. They thought it was a bunch of big talk. They had heard those promises before.

Cerra assigned her assistant to the dean, a woman who had earned the respect of all the faculty and generally was critical of intercollegiate athletics, to lead the new academic counseling unit. To her, the athletic department needed a makeover. The assistant to the dean had been president of the faculty senate three times and had written key parts of a faculty handbook. Together, they implemented the new policies, including notifying faculty every time a student got dropped for the next competitive event for skipping class. The assistant to the dean was like a cop over athletics because the faculty trusted that she was objective and impartial, recalled Cerra.

"You know what they say about friends and enemies: Keep your friends close but keep your enemies closer," Cerra said. "By the end of the first year the faculty realized that I was going to deliver everything I promised."

Other rules ensued. Coaches would be unable to intervene directly with any of the faculty about their athletes' academic shortcomings. Professors were tired of coaches who, no matter how well-intentioned, were construed as pressuring and pleading with them to change students' grades. Cerra wanted to simplify that communication channel and avoid any possible misinter-pretations. The faculty member and coach would now have to communicate through Cerra's assistant dean about any academic concerns. There were other difficulties.

Study hall was required for all athletes; nobody was exempt unless they had a 3.0 grade-point average or higher at the end of their first semester. Some of the better students griped about attending; after all, they were already performing adequately in the classroom. But Cerra wanted them to prove it, with the reassurance that it no longer would be required at the end of the term. The complaints fizzled out slowly and became pretty minimal by the end of the first year.

Cerra realized her policies were strict and unpopular. The school president thought she might be going too fast and urged her to slow down. But Cerra was unwilling to do that. She rejected parceling out those changes over multiple years. The only way to endure the controversy was to get it over as fast as possible. Even Sister Jeanne joked that she worried that Cerra might face some student dissension if she attended the end-of-the-year athletic banquet.

"I set a high bar and it was like the Stephens class—they had to meet it," noted Cerra. "And after that, they were fine." To her, it seemed like all the agony was over after the first year. The student-athletes welcomed the new approach. The teams were winning and were nationally competitive. The students' minds were clear. They were at ease and could perform well the next day in an athletic event without worries about flunking a class. That stress was relieved.

Results and improvements arrived gradually. A Southern Association of Colleges and Schools accreditation team visited the campus the following year and, as a part of its review process, spoke with some of the athletes. The interviews proved how fast the situation at Barry turned around. The athletes revealed their pride in being students first and athletes second. Administrators valued their academic success. They had access to academic grants that were previously unavailable. It impressed the accreditation team, which cited athletics and the Division of Sports and Leisure Sciences for honorable mention in its final report, the only academic area to receive that notation.

Cerra tackled financial goals as well as academics. Barry's athletic funding came directly from university coffers, unlike her previous experience at Division I, which had entire fundraising departments to finance athletics budgets. Cerra sought to provide the athletes with academic scholarships first, while athletic awards kicked in as a supplement. Barry University provided a presidential scholarship through the financial aid department to attract good students, granting free tuition and full room and board, essentially a full ride. She encouraged the coaches to focus recruiting on those good students who also were good athletes.

"That meant that we could stretch out those limited athletic dollars. Academic awards available to all students are exempt from the scholarship equivalency count in Division II," Cerra said. "They may be slightly less talented athletically, but because they were good students, they were high achievers and could learn systems quickly. They could improve from good coaching. I had to convince coaches to save their limited athletic scholarship funds for impact players, but only those who were committed to graduating. The coaches who listened to my advice did very well and became very successful."

Word spread that the athletic director and dean would apply the rules evenly for everyone, marked by her strong early stand in dismissing a star athlete. That turning point curtailed challenges.

"They realized that I wasn't going to be selective. Everyone knew and understood the rules. They were warned about breaking those and still signed off. They lost if they tested the system. It was tough," Cerra recalled. "After that, the student-athletes embraced the changes and respected me. It was just getting them used to a whole new system and a whole new set of priorities that were there for their benefit."

By Cerra's third year at Barry, faculty members frequently stopped her on campus to tell her to send them more athletes. They loved having them because they were the only ones who came to class. Cerra laughed at the memory. The change was like night and day.

"That's why I said, 'I'm going to get over this and I'm going to get over it fast, because I'm not going to be this stressed out for years.' I knew once we got over the hurdle, we'd be fine. Coaches are used to black and white—this is the rule, and if you don't follow the rules, you're out. Coaches make rules all the time with their student-athletes. They understand that process. You have to approach the faculty differently. Faculty want to be involved in the decision-making, they want to make sure they are heard, they need to debate it, talk it out. So, it takes a year and a half to do something that I can take care of in two months in the athletic department. But we became very successful on the academic side, too."

Barry University earned six national championships under Cerra's administration: three in women's volleyball, two in women's soccer, and one in men's golf. Since her retirement in 2008, Barry athletes have added more than twenty national titles in men's tennis and golf, rowing, and women's golf. The foundation was strong, and nearly every sport is competitive today at the national level. The number of athletes who earned term grade-point averages of 3.0 or above roughly doubled to 65 percent. Academic policies remained in place, and the same priorities were followed by the new director of athletics, Mike Covone.

Admissions: The Lifeblood of Any Institution

During the 1990s, enrollment problems at Barry caused budget cuts, impacting Cerra's goal to develop the School of Human Performance and Leisure Sciences. Administration officials asked her to consider helping with admissions because they valued her skill in team building. Recruiting new students was a two-year process, and, as Cerra said, they needed to get "cheeks in the seats." Cerra hesitated to accept the role. Reorganizing athletics had challenged her immensely, and overseeing admissions was ten times worse. She knew they were late in starting.

Cerra contemplated the move for an entire year while she faced personal issues with caring for her aging mother.

To prepare for the new position, Cerra hired highly recommended consultants and asked an all-important question: Will your system work if you have to deal with a person in charge who knows absolutely nothing about admissions? Cerra chuckled at the thought. The consultants responded that they loved it because she had no predisposed opinions about what worked. They were confident that they could teach her the necessary skills. Cerra declared that she would do whatever they asked. The consultants would be responsible if the attempt failed.

The dual roles in 1998 brought new titles: dean of the School of Human Performance and Leisure Sciences (HPLS) and associate vice president for Enrollment and Academic Services. The associate athletic director was promoted to athletic director to free up some of her time. Cerra motivated the admissions staff to work late nights in order to meet their enrollment goals by serving them dinner. Offering such a simple inducement impressed the administration. They were pleased that, after Cerra's first year in admissions, the incoming freshman class enrollment had doubled.

"They just needed the right person to focus them properly and get them working together toward a common goal," recalled Cerra. Their collective efforts added more than $12 million to the budget, which relieved the financial crunch. The administration wanted her to stay in enrollment services and preferred to fill her position as dean of the School of Human Performance and Leisure Sciences rather than seek a new dean of admissions. Cerra was committed to doing what was best for the university but was unhappy working in a very necessary but personally unmotivating job. She had taken on admission responsibilities primarily to build the university in order to ensure success for her goals in athletics and academics.

"I was terribly unhappy in admissions; it's not why I came to Barry," noted Cerra. She wanted off the demanding and frustrating treadmill of continually working toward and reaching overwhelming goals. University finances had stabilized, and Cerra wanted to focus on what she loved: the School of Human Performance and Leisure Sciences.

Sister Judith Encourages Cerra to Return to Her Passion

One day, Cerra sat in her office in admissions and realized how much she wanted to return to HPLS. Barry was just starting its search for her replacement as dean. She wanted a sign from heaven about what she needed to do and whether or not to stay. She prayed silently, and as she closed her eyes, a coworker rushed in to say that a retired nun had returned to campus and was looking for her. Sister Judith Shield, a former dean of the business school and one of the first persons Cerra had met on Barry's campus, had been a bright light of encouragement who regularly told her what a great job she was doing. When Sister Judith arrived, Cerra showed her around the office, which previously was her apartment when it was a residence hall. Then Cerra accompanied her as she left the building. Suddenly, Sister Judith turned to her and looked at her directly. Out of the blue, she spoke forthrightly, as though informed by angels.

"I'm going to tell you one thing: Don't let them make you do anything you don't want to do," recalled Cerra about those words. "I never had discussed anything with her. None of that came into our conversation." Sister Judith continued with her encouragement and repeated her advice.

"Don't let them make you do things that you don't want to do."

After poignant goodbyes, Cerra returned to her office in tears, struck by the realization that this might be the sign for which she had prayed. She knew that nuns live lives devoted to obedience and do whatever is required no matter what. They expect lay people like Jean to have the same kind of devotion. Sister Judith's remarks struck Cerra as instrumental, and she needed to act. She quickly called the provost, Dr. Pat Lee, and said that she wanted to see him over a personal matter. With renewed vigor, she went next door to his office and proclaimed that she was unwilling to stay in admissions.

"You need to hire somebody in enrollment services and let *me* go back to what I love, which is Human Performance and Leisure Sciences. You can take my title away, my cabinet position, cut my salary. You can do whatever you want to do. I just want to do what makes me happy."

The provost asked what had prompted that strong request. She described the story of Sister Judith and her insight. He was struck by that and suggested that, together, they go to see the university president. In Sister Jeanne's office, the provost proclaimed that Cerra was not going to remain in admissions because she wanted to go back to Human Performance.

Like the provost, Sister Jeanne asked what had prompted that. Again, Cerra told the story about Sister Judith. Sister Jeanne reflected on that momentarily before calling it unbelievable.

"You do what you want to do. If that's what you want to do, we'll be fine. You can still be vice provost and you can still oversee admissions, but you don't need to be the one running it."

Jean agreed. That was a deal.

AFTERWORD

Dr. G. Jean Cerra finished her career at Barry University by helping to obtain provisional accreditation for Barry University's law school. By the time Cerra had finished seventeen years in administration there, Barry athletics regularly finished among the top NCAA Division II programs in the Sears/NACDA (National Association of College Directors of Athletics) Directors Cup, an annual competition that gauges overall athletic excellence. In 1998 and again in 2002, Barry earned distinction nationally as the best private university in the Division II rankings. Eleven of the twelve varsity sports earned team GPAs of 3.0 or above. All but one student-athlete who completed four years of eligibility graduated during her tenure.

The university called her a generational leader and pioneer in college athletics, and she earned a coveted spot on its Wall of Honor, similar to Hall of Fame honors awarded by University of Missouri Intercollegiate Athletics, NACDA, and the Sunshine State Conference. In 2023, Women Leaders in Sports honored her with a Lifetime Achievement Award. It had been forty-five years since Cerra and ten others had founded the organization as the CCWAA.

Kathy Stevenson Turpin first observed what she called Cerra's caring, confident, and strong leadership while she was a student-athlete at Missouri. Before graduating in 1980, she had helped Missouri women's basketball to several top-twenty national rankings, along with a couple of conference championships. She recalled the importance of seeing Cerra in an athletic administrator role at Mizzou, stressing how "if you can't see it, you can't be it."

When Turpin attended her first NCAA convention, she discovered Cerra speaking on proposed legislation. At the time, Turpin served in athletic administration at Missouri's Truman State University. It had been over a decade since their paths had crossed, and she wanted to say hello. Turpin observed as Cerra returned to her seat and moments later approached Cerra's table to say hello. Placing her hand lightly on Cerra's shoulder, she began to introduce herself, unsure if the Barry University athletic director and dean would recall her from the University of Missouri.

Before Turpin could offer her name, Cerra turned with surprise, smiled, and said, "Hello, Kathy."

They stayed in touch, and six years later, Cerra hired Turpin as associate director of athletics and senior woman administrator. Their views on ensuring opportunities for both women and men aligned closely, along with similar passions for implementing Title IX's philosophy.

It took years for Turpin to grasp Cerra's national impact on sports, particularly her role as a founder of the Council of Collegiate Women Athletic Administrators. Learning about that history and the CCWAA's influence on bringing women into NCAA governance served to deepen Turpin's respect. The myriad opportunities available to women today were once unimaginable and can be attributed to Cerra and other trailblazers, Turpin noted.

"Although she is a Title IX pioneer, Dr. Cerra's efforts have always been for equal opportunities for both genders. She had high but fair expectations of anyone in her program. If you were fortunate to be a part of it, you learned right away that she would expect and accept nothing less than being successful in 'doing it the right way' and 'doing the right thing' for the institution, the department, students, student-athletes, and the entire athletics program."

Cerra encouraged Turpin to earn her doctorate while at Barry and inserted a clause into her contract that provided additional support for her teaching and administrative obligations. In 2007, Turpin founded a consulting company that conducts Title IX and athletics department full-program reviews, evaluates NCAA rules compliance, assists institutions transitioning to new conferences and national affiliations, and develops strategic plans. By 2009, Turpin, inspired by Cerra's trailblazing work and experiences, wrote about the impact of Title IX on the career paths of women in intercollegiate athletics in her doctoral thesis, earning a PhD in educational leadership and higher education administration.

"To this day, if I have a tough professional decision to make, she is my first call for advice. Dr. Cerra has taught me, and I have shared with so many young people, you never know who might be your future employer. The decisions you make today and the impression you make on all those around you may provide a life-changing opportunity in your future."

Turpin has the deepest gratitude toward her mentor and the foundation laid by the Title IX generation of women's sports trailblazers.

"My story is not possible without Jean Cerra."

Sold-out venues, nationwide media coverage, coaching salaries in the millions of dollars, and television commercials featuring women athletes are but a small part of the tidal wave of opportunities and unprecedented achievements today.

"Yes, it required vision and courage toward everything that we believed could happen and which most women in sport at the time either doubted or resisted," Cerra said. "We've come a long, long way, but it has taken more than fifty years, and that's a lifetime lost for our generation that was denied all of these wonderful opportunities.

"Thank God some of us have lived long enough to see it become a reality."

ACKNOWLEDGMENTS

I'm grateful for the support and encouragement of many people throughout this project. This writing adventure began following a chance meeting with Jean Cerra at the 2022 Celebration of Title IX and Women's Sports at the University of Missouri. She was one of the guest speakers. Cerra later told me how she hoped to find someone to collect and share her stories. I thought about that for a few months, then called to offer my services. We quickly got to work, and I'm deeply grateful for her thorough analyses and careful descriptions. Thank you, Dr. Cerra.

Weekly phone calls with her were inspirational, informative, and invaluable, sort of like a Mitch Albom *Tuesdays with Morrie* scenario. I first met Cerra while taking journalism classes during summer school when I was assigned to interview her for the *Columbia Missourian*. She had been hired in May 1976 as the University of Missouri women's athletic director. I was entering my senior year and playing two sports—basketball and softball—and eager to meet the new leader. The article remains in Cerra's archival material with the university.

I'm indebted to the talented editors who have shaped my words and refined my style, including Matt Proietti, my former editor at the *Mountain News* in Lake Arrowhead, California, who offered his expertise and time in synthesizing early drafts. Matt grasped the story's development, and this book would not be what it is without that perspective.

I'm also thankful to Sarah and Mark Kohnle, friends from my university days who listened to my initial excitement over the book. Sarah quickly caught onto important descriptions and suggested a working title.

Patti Baymiller and Geri Migielicz, Missouri School of Journalism graduates, were tremendously helpful with their observations and insights. Patti covered women's sports during the 1970s as a student reporter, and Geri, a basketball teammate at Missouri, is now a professor of journalism at Stanford University. Their assistance is much appreciated.

I'd also like to thank Mizzou sports archivist Bob Brendel, along with archivists at the University of Missouri's Ellis Library and at the University of Iowa.

I'm deeply thankful for CCWAA Founders Barbara Hedges, Linda Estes, Mary Hill, and Judie Holland, who shared with me their stories about the struggles of women's intercollegiate athletics in the 1970s and 1980s. This book benefits from their observations.

I'd like to thank other early leaders in the Title IX generation of women, including Merrily Dean Baker, Ann Marie Rogers, Sharon Taylor, Carole Oglesby, Judy Sweet, and Joan Cronan, for their thoughts and recollections.

I'm grateful to athletic administrators and coaches like Deb Duren, Dr. Lynn Lashbrook, Joe Castiglione, George Walker, Dru Hancock, Alexis Jarrett, Charles "Jake" Jacobson, Cheryl Lightfoot Levick, and Pete Hoener for spending time with me and sharing their reflections. Thank you.

Personal friends of Jean Cerra, like Genelle Fernandez Garverick, Gwen Riggs Nunes, and Pat Donatelli, helped with anecdotes. Former Missouri teammates Lisa Borcherding Housson, Kathy Stevenson Turpin, Julie Maxey Ferguson, Sharon Farrah, Suzanne Alt, Laura Harper, and Laura Jackson assisted with stories and research. I benefited greatly from the encouragement of longtime friends from Southern California. Stephens College athletes Diane Daugherty and Dana Caston Moore and Texas A&M's Brenda Crim helped me understand their personal journeys in intercollegiate athletics during the 1970s. Thank you everyone.

Family, including my partner, Ruth Villarreal, and my sisters, Sharon Rudolph and Nancy Rudolph Vanderlip, were there to pick me up when the project was overwhelming and listened to me read the early drafts. I'm so deeply grateful.

Finally, to the crew at Streamline Books in Kansas City: You are to be commended for a job well done. I so appreciate your insights and editing, which have made this project come alive. Specific thanks go to Stephanie Rondeau, Chloie Benton, Ginny Glass, Abigael Elliot, Kiska Carr, Alex Demczak, and Will Severens.

Thank you to everyone who listened to me share this largely unknown tale. You helped me refine the message about this eventful era when women sought full representation in intercollegiate athletics, both as athletes and as administrators, and went from cheering in the bleachers to donning the team uniforms. It truly was a remarkable time.

ENDNOTES

1 M. Mackenzie, "The U.S. Women's Soccer Team is Still Denied Equal Pay—So Title Nine is Writing Them a $1 Million Check," *Glamour Magazine Newsletter*, July 28, 2021.

2 L. Reeder, *Dust Bowl Girls* (Thorndike Press, 2017).

3 Title IX of the Education Amendments of 1972, 20 U.S.C. §1681–1688.

4 Personal correspondence, Linda Estes to AIAW presidents, October 9, 1973, University of Missouri archives.

5 Personal correspondence, Linda Estes to AIAW presidents.

6 Personal correspondence, Linda Estes to Mary Rekstad, October 10, 1973, University of Missouri archives.

7 Correspondence, L. Leotus Morrison, AIAW president-elect, to Linda Estes, November 14, 1973, University of Missouri archives.

8 G. Haney, "Women's Sports: How Far Will Dollars Go?" *Columbia Daily Tribune* (May 9, 1976), page 12.

9 Haney, "Women's Sports: How Far Will Dollars Go?"

10 Hill v Nettleton, 455 F. Supp.514 (D. Colo. 1978) August 30, 1978.

11 Title IX Self-Evaluation Report: UMC Intercollegiate Athletics; Mel Sheehan correspondence, July 13, 1976.

12 Title IX Self-Evaluation Report: UMC Intercollegiate Athletics, July 13, 1976.

13   *NCAA News.* vol 17, no 17, November 30, 1980, p. 3.

14   Jean Cerra letter to Chancellor Herbert Schooling, March 16, 1978, University of Missouri archives C 1/17/3 Box 13 f.13.

15   Scannell, "Women's Full Ride Restored," *Washington Post,* January 10, 1978.

16   Y. Wushanley, *Playing Nice and Losing* (Syracuse University Press, 2004), p. 118.

17   Minutes, CCWAA meeting, Stanford University, submitted by B Hedges, University of Missouri archives C 11/17/3 Box 13 f20.

18   J. N. Crowley, *In the Arena: The NCAA's First Century* (National Collegiate Athletic Association, 2006).

19   J. Holland, *Analysis of National Governance Systems,* December 6, 1976, University of Missouri archives, C: 1/17/3 Box 13 f.13.

20   G. E. Killian, "NJCAA's Highly Successful Women's Division," *Coach and Athlete Magazine,* November 1979, 14–16, University of Missouri archives, C: 1/17/3 Box 13 f.10.

21   First Report of the NAIA Task Force on Women's Athletics, September 1, 1978, University of Missouri archives, C: 1/17/3 Box 13 f.13.

22   Charlotte West to AIAW voting representatives and presidents of AIAW Member Institutions, October 31, 1978, University of Missouri archives C 1/17/3 Box 12 f.2.

23   University of Iowa archives; remarks by Christine Grant at the Fourth Annual Delegates Assembly, January 2–6, 1977.

24   *The Chronicle of Higher Education,* January 15, 1979, volume XVII, number 18, University of Missouri archives C 1/17/3 Box 12 f.14

25   *The Chronicle of Higher Education,* January 15, 1979.

26   P. Wunsch, "Title IX Threat to Women's Athletic Group," *Columbia Missourian,* March 4, 1979.

27   Ruth Lauver personal correspondence, September 14, 1978, University of Missouri Archives C 1/17/3 Box 12 f.2.

28   Barbara Uehling personal correspondence, November 21, 1978.

29   Jean Cerra personal correspondence to Barbara Uehling, January 31, 1979.

30   P. Wunsch, "Title IX threat to women's athletic group."

31   Charles "Chuck" Neinas in a Big Eight memorandum, May 15, 1979.

32   Linda Estes personal correspondence to Barbara Uehling, July 11, 1979.

33   Correspondence, William J. Flynn and James Frank to chief executive officers of the NCAA, March 7, 1980, C 1/17/3 Box 12 f.2.

34   Correspondence from Christine Grant to chief executive officers of the NCAA; University of Missouri archives C 1/17/3 Box 12 f.2

35   Correspondence from Christine Grant to chief executive officers of the NCAA .

36   Correspondence from Christine Grant to chief executive officers of the NCAA.

37   Minutes, Special Committee on NCAA Governance, Organization and Services; March 23–24, 1980.

38   University of Iowa archives, Christine Grant collection, box 5.

39   University of Iowa archives, Christine Grant collection, box 5.

40   University of Iowa archives, Christine Grant collection, box 5.

41   Memorandum, Henry Lowe to Big Eight chief executive officers, June 4, 1979.

42   Dan Kelly, "Sex and Sports: College Athletics Newest Problem," *Columbia Daily Tribune*, August 10, 1980.

43   Dan Kelly, "Sex and Sports: College Athletics Newest Problem."

44   Dan Kelly, "Sex and Sports: College Athletics Newest Problem."

45   1981 NCAA Convention Proceedings, Division I Roundtable notes, January 12, 1981.

46   University of Iowa archives, James Frank correspondence, September 15, 1980, to NCAA members, Christine Grant collection.

47 Correspondence, James Frank to Fred Davison, president, University of Georgia, University of Missouri archives C: 1/17/3 Box 11 f.31.

48 *The Chronicle of Higher Education,* January 15, 1979. volume XVII, Number 18; University of Missouri archives C 1/17/3 Box 12 f.14.

49 NCAA Convention Official Minutes, January 13, 1981, 175.

50 NCAA Convention Official Minutes, January 13, 1981.

51 NCAA Convention Official Minutes, January 13, 1981.

52 NCAA Convention Official Minutes, January 13, 1981.

53 B. Hedges and J. Holland, *Women's Collegiate Sports: AIAW to NCAA* (CreateSpace Independent Publishing, 2012).

54 Hedge and Holland, *Women's Collegiate Sports: AIAW to NCAA.*

55 NCAA Convention Official Minutes, January 13, 1981, 163.

56 M. Bechtel, "AIAW vs. NCAA: When Women's College Basketball Had to Choose," *Sports Illustrated,* June 14, 2022.

57 University of Iowa Women's Archives, Christine Grant, Box 5; Donna Lopiano to AIAW voting representatives and chief executive officers of AIAW Member Institutions, January 23, 1981.

58 University of Iowa Women's Archives, Christine Grant, Box 5; AIAW news release February 9, 1981.

59 University of Iowa Women's Archives, Christine Grant, Box 5; AIAW news release February 9, 1981.

60 University of Iowa Women's Archives, Christine Grant, Box 5, February 11, 1981, James Frank correspondence with Donna Lopiano.

61 University of Iowa archives, Christine Grant collection box 5.

62 Sperber, 1990, collection of Pam Gill-Fisher at University of California-Davis.

63 Correspondence regarding a merger proposal from Christine Grant to Donna Lopiano, et al; March 22, 1982. University of Iowa, Christine Grant collection.

64 Y. Wushanley, *Playing Nice and Losing* (Syracuse University Press, 2004), p. 118.

65   University of Iowa archives, Christine Grant collection, Gender Equity in Athletics, 1984 speech.

66   J. Gentry, "Low Profile, High Performance," *Missouri Alumnus Magazine*, vol 72, no. 3, January–February 1984, 22–23.